PANDEMIC EXCHANGE

HOW ARTISTS EXPERIENCE THE COVID-19 CRISIS

Theory on Demand #41
Pandemic Exchange
How Artists Experience the COVID-19 Crisis

Editing: Josephine Bosma

Production: Agnieszka Wodzińska
Cover design: Katja van Stiphout

Published by the Institute of Network Cultures, Amsterdam, 2021
ISBN print-on-demand: 978-94-92302-74-8
ISBN EPUB: 978-94-92302-75-5

Contact
Institute of Network Cultures
Phone: +3120 5951865
Email: info@networkcultures.org
Web: http://www.networkcultures.org

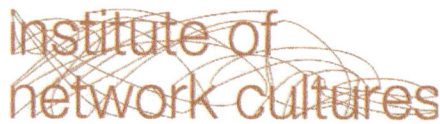

TABLE OF CONTENTS

INTRODUCTION

A few weeks into the second lockdown, or was it the third wave, of the COVID-19 pandemic, a desperate Facebook post by an artist caught my attention. I know the artist in question quite well. He is a mellow and smart guy, not someone to panic or complain easily. Now, at the start of the second lockdown in the Netherlands, he sounded exhausted and defeatist. He ended his post with 'See you in 2035!' His brief outburst somehow managed to stand out between the many news links, quizzes, vanity posts, and silly memes. This was the voice of a human, of a friend in need.

It wasn't the first frustrated COVID-19-related post I came across, of course. By this time, in January 2021, a vast number of fearful, angry, and other emotional outcries about the pandemic had already passed by on my various screens. The near flame wars about the need to take the virus seriously were often hard to avoid, fortunately occurring at ever-larger intervals but never fully subsiding. Fear and anger were alternated with boredom posts. Hordes of people forced to work from home, or to just stay home and do nothing, flocked to social media to engage in all sorts of time-killing pastimes together.

Amid all that, just about every art institution (and others, naturally) looked for ways to continue their productions online, with varying levels of success. From the first days of the pandemic, already crammed online platforms were flooded. The attention economy was shredded to bits, only to return restacked and contorted. The internet, which has been a vital part of my work field, my battlegrounds, and my social spaces since 1995, changed more in the first year of the COVID-19 pandemic than it did with the birth of the Web, the first social media platforms, and the app revolution combined.

There I sat, at home in yet another lockdown, watching it all unfold. I saw friends and colleagues struggle, some to the point of collapse while feeling increasingly frustrated and cut off myself. The artist's remark about the year 2035 became a haunting symbol for all time, all conversations, and all interactions already lost. I somehow had to fight the void this ominous '2035' represented.

This publication is one result of that fight. It is a very basic attempt to reach out and feel profoundly connected again to the art field I cannot do without. It took a few weeks for the idea to take hold. One month after the '2035' Facebook post, I asked artists in my network if they were interested in being interviewed about their pandemic experiences. I wanted to know how they were doing. I missed their representation in the news and in discussions around the pandemic and the lockdowns it necessitated. There was a lot of worry about the economy in national crisis committees and the media, but this worry seldom concerned cultural workers of any kind. And whereas most people working in art institutions, from janitor to director, still retained their income, artists generally are in a more precarious position.

Unfortunately, particularly for this project, my network thus far includes few artists from Asia and none from Africa. I am aware of this gap and hope others will fill it, or that I will find a later opportunity to do so. Even in today's hyper-connected world, among the issues here are techno-cultural and language barriers and my preference for working with artists I have met face to face. Online presences can replace physical meetings rather well at times, but relationships that form there also need time to grow.

One of my aims for this interview project, albeit not in a perfect way by far, was to somehow capture the spirit of art and artists, even if all I can do is pass on their voice or offer a slight glimpse into a much larger and much more diverse world of art. There is a certain sensitivity and originality in the way artists approach the world that is valuable, also in times of crisis. This collection of interviews shows many fine examples of such sensitive and original thinking, living, and working. As is often the case with interviews, reading them can make you feel very close to the person who is 'speaking.' In that sense, this is a collection of encounters, a way of meeting the artists and entering their sphere.

Method

My approach, from the initial questions to the ordering of the content of this publication, has been more intuitive than academic. Most interviews were entirely conducted through email. Some artists gave very brief responses, while others wrote long reflections. Some artists received additional questions, but most did not, and in two or three cases this happened through some kind of video conferencing software (Skype or Facebook chat). One artist suggested an additional question, 'How real is the COVID-19 threat to you personally?,' which I did not forward to all artists as it did not always feel appropriate. The questions were edited out of the final texts to achieve an easy reading experience, less repetition, and a smoother flow. What you see before you, therefore, looks like a series of monologues. This format, I hope, also strengthens the experience of individual voices and meeting the other. Because most artists give detailed descriptions of the local or national situation concerning COVID-19 in their responses, the interviews offer a broader context to the circumstances under which artists have worked and continue to work during this pandemic.

Additionally, I asked the artists for pictures they thought would fit with their interviews. I received a mix of new and existing portraits of the artists, photos of their work, of their homes, studios, and environments. One artist, Archana Prasad, could not provide any. I took stills from her video interview and a public domain Wikipedia photo of the community workspace in Bangalore that she has co-initiated.

Artists

Many readers might know the main focus of my work is on art in the context of the internet, net art in the broadest sense of the word, because I find this a most relevant area to explore. My work as a critic and researcher of art in the context of the internet was initially triggered by a lecture about Marshall McLuhan by Derrick DeKerckhove in 1991, more specifically McLuhan's idea of media as extensions of the nervous system. Understanding the interchange between social bodies and their technology as it accelerates through the development of relatively open networks seems ever more urgent, and for me, an understanding of this interchange begins with exploring its art. Most artists interviewed for this project therefore work with technology in some way or the other, or at least are not unfamiliar with it. They use it in dance, performance, activism, community projects, installation art, visual art, conceptual art, and music. Some are well known, others less so. I reached out to artists I was curious about at that moment, because of their social media activity or lack thereof, or just because I hadn't heard from them in a while. At some point, I had to stop reaching out to more artists, simply to be able to handle the number of exchanges.

What came back to me was often surprising, and not only am I moved by the content of many of the interviews, but also by the generosity of the participating artists. There is much overlap between the interviews, of course: nearly everybody had exhibitions and jobs canceled, was cut off from their social circles, and had to find ways to fill the long days at home. Not everyone experienced this as a problem, to the contrary: for some, lockdowns offered a chance to step back from a hectic life, exhale, and recharge their energy. Yet many struggled, on varying levels, with the lack of income, feelings of isolation, various stress-related issues, or with the dreaded virus itself. Projects were abandoned and new inspiration came. Self-isolation produced a lot of self-reflection, but also reflection on art, life in general, and the world. I discovered that some artists are gifted writers. The power of these interviews often lies in the details, though sometimes it's the entirety of a story that blows you away.

The interview with **Archana Prasad** is an example of the latter. Prasad is an artist-activist and organizer from Bangalore, India. Her text is filled with personal details about her family and health. Prasad is the co-initiator of the collaborative communities project Jaaga, co-developer of the DARA network app, and co-organizer of the BeFantastic art and tech festival. The pandemic forced her to switch from being a highly independent professional to taking on a balancing act between working from home, homeschooling her son, and acting as caretaker for her parents. Prasad is one of two artists in the book who got the virus last year. She told her story in a series of videos because she had trouble typing due to loss of vision in one eye, most likely a result of 'long Covid.'

Similarly, the interview with **John Duncan** makes you feel the devastating effect of being cut off from work, left with no income, and having to live on scraps. Originally from the U.S., John Duncan is an artist, performer, and musician who lives in a large shared former farmhouse in the Italian countryside. Pre-pandemic he earned most of his living from music performances around the world. Lucky for Duncan, he found support with his neighbors.

Another moving text comes from Brazil. **Lucas Bambozzi** tells us the harrowing story of the situation in his country, where the president undermines all efforts to keep the people safe. Bambozzi, an artist-activist and filmmaker, is involved in various initiatives and actions across São Paulo. No other text is more exemplary of how politics and health are connected and how artists can be at the forefront of change. It took a grassroots movement including artists like Bambozzi to help the Brazilian people protect themselves. His elaborate text closes off the book to emphasize its urgency.

Some artists write deeply insightful analyses, combining personal reflections on the lockdowns with their politically engaged art practices. Artist-activist and researcher **Michelle Teran** travels between Germany and the Netherlands, and in her text, she carefully interlaces her experience of a social conflict in a community garden group in Berlin with that of a collaborative writing project on community-engaged work and collectivized learning practices in Rotterdam. The writing project is vandalized; the community garden group likewise needs to reboot. Teran shares an excerpt of the Rotterdam document, 'The Social Practices COVID-19 Teaching Resources.'

Pandemic Exchange offered the opportunity to finally take time for reflection. Infrastructure artist, curator, and writer **Nancy Mauro-Flude** gives the most detailed description of the first reactions to the pandemic in Australia, where she works, and Tasmania, where she lives. Like Teran, Flude captures the initial shock well, but with a hint of irony and sarcasm. She describes her struggles with the university's bureaucracy, the fate of her students, her struggle to combine her work with caring for her family, and several works she made over the course of 2020. Among those is an ongoing writing of a feminist critical internet theory.

Another view on the situation down-under comes from artist, writer, and curator **Melinda Rackham**, who lives in South Australia across the bay from Kangaroo Island, where bush fires killed billions of animals just before the pandemic hit. Though Rackham also describes the difficult times many in Australia went through, she is one of the artists for whom the lockdowns were generally beneficial. Australia's strict interstate border policy isolated her from her family, but the forced self-isolation enabled her to finish a new book and create a series of remakes of art by women artists Rackham admires. Among them is VNS Matrix, the Australian art collective whose 1991 Cyberfeminist Manifesto Rackham revisits.

Others found the sudden self-isolation and new work mode a bit harder to digest. For artist and musician **Ben Grosser,** from the U.S., whose works are often critical reflections on how we use new media and software, not much changed in terms of his art practice. Yet, even for the introvert he says he is, social isolation took its toll. After an initial paralysis, Grosser reinvigorated himself with a lighthearted web-based work entitled *amialive.today*, and then made one of the most timely net art pieces of 2020, *The Endless Doomscroller,* a work that represents the gloomy everyday pandemic social media experience by just showing the headlines of news articles.

Both Ben Grosser and Canadian media artist and activist **Garnet Hertz** teach at art or design academies. Hertz had to dismantle his studio on campus but found radical ways to keep supporting his students. One of the things he did was hand his mobile phone number to his students and tell them to call anytime. The lockdown made Hertz experiment with activist art tutorials on social media, a pastime that helped him get over a brief disillusionment in art during the first lockdown when a techno-culturally ill-informed mainstream art world flocked to the internet. Hertz also describes lockdown brain fog, the art of skateboarding, and the undervaluation of the work of artists in academia and tech.

Though online teaching helped many artists survive the lockdowns financially, it wasn't always easy. It could even be downright impossible to make the switch from classroom to screen. Dutch artist **Dennis de Bel** experienced the beginning of the COVID-19 crisis in China in January 2020. When he and his Chinese partner started wearing facemasks during the first virus breakout in the Netherlands in March 2020, the couple became the victim of insults and racist slurs. De Bel describes the exodus of Asian students from Europe, the nightmare of online teaching due to Dutch academies' obstructive Microsoft addiction, and cannot hide his longing for the orderly approach to the pandemic in China.

Some are surprised by the fast pace of the developing pandemic. Only one week after returning to New York for his Ph.D. research, Egyptian dancer and choreographer **Adham Hafez** suddenly finds himself facing four walls in the lockdown. Hafez writes about the impact of such a restriction of movement on a dancer, how he managed to perform online, and how travel restrictions are nothing new to someone from the Middle East.

Uruguayan artist and musician **Brian Mackern** was also traveling when the lockdown started. After an adventurous trip back to Montevideo, he gave talks, presentations, and concerts from home. Oddly, these pay a lot less than a physical performance would, while preparation and stage time stay the same. Like many others, Mackern finds it difficult to focus, and he develops a special routine to keep up his health and sanity.

The situation differs greatly from country to country. A text that weaves together harsh reality, near science fiction, and dreams comes from the Greek globetrotter and Neen artist **Miltos Manetas,** who currently lives and works in Bogota, Colombia. His text is a critical and ironic commentary on the great social inequality in his new country of residence and the world at large, an inequality that creates huge differences in individual levels of suffering from the pandemic. Manetas' self-awareness of being what he calls 'plus-privileged' and his scuffs at the art market make for a fun but also sharp read.

In contrast, Japanese multimedia artist **Sachiko Hayashi** lives in the welfare state of Sweden, which has a controversial approach to the pandemic. Hayashi describes how the country's natural herd immunity strategy divided the nation to the point that friendships broke and some individuals even left Sweden. The artist finds herself in harsh disputes in which she is called a right-wing populist for asking for stricter measures, the opposite of how discussions about pandemic measures play out in most countries where it is exactly right-wing populists that want measures to be loosened. Hayashi's health forces her to self-isolate, a period she uses mostly to update her technical skills.

Among the relatively unscathed is French visual artist **Tiny Domingos,** who lives and works in Berlin, Germany. He takes us on a trip through the city, explaining the historical connections between disease and urban planning. His tone is upbeat. Though several of his shows were canceled, Domingos enjoys his time with his children and the opportunity to delve into new research and work. He offers one of the most beautiful metaphors for living through a lockdown with homeschooled teenage children.

Also in Berlin, but with younger children and thus having more difficulty balancing homes-chooling and work, are **!Mediengruppe Bitnik**, the artist duo Carmen Weisskopf from Zurich, Switzerland and Domagoj Smoljo from Island Vis, Croatia. The duo was in Shanghai in January 2020 to prepare an exhibition when this huge and bustling city suddenly went into lockdown. Back in Berlin, they immediately prepared for the lockdown they knew would come. The pandemic inspired !Mediengruppe Bitnik to develop a new work around the ambiguity of data.

Also in Berlin and doing relatively well is Estonian visual artist **Ivar Veermäe**. Half a year before the first lockdown in Germany, Veermäe had become a father. When the city stops in its tracks he goes on endless walks with his daughter, exploring the city. The pandemic and his young daughter make him think about how we relate to other species, also those that live within us.

Similar reflections come from the Mexican multidisciplinary artist and curator **Arcángelo Constantini**. For many years his work has revolved around bacteria and mutualism, the ecological interaction between species. In addition to telling us about his ongoing project, Constantini describes the lack of support for the arts in Mexico and paints a lively picture of a Mexico-City street during the lockdown.

An artist who experiences the unpredictable and disabling effects of long Covid is a Dutch artist and 'mind-shifter' **Jennifer Kanary**. She contracted COVID-19 in March 2020 and still suffers from relapses one year later. Kanary describes what happened when the pandemic measures closed down her main source of income, her child needed homeschooling, and COVID-19 kept knocking on the door.

The year was much easier for Canadian .gif artist **Lorna Mills.** A true optimist, her biggest change was probably going from being an active socialite to rediscovering her true introvert side. Seizing the moment, in March 2020 Mills co-curates the successful online exhibition *Well Now WTF*. Most of her work already always takes place online, but the lockdown brought her an unexpected new collaboration with a teenage DJ for a neighborhood street performance.

The lockdowns force everyone to rediscover their local environment. Like so many artists traveling a lot between countries, queer feminist artist and activist **Mare Tralla** had to deal with multiple pandemic situations in both her motherland Estonia and in the UK, where she lives. She made sympathetic small works and interventions around her home to honor the scientists developing the COVID-19 vaccines, and made one-person-crew films in the empty streets of London. Strict rules for government support make Mare Tralla struggle financially.

The self-confinement during lockdowns also forces a reevaluation of the home. A thoughtful suggestion on how to do that came from Italian artist **Daniela de Paulis**, who lives and works in Rotterdam, the Netherlands. De Paulis, originally trained as a dancer, recalls the merging of home and body in Chantal Akerman's *No Home Movie*. Like so many, Daniela de Paulis went from an initial involuntary self-reflective state to developing new work, often inspired or influenced by the pandemic, and returning to an older work that had been started in 2015 but needed the time for reflection the lockdowns offered.

The shortest interviews say a lot about how the pandemic impacted individual artists as well. **Igor Vamos**' text says all it has to: the lockdown brought Vamos much-needed quality time with his family and time to start writing again after decades of constant traveling across the planet. Isolation here comes as a relief. Vamos is one of the **Yes Men**, the artist-activist group he formed with Jacques Servin in the 90s (first as RTMark), who have taken on large institutions and corporations ranging from the WTO to ExxonMobil and Shell.

Early multimedia artist and filmmaker **Lynn Hershman Leeson** gives us a glimpse into her busy life. This workaholic achieved more in the first few months of lockdown than most would in years. Her body quickly asked for mercy, but after a short period of recovery, she tirelessly returned to work, and at the time of the interview had received her first vaccination.

Of a younger generation, post-digital artist **S()fia Braga** describes the near traumatic experience she has when suddenly being locked inside the apartment that is her home but where she barely spent time before. It would change her work profoundly from light to dark. Braga takes inspiration from Kafka's 'The Metamorphosis' as the walls start closing in on her.

Net artist and performer **Annie Abrahams** finds herself in a strange place when the push towards online meetings and online art events creates a new interest in online performance and bodily presence. She has to balance her personal sensitivity and attentive performance work with firmly re-positioning herself in a renewed art discourse, one in which historical awareness about art in the context of the internet is seriously lacking.

Last but not least, I am very grateful to have received a response from the U.S.-based artist **Tina La Porta**, an artist I know from her online performances and art explorations of human connection in the mid-90s internet. La Porta was later diagnosed with schizophrenia. She now makes art about mental illness and its treatment. The pandemic and the lockdowns made her fall into a depression for which she found little understanding from the art institution where she was to host her solo show.

Finally

The effects of the COVID-19 pandemic will be the topic of many discussions, documentaries, and research papers for years to come. Thus far, most analyses concern macro-economic and public health effects, documentation that consists mostly of statistics. The pandemic sweeps across the world in such an all-encompassing way that one easily loses sight of its impact locally, individually, and even for entire networks, sectors, and communities. We may learn only in hindsight how problematic it can be to lose track of the subtleties of the bigger and smaller dramas and changes that unfold. The language used around the COVID-19 measures feels limited. We are divided into 'essential' and, so one might deduce, 'non-essential' workers. Vaccinations are expected to 're-open' society as if it were a shop.

Though it was not the main reason for this interview project, I am worried about how, at least in Western Europe where I live and where vaccines are slowly 're-opening' society, a political discourse and new hierarchy seem to develop around the initially helpful and necessary concept of 'essential workers.' Somehow the protection of public health became the protection of a 'healthy economy,' and its definition and shape can be disputed, to say the least. Here, a populist notion of economy dominates, a view in which cultural expression and mental health have little value.

Now the pandemic seems in its last phase thanks to vaccinations in many parts of the world and a year of COVID-19 measures has severely impacted people's income and wellbeing. A struggle about who is first in line to return to their old life and work practices begins. This is when we see how artists and cultural workers are affected by the vague status of all who are not 'essential workers;' their position seems to weaken. Illustrating this is for example a much-criticized recent Singaporean poll in which 71% of respondents place artists at the top of their list of non-essential workers, or how today, at the end of the second lockdown in the Netherlands, just about every sector is allowed to re-open long before museums and theaters. Though *Pandemic Exchange* wasn't inspired by these recent developments, the near invisibility of the arts sector in most COVID-19 pandemic crisis management debates was definitely an inspiration, and this invisibility seems to have led us to where we are today.

But *Pandemic Exchange* is also about reaching out to the artists and hearing about how they have been. It also became a journey or an exhibition of sorts as well. The combination of local pandemic situations, different national responses to the crisis, and the way the artists react to them makes for a powerful and at times moving experience. Some of what is in the interviews is relatable, and some of it surprises or even amazes. It would be good to learn more, to see other initiatives around art and the pandemic in which the focus is not just on individual works about these trying times, but on the artists that make them and on the circumstances in which they work.

For now, I hope *Pandemic Exchange* offers at least some form of representation of how artists experienced the COVID-19 pandemic. I thank all artists for their generosity.

- Josephine Bosma, May 2021

QUESTIONS

1. In many countries the authorities were late to acknowledge the severity of the pandemic. How was the situation where you are (can be as local as your city or neighborhood, anything that is important to you) and how did/do you experience it? Can you describe what happened and is happening now?

2. COVID-19 measures gravely affected the movement of people and goods. It changed the way many people had to work, and many even lost their jobs or livelihood. What happened in your life? Did you manage to continue working, and if so, how? Were you able to adapt to the new circumstances easily?

3. Artists generally don't produce consumer goods or simple, easily marketed products. They work and think along idiosyncratic paths, often creating objects, installations, events, or situations that reflect on or react to the world. At the same time, their work process can also be vulnerable to outside influences, even to the point where it gets blocked. I wonder if the situation around the pandemic inspired or influenced you in specific ways. What have you done or created during the pandemic? Has there been a development in this over the course of the past year?

Additional question suggested by John Duncan:

4. How real is the COVID-19 threat to you personally?

One artist, Dennis de Bel, received different questions:

- Hoe is de situatie waar jij bent sinds de pandemie is begonnen? (What is the situation like where you are since the pandemic started?)

- Wat voor impact heeft de pandemie op jou en je werk gehad? (What impact has the pandemic had on you and your work?)

- Als je nog hebt kunnen werken, wat heb je dan precies gedaan? (If you were still able to work, what exactly did you do?)

- Hoe zie je de nabije toekomst voor jou en je werk? (How do you see the near future for you and your work?)

BRIAN MACKERN

My art has become more introspective and delves into ways of self-being awareness, involving rituals while producing the sounds. This way of doing things has always been part of my workflow, but it has a strong presence nowadays. I feel it's kind of a self-defensive way of trying to keep my sanity in the middle of this huge storm of info contamination.

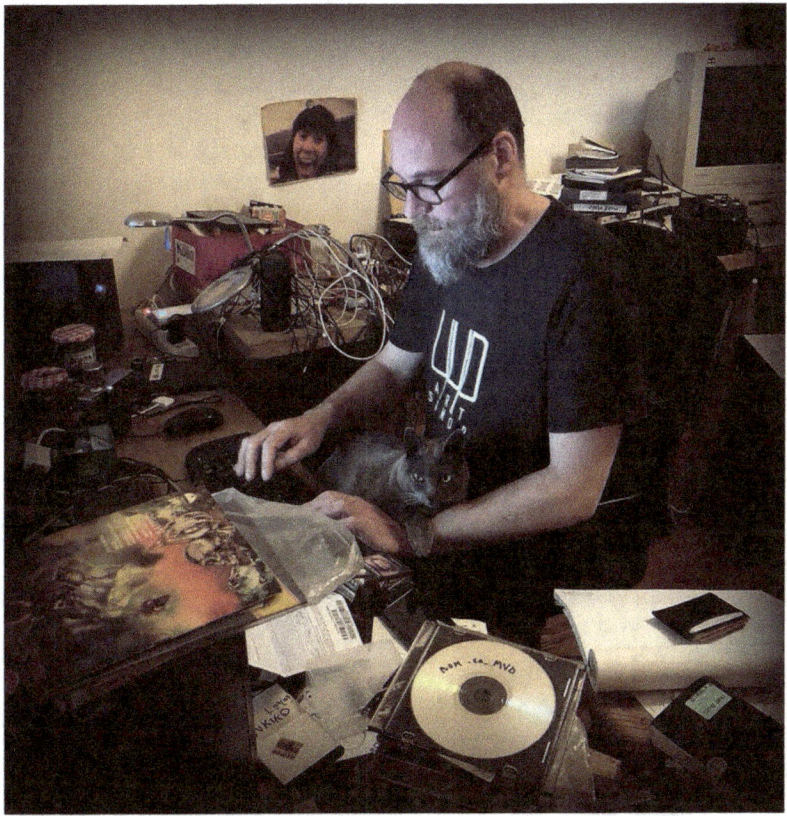

Figure 1: Back at my home studio, with my cat Murmullo (photo by Anita Crescionini.)

During most of 2020, things in Uruguay were rather quiet. The first documented COVID-19 case was on the 13th of March (a Friday the 13th!), and from then on, the main idea that authorities carried on in their discourse was one of 'responsible freedom.' Words that sound very nice if you also develop lots of economic measures for society to take that responsibility. If you don't have the economical means to stay at home or to do teleworking, then you don't have any 'freedom' to take that responsibility. Everything went fine until the cases and the curves started to explode. We managed somehow to have a very low number of cases during most of 2020, missing the first wave (roughly 10/20 cases per day) while being between two countries – Argentina and Brazil – where infection numbers increased exponentially.

It is not clear why this low infection rate in Uruguay happened, but for sure it wasn't because of responsible freedom... Maybe it was because we are a very small country with a very low density of population, or maybe because we were lucky. So, there weren't many measures taken to prepare for the wave to come (which for sure was coming, watching the tendencies around the world). People felt safe. That is over now that we are having peaks of 3,000 people infected per day, and we are very close to having intensive care units saturated. We are count-ing on vaccines that are already arriving, and maybe the lucky timing will help us once again.

I have some anecdotes: the pandemic was declared while I was mounting a fairly ambitious exhibition in Chile: *mundointerior.net*, an exhibition that remixes collections of archives from a 2004 hard disk I have. It is part of a series of multi-format exhibitions that I've been doing in many different forms since 2008, beginning with *The Rotten Machine* from 2008. So, I got stuck there in Santiago. There was a very tight curfew declared and all flights canceled, until the Uruguayan embassy, in collaboration with a religious group that just happened to charter a flight to bring some of their congregation to Uruguay, made it possible for me and for other Uruguayans to come back to Montevideo. It was a super emotive flight: the airport in Santiago de Chile was a desert, all the info billboards still working, showing that all the flights were canceled, it was like an apocalyptic movie... And the trip to the airport from Valparaíso to Santiago was quite an experience. It involved *laissez-passer* documents from my embassy and passing through some rather scary control roadblocks on the route in the middle of the night.

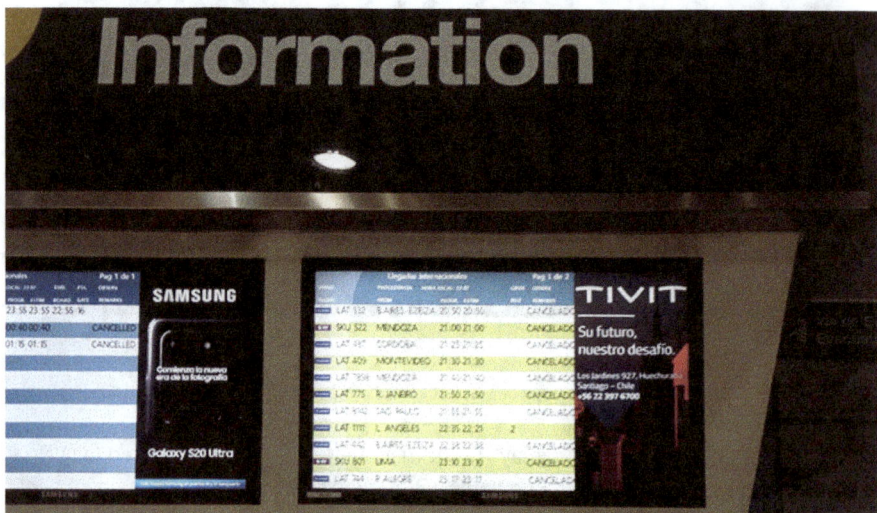

Figure 2: Billboard of canceled flights, Santiago de Chile airport.

Here in Uruguay, the economic situation is terrible. It hasn't fully touched me yet, because I have a formal job at a museum (where I have lots of work nowadays because of the migration of content to online platforms due to the closing of museums). Still, what I earn here is only a small percentage of my normal income, which mostly depends on my artistic practice... This part of my income I practically lost, because my artistic practice mostly depends on being somewhere in person, i.e., at concerts, performances, workshops, talks, etc. But I can't complain. I have friends whose income depends entirely on events and show business: VJs, DJs, producers, also small, one-person companies that lend audio gear or projectors for shows. They are having a very tough time, even having to sell equipment for very low prices to manage to make ends meet. There is lots of anxiety and depression...

As for my own talks, shows, and performances, I managed to carry on with my projects and have a small income through them, though not the usual figures. Institutions pay much less for Zoom participation or online presentations. It works for artists that are in some way inside the academy, institutionalized: they already have their salary, and their participation helps grow their line of research and their CVs. But that doesn't work with artists who are outside of that market.

I managed to make ends meet by cutting all possible extra expenses. Meanwhile, what I did was take the idle time I was left with to document many old works of mine and develop some lines of personal research, taking this economical hiatus as a personal investment.

I finished works that were already half produced and semi-abandoned because of lack of time, and I re-worked some others which were thought of as physical installations for shows online. These re-workings were not only adaptations to online formats; they also involved a lot of thinking about what, how, and why to adapt and/or migrate certain things. I would ask myself whether these adapted works are just as effective in the shape of an online exhibition, or as a video, etc.

They aren't.

My work at the museum includes migrating and adapting content to online platforms, and for this, you need to re-think everything depending on which online platform you choose. Each platform has its strengths and weaknesses, and that generates different targets in ways of communication. So, you need to work with a 'concept umbrella' under which different products are delivered to different platforms. The same content but communicated differently for each platform involves a lot of extra work.

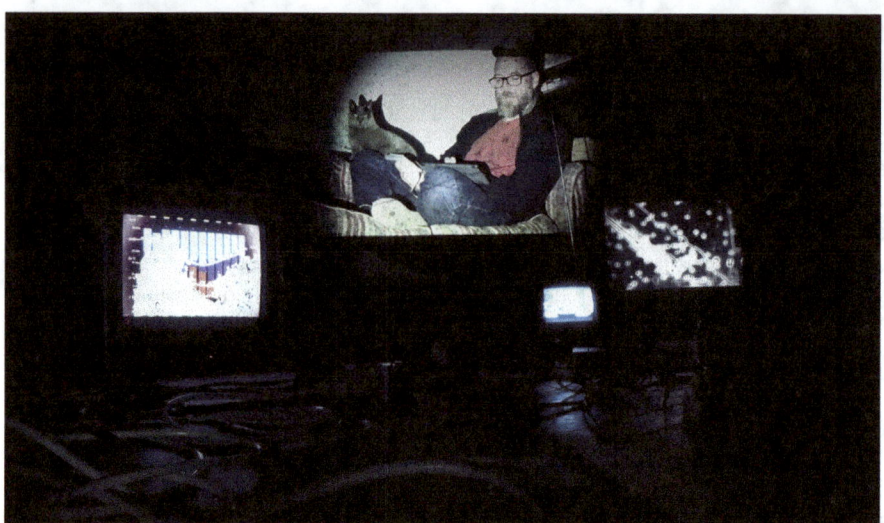

Figure 3: Temporary studio in Valparaiso (with cats Rucio and Koshka)

At first, it looked very promising that everything had to go online. Being part of the old net.art movement, I thought that many new ways of experimenting with the web would arise and shine. I expected that new generations of designers, programmers, entrepreneurs, and artists who grew up already immersed in this physical/virtual world would come up with some revolutionary ideas but in the end, you see that everything is stuck on the idea of the internet as a publishing platform. There are not many visions about what's under the hood. And 'the new' looks a bit like 'the old,' just refurbished.

I didn't have that many problems adapting to teleworking because my line of work always involved being online. What is really stressful is that now everything goes through net connections, and you start to lose track of the difference between what is work and what is not. You need a lot of discipline keeping them separate while at the same time trying to avoid the noise that social networks are constantly delivering. I think the info contamination about COVID-19 was the main thing this last year and it has been very disturbing for everybody. We are living in a very chaotic moment in terms of information, and we have to deal with the sensation social media algorithms create besides social media fragmentation: one of a very pessimistic and unsafe future for the whole world.

At first, I was full of energy to do online events from home: I did talks, presentations, and concerts I prepared as installations with synchronized TV sets. I tried rather complex technical sets. As for my projects, one of my lines of research lately is sonifications, a technique that consists of compositions based on the conversion of data tables to sound. I noticed that although I was already working with healing frequencies and composing sound ambiances for meditation, now everything I do goes in that direction. My art has become more introspective and delves into ways of self-being awareness, involving rituals while producing the sounds. This way of doing things has always been part of my workflow, but it has a strong presence nowadays.

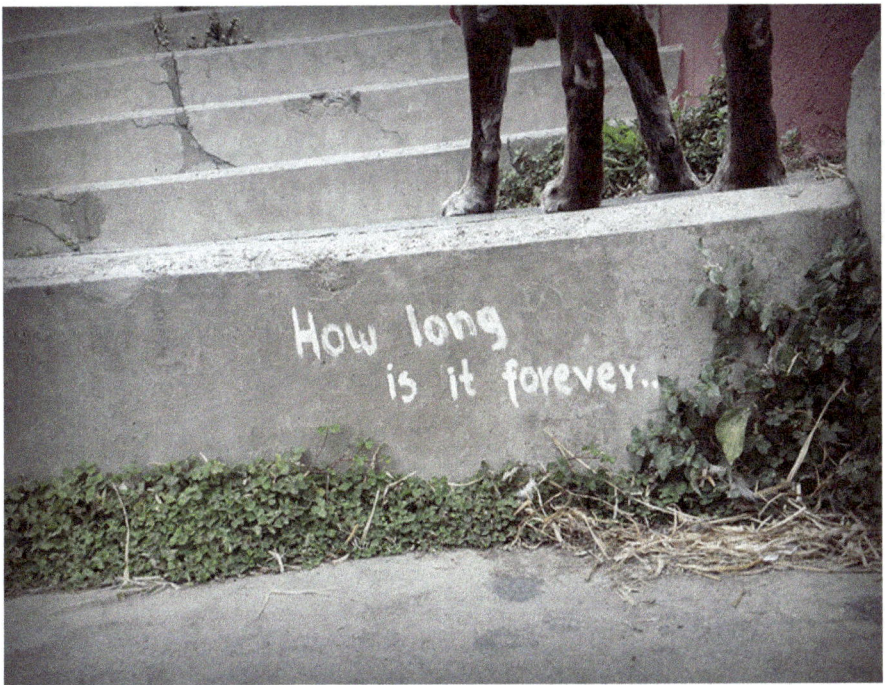

Figure 4: Graffiti in a staircase in Recreo, Valparaiso where I got stuck waiting for a flight to Montevideo.

I feel it's kind of a self-defensive way of trying to keep my sanity in the middle of this huge storm of info contamination. My evolution while coping with confinement and full-day net-working has been from a very extroverted state at first, to an introverted phase these days.

I am vaccinated already, so for me, the virus is not much of a threat, supposedly. My main preoccupation is my mother. She is 92 years old, and although she is healthy, active, and managed to change her gym and Tai Chi sessions and 'girl meetings' to Zoom and online platforms, undoubtedly keeping her safe is my main concern. Even though we are lucky that we continue to live our lives and maintain contacts and activities online, it is not the same.

In these last months, it has become increasingly difficult to focus on my workflow. Mental strain is already showing up in different degrees with people I know and with myself, i.e., lack of focus, difficulty to maintain routines, and to stay self-disciplined in our daily lives. There is too much info-noise.

I try to maintain a routine of daily activities, healthy diet, and exercise routines (mainly Chi Kun and Tai Chi) to keep fit, and that helps a lot, but sometimes it's difficult to maintain a timetable for each activity. It's very easy to lose track of yourself when you are online all the time, in the middle of this hurricane of network meetings, social network notifications, etc.

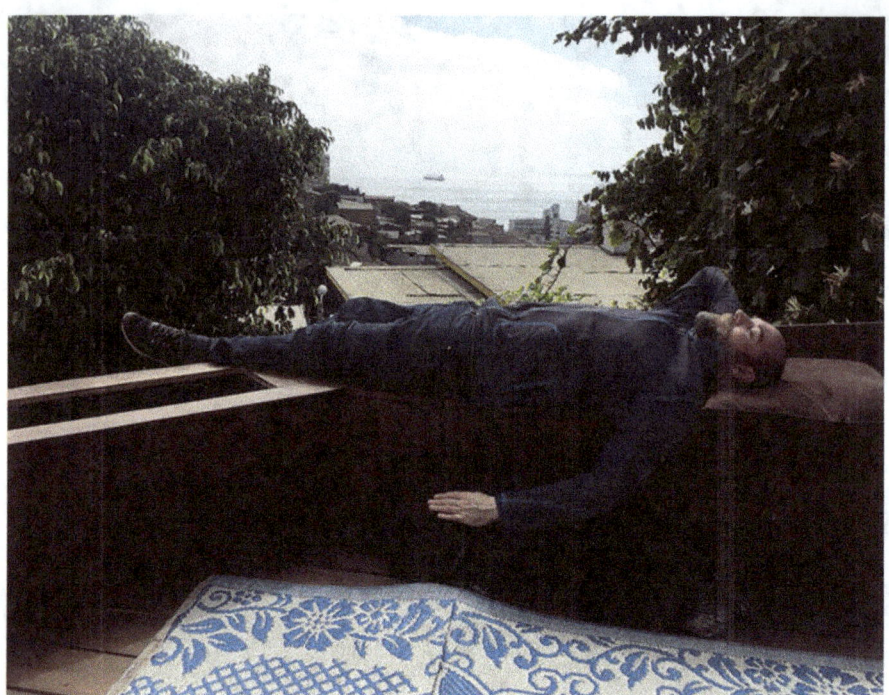

Figure 5: Waiting for flight news in Valparaiso with Rita (photo by Valentina Montero).

Sometimes I fall into a kind of self-indulgence laxity, which develops into a strange and uncomfortable sense of guilt. Sleep regularity also has been a problem lately, although that makes me somehow more aware of my dreams, which I am keeping track of.

I feel that the real threat for me is not the COVID-19 itself, but all the social media construction of chaos, hate, and pessimism derived from this pandemic, the excess of hours spent online, with screens, and the lack of personal, face-to-face contact with others.

MARE TRALLA

It took a lot of work to keep the momentum going and to stay motivated for yet another 'online' action in social media.

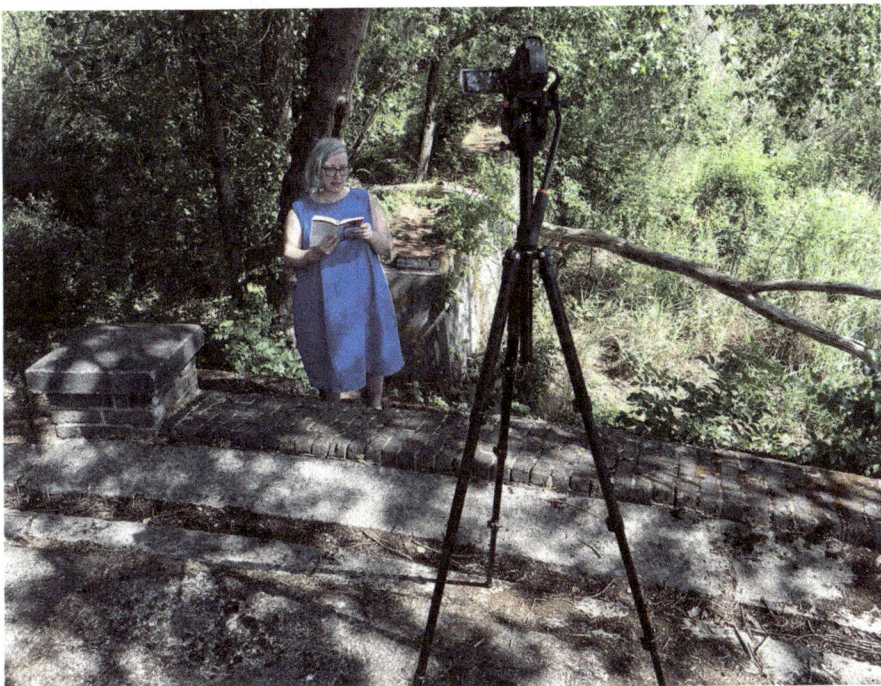

Figure 6: Mare Tralla doing a film shoot in a London park during lockdown, with a one-person film crew.

My professional life connects to two countries: Estonia, where I am from, and the UK, where I have been living for two decades now. And how both countries responded to the pandemic affected me. In Estonia, they went into lockdown very fast and early. I had a few professional trips planned to Estonia that got canceled; this affected my income without getting any compensation. In the UK, they were very slow to react at first. When they finally did, it took a very long time to get any support.

With the first lockdown, everything really seemed to stop at first. The streets were empty and people stayed indoors. I have a few bits of footage we filmed during the first month of lockdown in London and the streets are totally empty, very weird. Later lockdowns were different. At the same time, all the green spaces, where we were allowed for an hour of exercise, were full of people and did not feel safe. During the first lockdown, I felt pretty depressed and found it hard to go out. I essentially locked myself into my house. Having a tiny garden helped a lot, and people in the small street where I live in Finsbury Park were chatting in front gardens while we were doing small spring jobs. I think everyone did a little more in their garden than in previous years. The local neighborhood feeling at that time was pretty much that we are all in this together, and people were very eager to offer help to those who needed it. There is a neighborhood app, which many used extensively at that time. So, the positive side to the pandemic initially was that we saw how kind people in our local neighborhood people are. Still, a lot has changed through the various lockdowns.

How the UK government handled the easing of the corona measures — relaxing the rules for the Christmas holidays, and then afterward introducing an immediate full lockdown — was super hard to deal with mentally. All the later lockdowns were not as total as the first one. Many types of businesses were allowed to keep working. When deciding on which types of businesses can operate, the UK government put profits of rich land and corporation owners first, and the needs of the people last. The fact that construction businesses, including every type of building works and maintenance works, were allowed to continue shows how strong the lobby of these industries is. There has been an enormous amount of house improvements and building projects completed in my neighborhood during the last two lockdowns. These industries are mainly male dominated; areas where more women work, like the service sector, were totally closed down.

Sadly, during the later lockdowns, it looked like there was much more crime in the neighborhood. It would get reported more and more on the app and people seemed to become less trusting and seeing negative everywhere. I think we are all very tired now.

We are seeing an easing of the last lockdown at the moment, but there is nothing gradual about it. As soon as one rule is relaxed, people take it to the extreme. Since Monday, non-essential retail opened and we were allowed to meet up at outdoor venues, including beer gardens and restaurants. On Wednesday evening, I cycled sixteen kilometers across London from South to North, every pub and restaurant on my way was full to the max, it felt like a Friday evening at normal times. Some of us have had our first dose of the vaccine already. I do see how people start relaxing a bit more and feel hopeful that the situation will change permanently for the better.

Personally, I had no money coming in for more than five weeks when the first lockdown happened. I get my income from doing art and cultural projects and also selling some crafts at craft markets, which is also a kind of long-term art project. At the start of the pandemic, a project in Estonia and visiting lectures there immediately got canceled, the market closed here, and I had absolutely no money coming in from anywhere. For the first time in my life, I applied for Universal Credit. It takes five weeks in the UK to get any support from the moment you apply. It took the UK government very long to get any support schemes for self-employed people in place. Even though I have been self-employed as an artist for more than twenty years, I did not qualify for self-employed support, because in the last three years I had made a little more money on contract jobs (various international projects), which were not seen as self-employment. So, I only qualified for Universal Credit. It has been very hard financially.

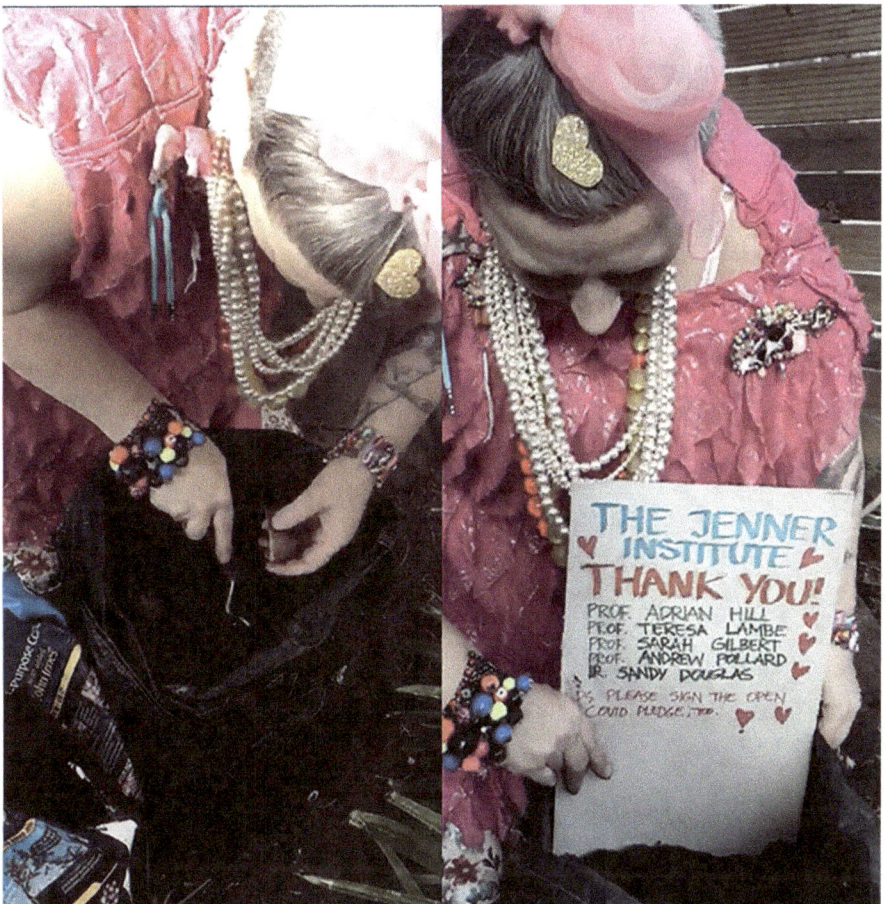

Figure 7: Covid Plants Action, front garden activism, a part of Free the Vaccine campaign. We planted and dedicated plants to COVID-19 vaccine researchers. The images were used on social media. We also sent direct messages to the researchers, thanking for their work and asking them not to sell out to Big Pharma and instead support the pledge for affordable global vaccine access. Here, Mare is planting potatoes for the Jenner Institute researchers, who developed the AstraZeneca vaccine (Lockdown, spring 2020).

More or less all projects for that year got canceled or postponed. Some postponed projects are now happening a year later only virtually, like Zoom events or web exhibitions. Only one exhibition, planned for last year, took place physically. That was in Estonia. I could not travel and had to produce a work that was a simpler, video-based installation instead of fulfilling my initial plan. This way, I did not need to go there. For this work, I had to film performances in the green open spaces of London during lockdown. I could only work with someone who lives in the same house as me. Every time we went to do a film shoot, we were slightly nervous as we were breaking the rules. I could not get a sound engineer to come with us as it was impossible. It was not feasible to rent equipment either. I would have loved the sound to be better in this work, but I am so grateful that I could make it at all.

It has been more challenging with some other projects. Firstly, in recent years I have been involved in a lot of creative activism and community activism. It took a lot of work to keep the momentum going and to stay motivated for yet another 'online' action on social media. WhatsApp and Zoom have ruled my days. I think we took for granted how important meeting in physical space really is for all of us.

Secondly, there is a film being made about me in Estonia commissioned by Estonian TV. It has been weird to do a lot of self-filming and self-reflecting for the film throughout the year because the film crew cannot travel to London, and I cannot travel to Estonia. So, the film will take at least an extra year to finalize.

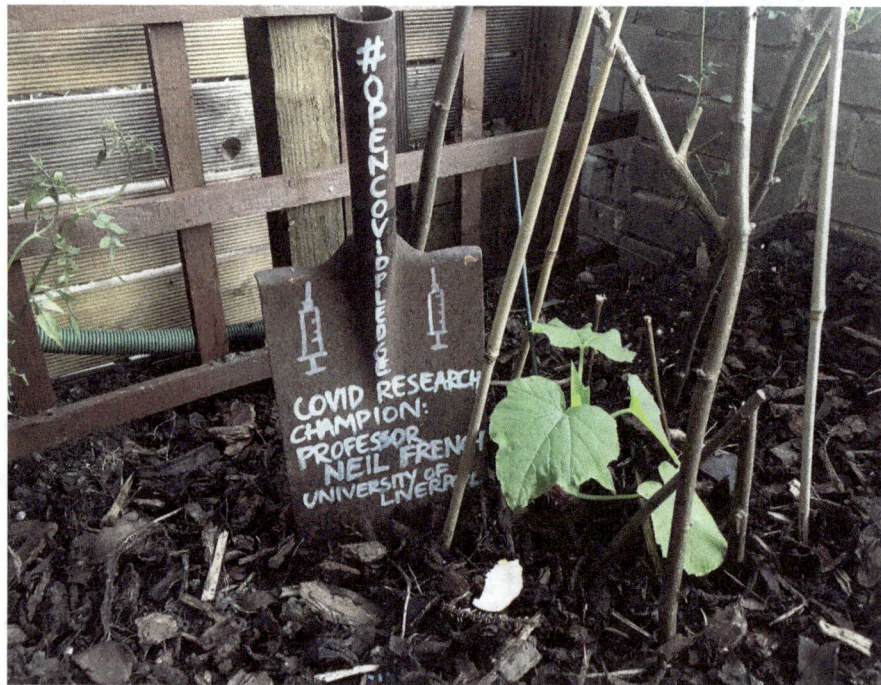

Figure 8: Covid Plants action. Here is a zucchini plant dedicated to a researcher from Liverpool University. It has the hashtag #opencovidpledge on it.

It hasn't been all so negative professionally, though. The pandemic allowed for some time to re-evaluate what I am doing. It also created some new connections, and I have started working through a lot of personal archive materials (videotapes, old files, photos, printed materials, and all sorts). Working with archive materials re-connected me with a few people who make independent media art since the 90s. We are now working on a project together. I also wrote many more art funding applications than in previous years, and I am really pleased that one of them was successful. At least for next year, I have a bit of funding to continue working as an artist.

I have had much more time to think over my creative practice and what I possibly want to do in the future. It could even be that this time has helped me to appreciate my work a bit more and re-energize me creatively. Currently, I am working on a new project, which has been mentally in the making for over twenty years. It took the pandemic to finally force it out of me. I do have to travel to install it in Estonia in July. I feel very apprehensive about traveling though. The trip may still be canceled as both the pandemic and the responses of various governments are unpredictable.

LORNA MILLS

I do know that some artists went through a pandemic paralysis, but my shock over the situation was very short. I'm too aware of my own mortality to waste much time anymore.

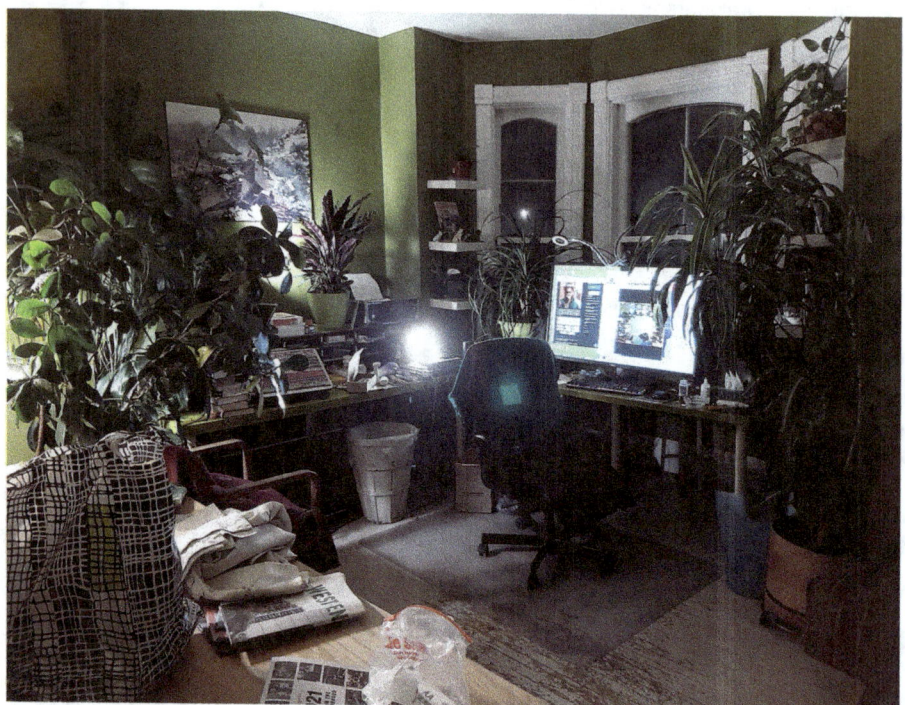

Figure 9: Lorna Mills' studio.

In Canada, a few COVID-19 cases were discovered in January 2020. In Ontario, where I live, the first lockdown started in March. Access to PPE was spotty for health care workers, and an appalling number of infections and deaths unfolded very quickly in Long Term Care institutions, with higher infection numbers and death rates in privately-run LTCs. We are currently in a third/fourth wave of infections and death with our hospital system under a lot of strain.

Before the pandemic hit, I used to host out-of-town artists and entertain a lot of friends. That's gone and I miss it, but it is a small price to pay compared to what so many people have gone through. I am also really a work addict and I thrive on being alone. Friends visit me on my doorstep now and I am still in touch with people around the world online. I have a house in downtown Toronto and my neighbors have been very vigilant about social distancing. I have a 175 lb. [circa. 79 kg] dog, a Neapolitan Mastiff, so I do get out at least three times a day and converse with many strangers since walking him is like walking a unicorn and dating a rock star.

I've always worked from home so there were no changes there. The only change I experienced was in terms of income: next to my art practice I do video editing and related tasks for different clients, and my main client lost most of their commissions. The majority of their work is in education and air travel, which collapsed almost entirely. Luckily, I own my own house; there is no exorbitant rent to pay, and I can do renovations myself. This is one of the things I have started to do since the crisis began. I had some income from art commissions that were already in the pipeline, events that were not canceled but changed to fit the pandemic measures: exhibitions took place outdoors, for example. Also, the Canadian emergency funding for businesses affected by the crisis was a great help.

Gallery shows are on hold, and I don't mind that, though I have been producing work for future real-life (not online) screen-based installations. I do know that some artists went through a pandemic paralysis, but my shock over the situation was very short. I'm too aware of my own mortality to waste much time anymore. I'm also a bit of a Pollyanna, and always hopeful about the future. It is probably a misplaced faith, but it keeps me happy.

Last March, when the pandemic shut down so many art spaces and the internet became the most important means to communicate and produce new art events, I co-curated an online exhibition called 'Well Now, WTF.' It was a direct response to everything shutting down: schools, museums, the whole world seemingly coming to a halt. The other curators were Faith Holland and Wade Wallerstein. The exhibition included over 100 artists, who were entirely free to decide what to show. We received funding from Giffy and later also from the Refraction Festival, an online music festival that took on a part of our exhibition. We decided to give all of the funding to the artists and not to take curator fees. We asked artists to consider waiving a fee if they did not need the money: if they had income from elsewhere, the funding could go to those that really needed it. Many artists responded positively to that and did not ask for fees, which was of course fantastic. We had a PayPal donation button on the site that brought in some money for fees as well. The show became a huge success: the media response to it was surprisingly over the top! I guess it was the right place and the right time.

Next to 'Well Now WTF,' I worked on several shows that were planned ahead of the pandemic. An ISEA 2020 commission I was invited to by the Montreal curator Erandy Vergara before the pandemic hit was adapted to fit the new COVID-19 rules and took place outside. A GIF work I created for this project was displayed on trucks with LED screens. Similarly, one of my animated works was shown on the outside of Kunstlerhaus Bethanien in Berlin as part of Robert Seidel's Phantom Horizons project. Also for a gallery in Berlin, I created stickers for a web project called stick.t.me. This was an online and on-site group show at Panke Gallery curated by the Zentrum für Netzkunst, run by Tereza Havlíková, Paloma Oliveira, Anneliese Ostertag, Tabea Rossol, and Panke gallery director Sakrowski.

I collaborated with the Roehrs & Boetsch Gallery in Zürich on a crypto art advent calendar. Each work was minted as an NFT, meaning it received a unique place on the blockchain. Currently, I am participating in another NFT/hybrid project called 'Pieces of Me,' curated by Kelani Nicole and Wade Wallerstein. (Since NFTs are now the subject of Saturday Night Live skits, I will spare you the details of the latest internet art frenzy.)

My good friend, the brilliant Sally McKay, and I were commissioned for an ongoing Emily H. Tremaine Foundation series, curated by Rea McNamara, to create a web project for Hyperallergic. We ended up with *Boost Presume I'm Gonna Breathe Grieved,* a mixture of scrolling gifs and word salads with a sad, wistful song from the Carpenters.

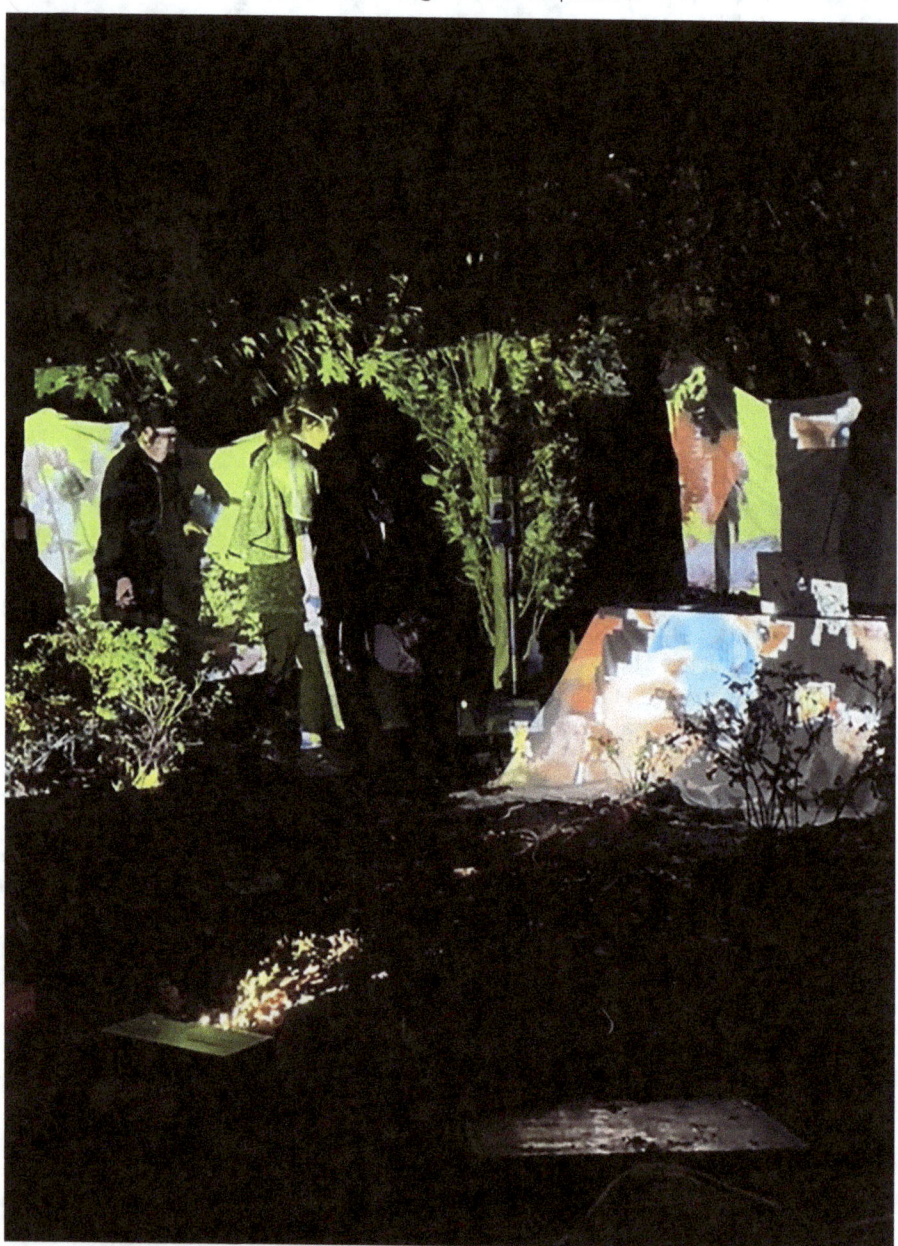

Figure 10: Lorna Mills' collaboration with Kes.

With the exception of 'Well Now WTF,' most of these projects would have happened in a normal year. But there was one more pandemic art project that was very close to my heart: a local collaboration in my neighborhood. At the suggestion of their parent, I collaborated with a 15-year-old neighbor, Kes Lake, who turned out to be a brilliant composer and musician. Over the summer we did three short evening concerts in the park across the street from our homes for neighbors and friends. Kes made music on their laptop, while I projected my GIF works on the surrounding trees. The events were small but absolutely joyful. Malsolm Levy, the curator from the Refraction festival, who had also supported 'Well Now WTF,' included one of the concerts in the festival, and Kes Lake, my teen collaborator, got their first artist fee.

JOHN DUNCAN

Meetings with friends, usually with some specific purpose or project in mind, take on an unspoken undercurrent of joy that I savor, simply because we're in a room together.

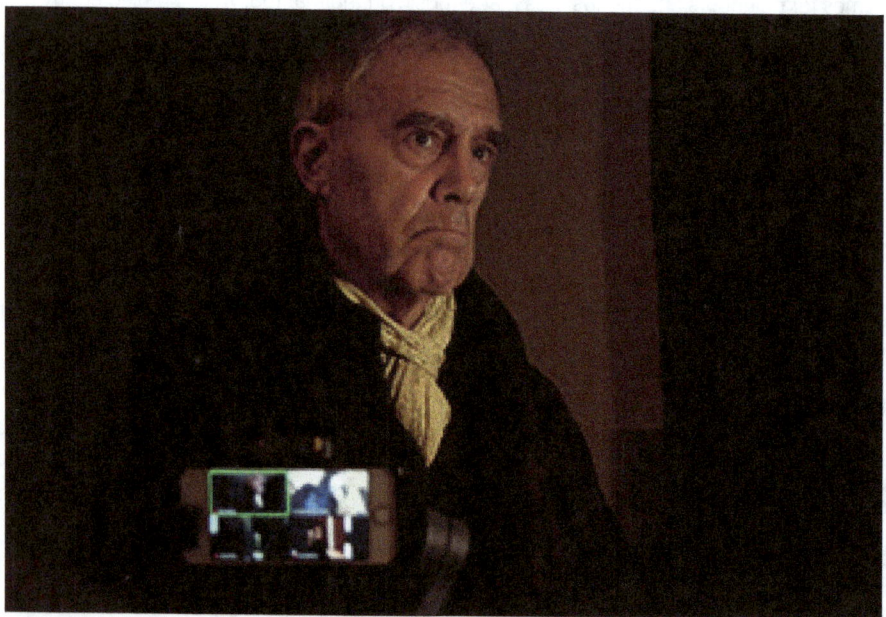

Figure 11: John Duncan as Joe in Samuel Beckett's Eh Joe, produced and directed by Luz Maria Sanchez who also plays Voice. Streamed live from Mexico City and Bologna.

When the lockdown was announced in Italy it was introduced by zones, then provinces, within days of each other; I monitored it carefully and planned the end of projects around it. Then, overnight, the entire country was in full lockdown. Boom. No movement whatsoever without written permission. The day it happened I was furious. Like tapping a click, my entire income was canceled for the foreseeable future. The bills were not, of course. The following day I started smoking again.

Fortunately, supporters were understanding and generous enough to accept making preorders until it became possible to finish the projects that were within days of being ready. Then their incomes became threatened as well.

Then summer arrived. I live in an apartment in a complex of nine, in a remote mountainous area outside Bologna. None of us could work or go anywhere apart from walks in the fields and wilderness around the complex, which turned out to be a luxury. We have long had a practice of helping each other and accepting each other's more eccentric characteristics, which helped a lot as well.

Because we were isolated, we stayed among each other and often did things together. Which also turned out to be a major luxury and a formative learning experience.

Lockdown became a motive for us to rely on each other more than ever, to pay attention to each other's needs and moods and offer help when needed. It also encouraged us to be more conscious of what sort of help was needed and when to offer it. And to accept it. When trips to the supermarket meant waiting in line for up to an hour to be allowed in, we took turns going there with everyone's list, each list kept to a minimum, and the expenses covered in favors returned rather than cash. We visited each other on whims. One couple started holding weekly 'pizza night' gatherings where everyone was welcome. All of that continues now.

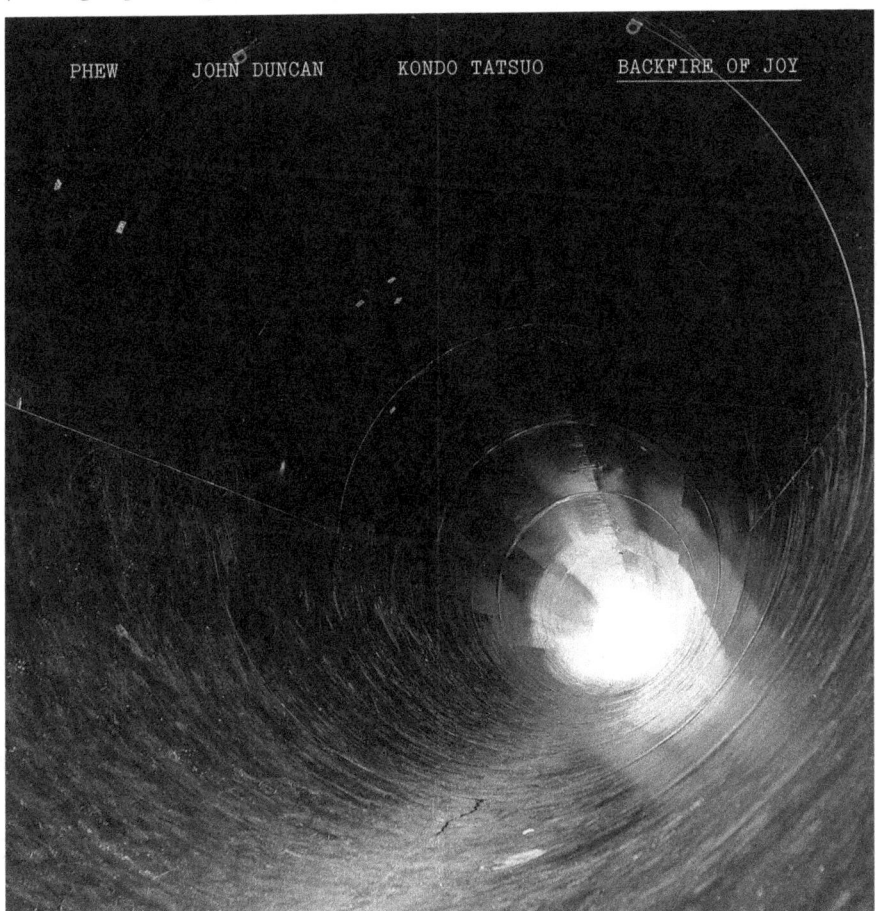

Figure 12: BACKFIRE OF JOY. Phew, John Duncan and Kondo Tatsuo live at Hosei University, Tokyo. Released by Black Truffle.

The conversations, both private and at these weekly gatherings, often become philosophical, with links to books, films, and music. They often end with me thinking about a perspective I hadn't considered or at times imagined. They inspire discussions and private thoughts about community, about the dynamics that explain why this is such a positive aspect of daily life here. Two or three times, we were presented with a situation and asked to decide on it democratically, which always fails. It brought aspects of our characters that sparked irritation in others and was eventually resolved in a way that doesn't involve the group. What does seem to work is looking for ways to show respect, finding a balance between that and doing what each of us wants or needs to do, to avoid stifling one with the other. A part of that is accepting eccentricities within ourselves and each other, and assuming that each of us is a bit mad.

The time routinely given over to income work was devoted to art and research, mainly following up on news reports – especially covering astronomy, aviation, and space exploration – watching and studying films and series of all kinds, often several times, focused on different details. Studying Russian. I jumped at every invitation to record new work, often finished in a day or two. In a few months, music labels and producers I work with started getting so overwhelmed with albums I was sending that they started to lose track.

Daily routines didn't change much. Throughout my adult life, I've been compelled to be stringently frugal. By now, the strategies and regimens for that are familiar territory. So are the ones concerning sleep and eating patterns, satisfying the urge when it comes, regardless of the clock.

One unexpected influence was a result of friends cleaning out their closets. Two friends found recordings of concerts and sessions we'd recorded decades ago that I've always loved and felt they didn't. Both listened to them again and suggested proposing them to labels to release them as LPs. Both projects are at the pressing plant as of a week ago. Cleaning out my closet inspired me to get out the sewing machine and play with scraps, starting with little things, sachets full of lavender, tobacco pouches, growing into clothing for summer based on an expanded caftan design. Now I focus mainly on making artworks: an anarchist banner covered by secondhand panties and boxers sewn onto it inspired by patchwork quilts, and another called *Veneration* that's more along the lines of a Voudoun altar, delta-shaped with a net of secondhand lingerie suspended in front of it in an installation that will probably involve audio as well.

Special limited editions that provided income to cover basic expenses this time a year ago no longer do that, since most of the supporters of my work who ordered them can no longer afford to do so.

Neighbors are kind enough to share vegetables from the garden and get together for occasional meals. Travel is rarely necessary, so a tank of fuel in the car lasts for weeks or months.

Part of the frugality regimen means making art with materials I already have or at least have access to. It often involves exploring an approach that is relatively new to me, spending as near to zero as possible in the process.

Living alone and staying single also helps immensely.

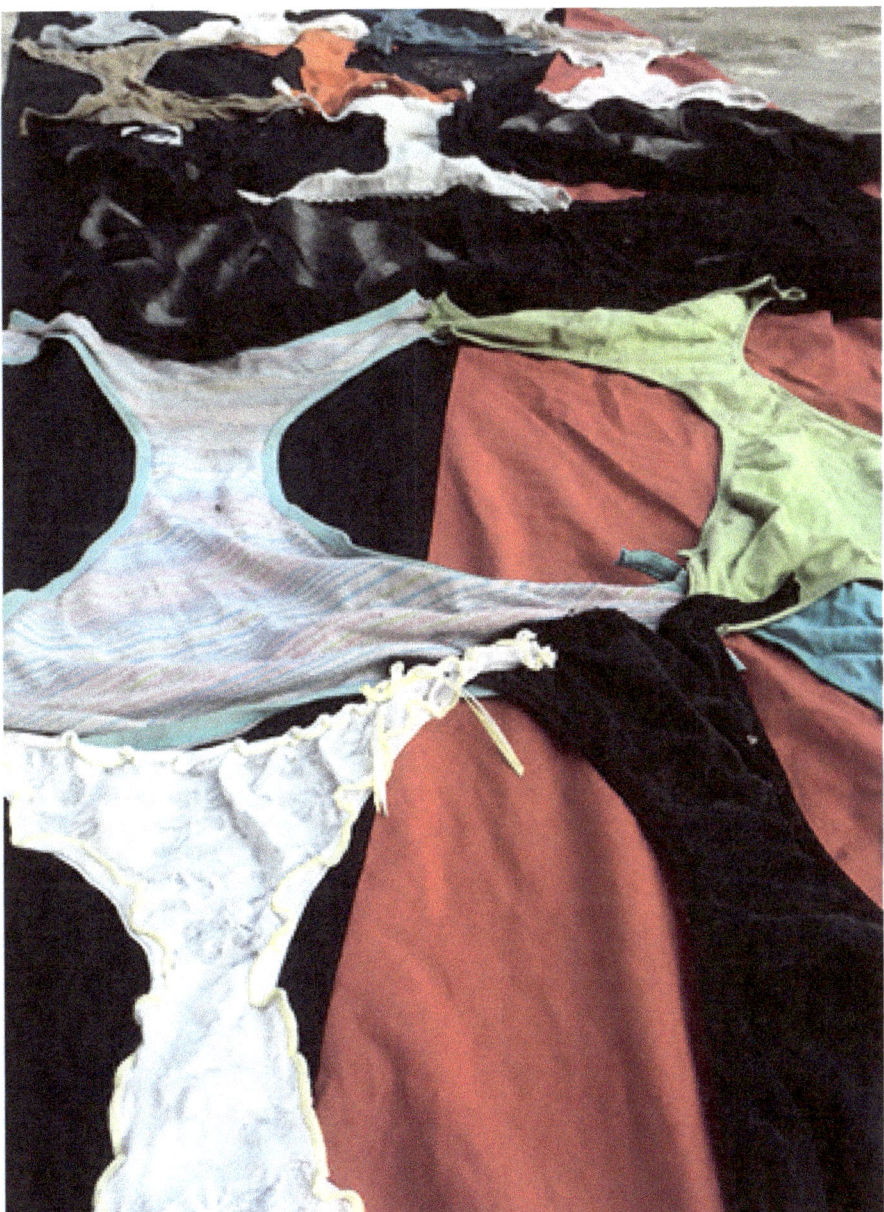

Figure 13: Detail of Patchwork (anarchist flag and secondhand underwear), 2020.

On the topic of how real the COVID-19 threat is to me personally: even before the onset of COVID-19, several close friends had already died from a variety of causes, from cancer and drowning to suicide... Several artists I respected have died from it over the past several months. Life can be finished with you in the snap of a finger.

At this point, the longer I'm alive, the more my time is limited at best. Knowing this leads me in unexpected directions, becoming far more of a positive force than it ever has.

Meetings with friends, usually with some specific purpose or project in mind, take on an unspoken undercurrent of joy that I savor, simply because we're in a room together. I dance more, mainly on my own at home, sometimes inviting neighbors, at the spark of the moment with music blasting. I tend to focus completely on a project nonstop from start to finish, sometimes going without sleep. Ones that depend on a producer to complete have always made me very impatient, exposed to the possibility that I might never see the final result; now that feeling of vulnerability is especially acute. The direction I least expected, sewing, is turning into a sort of zen balancing of that, an aspect I would not have ever imagined.

ARCHANA PRASAD

To be honest, as a woman, it was and is a very trialing time. You have to be present emotionally for everyone who is struggling with this very difficult shift.

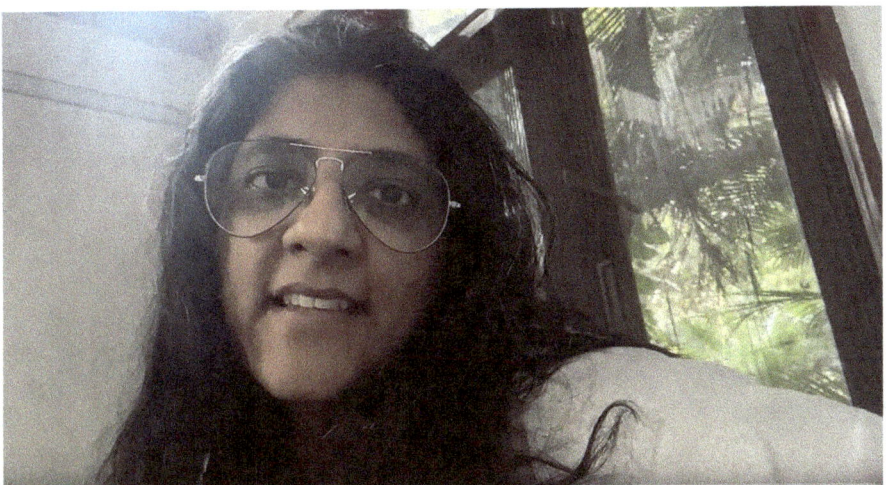

Figure 14: Video interview still, February 2021.

We went into lockdown as a nation in India on the 22nd of March 2020, but my family and I started taking precautionary measures for COVID-19 already in mid-January and early February. Part of my family lives in Seattle, and my partner had traveled back from Seattle via China. This experience made us (my partner, me, and my 6-year-old son) aware of the situation quite early.

On the 4th of March, we had an event as part of the DARA network project that I was supposed to host in Dortmund, Germany. My tickets were booked, and I was about to leave the country on the 1st of March when my son refused to let me go. He is widely traveled and normally does not make a fuss about these things. But he was very distraught and said he was afraid that if I went, he would not see me again. His outburst was so intense that I canceled my flight. My 85-year-old father had just had a minor heart attack at the time as well. I am glad I canceled. Had I gone, I might have been stuck abroad for a couple of months because of the sudden decisions our government took. It was very short notice. People had less than a few hours to prepare for the lockdown. The entire nation went into paralysis.

I think India had one of the most intense, hardcore lockdowns at the time. There was a fair bit of panic and confusion. Since we had been thinking about the looming danger of a possible pandemic for longer, we were well prepared. We live next door to my aging parents, so we made sure that they were well stocked ahead of that announcement. We live in a small house, 650 square feet [circa. 60 m²], and we have a large garden, which proved to be excellent for us. We set it up so that nobody from the outside could come in and none of us could step out.

We ensured we had provisions to last us, and my parents, a month. We set it up so that we could take care of each other. With a good internet connection, work and such was fine. My child's school went online in under a week. It took a while until we had the resources to meet an online school requirement, like a dedicated laptop, something we never envisioned to be necessary so quickly. We found a second-hand one that we could use.

I think, honestly, we were all hit in different ways. My husband is very social, so the lockdown certainly affected him quite deeply. My parents also are very social. My mother runs a traditional silk sari business started by my grandmother, so it is about a 75-year-old business. It is a small boutique she runs from home. It is something she has done all her life, and suddenly she had to stop. It was hard to convince her of the importance of not allowing people to come in. I think it broke something in her. That boutique was her way to be social, to engage with the world, and to contribute to it, designing the beautiful saris she makes... My father is pretty solitary, so he managed to go into lockdown quite gracefully, except that he was due for heart surgery on the 20th of March. It has been postponed for a whole year now.

It is odd: the one thing my parents found difficult to stop was visiting the bank twice a week. For people in that generation, and I did not even know this until COVID-19, going to the bank seems to be an important social and reassuring activity. They go, check their bank balance, talk to the manager... It is a very 'in-person thing.' When they were no longer allowed to do it because of the lockdown and later because we stayed in lockdown mode due to my father's heart condition, I took it on instead.

My husband and I took our work entirely online. This transition was easy for us to do; we were already used to it. We are quite comfortable with that space. For my organization, Jaaga, we had to shut down the co-working. That took a very big hit because we could no longer ask our co-working members to pay. We were afraid we would have to shut it down. 2020 was its tenth year, so that would have been a shame. Several urban art projects had to come to a grinding halt mid-way, and our flagship event, a tech art in public space biennial, had to pivot into an online program for that year.

So, there was a lot of work to do. A lot of online exploration for me, and a lot of work for a six-year-old online. About the latter: I am not convinced that online schooling is the best way for children to learn, but it is better than nothing. And my parents, at that age group of octogenarians, were badly affected. Moving online was something they could not wrap their heads around. They went from being very independent social entrepreneurial people to become quite dependent on us in terms of that groceries would arrive and things like that. To be honest, as a woman, it was and is a very trialing time. You have to be present emotionally for everyone who is struggling with this very difficult shift. You are the primary caregiver to your children, to your parents, to your spouse, so while I had to figure out how my organization would pivot and survive, I also had to make sure all these people around me were cared for, and their needs were met as well.

Since the start of the crisis, I have stepped out into the city maybe ten times. Today, almost a year to the day, the city feels quite normal except that many people wear masks. There has been a lot of road work this last year, I noticed. Roads were dug up, mounds of dirt everywhere, in various neighborhoods across the city. On the street, pedestrians wear masks and drivers keep windows up and masks on; it is mandated by the rules of the state.

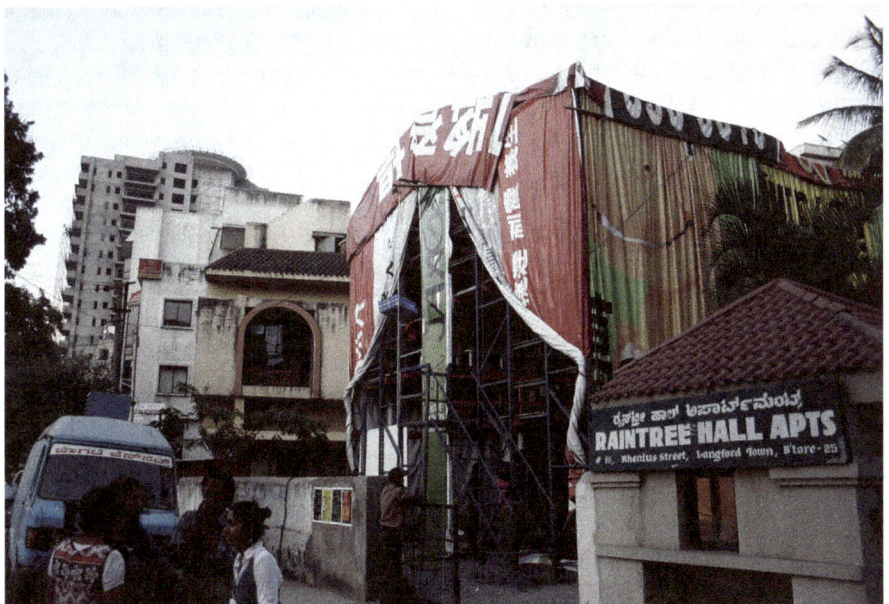

Figure 15: The Jaaga building made of pallet racks. Image source: Wikipedia.

Ten months of lockdown happening on and off, on and off, had its effect on our business. Jaaga consists of two parts: one is commercial and the other non-profit. The commercial side takes care of the tech art in the public space festival *Be Fantastic*, as well as the arts-related practice and workshops in the city. We do a lot of work with communities in public spaces. The for-profit commercial side is a non-profit at heart. We collect membership fees, which enables our members to have a co-working facility and a group of, let's say, 'peer mentors' of about 85 people at any given time. That is the number of seats we have. During the pandemic, over the last ten months, we have reduced our capacity for health and safety reasons to only 35 seats, 40 at most. For the first six months, we ran with about 15 to 20 people who came in. Even the people who came in did not come regularly, or daily as before. They came maybe once a week. It was pretty empty for a long time.

In the last month or two, we saw a large resurgence of people coming back to the co-working space. We still maintain a pretty strict health and hygiene code. People wear masks, there are sanitizers everywhere, and we keep the regulatory distance between seats. People in the private spaces are asked to keep that social distance as well

As a business, we have suffered significant losses. We have had the gracious support of our landlady. Because of her kindness, we have been able to retain our space gracefully and we will probably be able to continue that arm of the organization.

With *Bengaluru Fantastic*, the tech art festival in public space, we did a pivot. Instead of doing a festival with existing work by artists, we rethought the entire thing. With the support of the British Council and Goethe Institute, we were able to run a fellowship program for 23 selected fellows from 168 applicants. The festival was a one-month program. It started with two weeks of active, full day Zoom workshop sessions, in which people, for example, learned to code. Many were new to art and technology. We took them on a journey that allowed them to create projects collaboratively, leveraging some of the most cutting-edge AI tools and techniques. I have to say I am really proud of that pivot. We were able to get German and British people and people from across South Asia to work together in a close, meaningful way. They learned together and then produced eight projects successfully at the end of that period. All of that is online at *befantastic.in*.

It is one of those things the pandemic forced on us all. Otherwise, we wouldn't have pivoted in this way. We did it because the core groups we most wanted to support are creators, designers, and artists. We thought: what can we do with them and for them during such a difficult time? Something my co-founder Kamya Ramachandran and I felt very strongly about was the importance of supporting artists who are eager or curious to learn. Could we support their learning journey and help them create works that can later be showcased in public space? The festival took place in October, and we were able to show the projects to the world. We hosted four amazing dialogues between experts in the fields of technology and art practice and discussed the intersection of art, technology, and society. We had fourteen speakers in total and a great attendance online.

I think my work in particular lent itself very well to moving online. My team worked remotely across the country, North, South, West, and we even worked across time zones. My co-founder had shifted to Singapore, so we worked with her across time zones and somehow managed it. The biggest thing that came out of the pandemic for me, and Jaaga, is the DARA project.

We initially conceptualized DARA as an AI-based chatbot that would help creators and cultural producers find each other across borders of geography, discipline, and time. Through an arts grant from the British Council, we were able to conceptualize and code out this chatbot in 2018. From 2018 to 2020, we saw DARA mainly as an online art project creating a curated network, hosting live events, but always as a chatbot. It could host events, moderate dinner sessions so that dinner conversations are meaningful and valuable to everyone at the table. We finished the code just before the pandemic hit, and then we started to see this online art project as a very interesting online-offline thing!

When the pandemic hit, we got the chance to really think through what we were trying to do. Something that became clear to us was that DARA could be of great value to artists and designers in countries that were very badly hit, like India, where we don't have any state-level support in terms of social security. Artists and designers are among the groups that are certainly struggling. The one thing we could do was help people to connect better, to find each other. We pivoted DARA to become more of a mobile app that is also browser-enabled. We started supporting alumni networks, residencies, fellowships, and colleges, anything that involved creators. Even changemakers and social activists are using it now. It has become a directory of some of the best networks out there. It enables them to share events, projects, and work that they are currently doing, to keep in touch directly with someone, to leverage the value of their networks, and to also be inclusive to people they do not yet know.

We built DARA from April to July and launched it with the South Asian Network for the Arts (SANA), a solid network of cultural managers, producers, leaders, and artists that is run by the Khoj folks in India. It is a fabulous network of about 200 cultural leaders and producers. We launched with them as our first partner, and since then, we've grown from more than ten partners to more than a thousand, with more than 23,000 messages exchanged inside of our network since its inception. DARA went from an art project to a really meaningful service. It has been quite a journey doing that, and it feels needed!

On the 15th of July I fell severely ill. It came very suddenly. I spent a week touching a 104°F temperature [40°C]. It knocked me out for a month and a half. We were in lockdown, so I had to isolate myself from my family and then care for myself because the conditions in India were very scary at the time. Hospitals were overflowing with patients. I did not need to go on a ventilator, so I count myself as one of the lucky ones. But three days ago, I lost vision in my right eye, and though many factors might have led to it, the doctor says some research connects these vision-related issues to COVID-19. So, it is felt in a very real way. Physically, COVID-19 continues to be a very real threat to me. It has also set up some kind of rheumatoid pain in my joints that still hasn't left me after half a year. It is one of the lingering aspects of that sickness that is still with me.

My father has not been able to have his heart surgery. He has a valve that needs replacing, but when it was supposed to happen, the country shut down. After that, we have been too scared to have him go into a hospital. We hope we can take him in this year. He feels he needs the operation now. Luckily the rest of my family seems to have held up well, touch wood. I believe they will be all right if they continue to take on the precautions we have set out for ourselves.

Financially, we have done all right. My husband works in the IT sector. His work hasn't been disrupted at all. Mine has suffered some significant changes, and in some parts, we have under-profited, to put it gently, but we are still lucky.

My mother's store, unfortunately, took a huge hit. We're trying to pivot it into an online store, but a traditional silk sari heirloom boutique is just one of those things that do not move online easily. It takes a significant amount of work and mental juggling to get it there. Over the next few months, we will see whether we succeed.

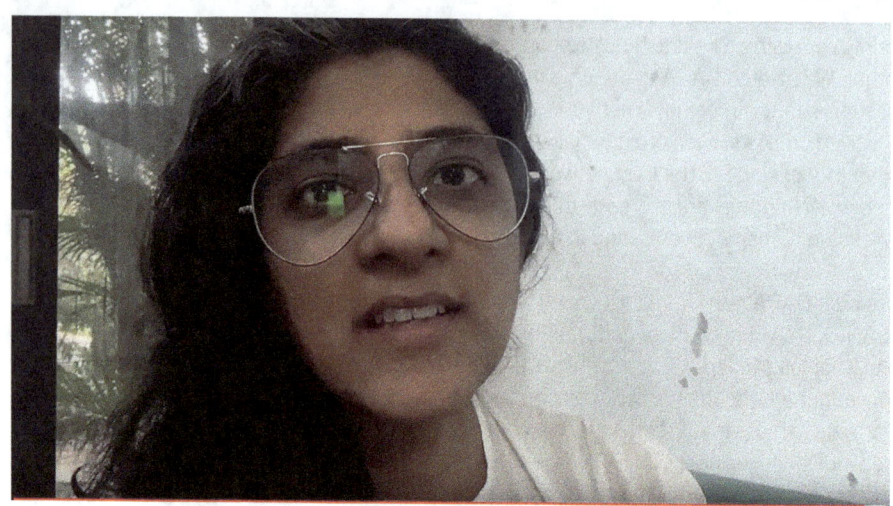

Figure 16: Video interview still, February 2021.

!MEDIENGRUPPE BITNIK

There have been incredibly unfair strains put on artists by the institutions that should be protecting them.

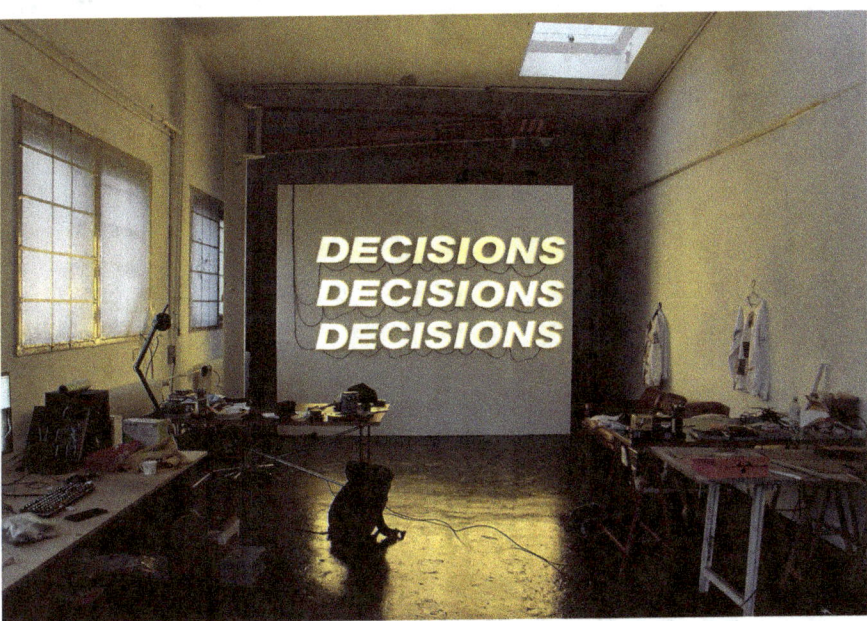

Figure 17: Production shot 'Decisions, Decisions, Decisions,' studio !Mediengruppe Bitnik, Berlin, 2020.

We are based in Berlin, Germany, and perceived the early response from the authorities to the pandemic as adequate and well-thought-out. Doma and I were actually waiting for everything to shut down all through February. In January, we started work on the show *crypto_manifold* with the team at Chronus Art Center in Shanghai. It was originally planned to open in March 2020. So, over the course of many video calls, we saw how the team at Chronus Art Center started working from home and then how all of Shanghai went into full lockdown at the end of January. It was eerie to watch how such a vibrant city came to a full stop. We had little doubt that the pandemic would hit us too, and so for the first time in our lives, we stocked up on food and other essentials.

Here in Berlin, the cultural field came to a full stop last year and has had a very stop-and-go existence ever since. Planning is hard. Travel is impossible. All the shows and public events we had planned for last spring and summer were either canceled or postponed. Some have since been able to happen, many have not. Never knowing whether the work we were struggling to realize under difficult conditions was actually going to be shown has been demotivating.

But at least we realized some of the projects we planned, and got paid for them. Because that's the crazy thing: as artists, we only get paid for commissions, shows, talks once we have realized them.

When everything got canceled last year, I think it left a lot of us with unfinished work or work that we had finished but couldn't show. Many times this meant that we would not get paid.

As artists based in Berlin, we were lucky that the state has come to the rescue with several direct subsidies for artists and institutions. Already by May 2020, the city of Berlin had paid €4,000 financial aid to every artist who needed it. Having a guest professorship at an art academy here in Germany, we did not need to apply. But many artists are still struggling. And there have been incredibly unfair strains put on artists by the institutions that should be protecting them. There have been reports of the Artists' Social Security and Welfare Fund called 'Künstlersozialkasse' excluding artists during the pandemic. The fund made claims that the artists excluded were no longer artists because they had taken on temporary jobs outside the art field to support themselves when their incomes dropped. Suddenly, they were no longer considered 'professional' artists. They not only lost their status as artists, but they also had to now shoulder much higher social security costs outside the fund. These cases seem like a bad joke when the fund should be lobbying for the cultural field instead.

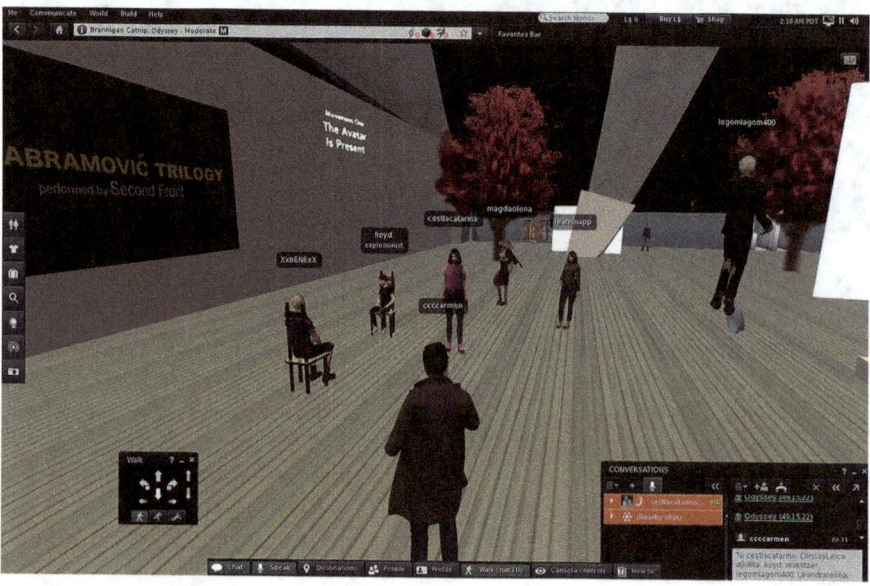

Figure 18: Klasse Brenner, class meeting in Second Life, Stuttgart State Academy of Art and Design (ABK Stuttgart) where !Mediengruppe Bitnik taught as guest professors in 2019/2020.

It looks like we all urgently need to step up our lobbying game. The artists, the clubs, musicians, DJs, theatre people. While the car industry, airports, the airlines were all supported because they are central to the economy, our field was only partly supported. Museums and non-commercial art spaces in Germany were classified as leisure, not education, and have been closed for much longer than the commercial galleries, which were classified as businesses. Financially, we are lucky, as the pandemic measures did not affect us too gravely. We have been very fortunate to have teaching positions throughout most of the pandemic. This means that financially we did not have to depend entirely on commissions and exhibition fees.

What has affected us personally most, though, was the closing of schools. We have an eleven-year-old son. Since March 2020, except a few weeks in autumn, he has been at home for most of the year. The teachers have done an admirable job of keeping the kids interested. But even so, it is hard and studio time is rare. Nevertheless, we have also been lucky in that being a couple, we can accommodate our art production, online teaching, and our son's schooling needs quite well between us.

In our view, the pandemic heightened interest in digital and networked practices within the arts. We sold two larger works into public art collections last year. We do believe that the pandemic helped direct these institutions' attention to internet-based art.

The pandemic helped inspire a proposal for a research project. The project looks at the ambiguity of data. We look at how the underlying data used for data-driven analysis and decision-making does not necessarily produce a reliable view of the world. Data is often murky, full of bias, the output of opaque black boxes. We want to think about how we can find ways of describing and working with the inherent ambiguity of data. Our part in the project will be called 'Unreal Data' and specifically investigates how data produces new realities.

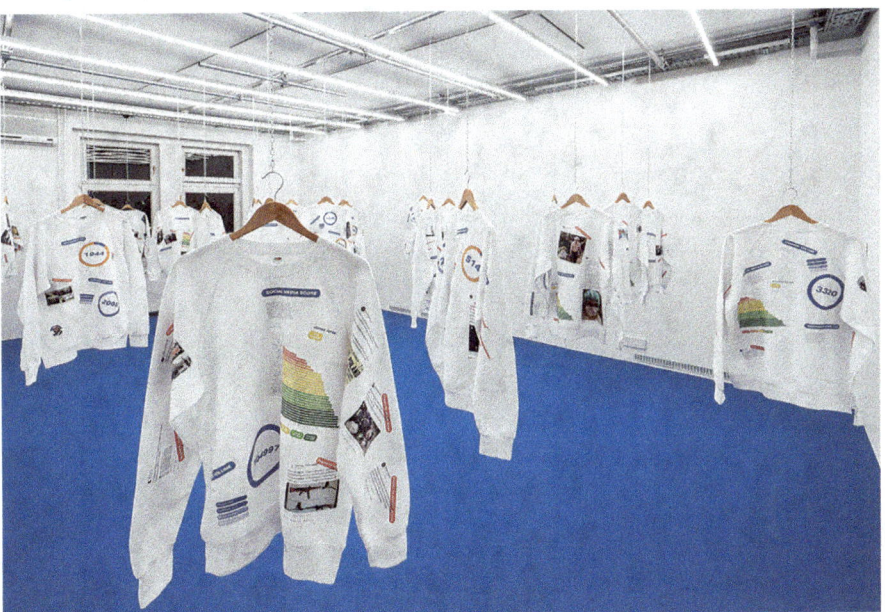

Figure 19: !Mediengruppe Bitnik, Flagged for Political Speech, exhibition view Delta Lab Rijeka, 2020. Photo credits: Tanja Kanazir/Drugo More.

Last autumn, we handed in a proposal, and a few days ago received the news that the research project is approved. So, starting next September, we will get to work with an incredible team of artists, a media theoretician, and a data scientist on these questions that have also become so relevant during the pandemic. Cu in 3 years. <3

JENNIFER KANARY

We are a non-profit, so lost income equals no food on the table.

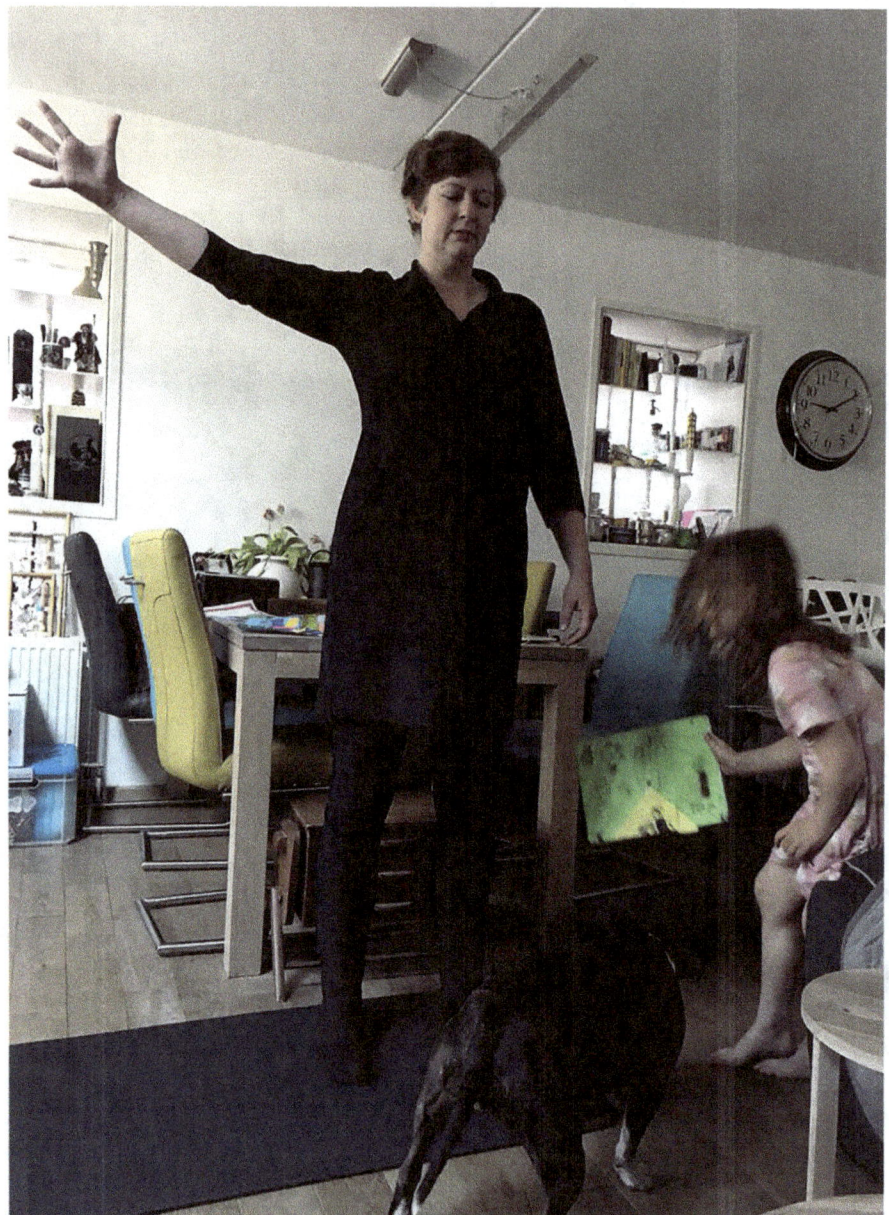

Figure 20: Jennifer Kanary tries to do yoga next to homeschooling during lockdown.

On the 22nd of February, I still had a care-free dinner at the Eye in Amsterdam followed by a movie with a friend. Rumors about COVID-19 had been in the news for some time. On the 27th, the first official contamination was reported in the Netherlands. On the 28th, there was a Ph.D. presentation that I wanted to attend in the De Waag Society. I remember very well that I was already considering whether or not to attend, and also asked my intern if she still felt comfortable coming. I remember I already washed my hands more often. It felt as if the government took it seriously, but that most people still laughed about it and thought it was all exaggerated. Of course, I took the journalists and scientists seriously. I also remember that on my way to De Waag there was a tourist in the streetcar (part of a group with suitcases) who sneezed very wetly at a short distance from me in this crammed space and did not cover his mouth. That this not only unsanitary but also already triggered the thought of 'corona' in me. On the 29th of February, I told a colleague that my body was fighting against something. It wouldn't, would it?

On the 9th of March, I received word from a new colleague that she was not coming to work and that she would be going into lockdown. She returned from a ski vacation in Trentino that day. It wasn't a high-risk area, but because infections were happening so fast, she was cautious. March the 12th, I received word that they fell ill, so they were tested for corona. March the 13th, they had the result: positive. That is when it came very close.

On the 13th of March, our daughter turned six. We deliberated with other parents via Whatsapp whether or not to go through with the birthday party. There would be a celebration in an indoor playground. There was a limitation of 100 visitors per day at the time. This indoor playground was small and only had a capacity of 60 visitors per day. Since the children were still playing with each other in class in the morning, we argued that they could still play together in the afternoon. The kids had a great time but did find it odd that I stayed away from them and that they had to wash their hands so often. We cancelled all friends and family visits for Saturday and Sunday just to be safe. That same evening I felt weak. I thought I was just tired from the party...

The next day was Saturday. I had flu symptoms, muscle aches, fatigue, and a fever. On Sunday, the government decided that schools would close. I seemed to be all-better on Sunday, but later unfortunately the virus struck me down hard. You couldn't get a test back then in the Netherlands if you didn't have a fever. I did not suspect it was COVID-19 until my smell and taste changed. First, everything tasted like smoke or metal, and then I lost my sense of smell and taste completely, even though I didn't have a stuffy nose. There was some speculation about smell and taste loss as a symptom on the internet, and my colleague reported to me that she had experienced it too.

My doctor confirmed it. For five weeks, I suffered from prolonged severe fatigue, nausea, occasional headaches (to gag from), severe muscle pain in my neck and shoulder blades, and cold chills. I took a hot bath four times a day because one moment I couldn't get warm under two blankets, and then I had hot flashes again.

Later, I developed shortness of breath when walking to another room. These symptoms are still listed under 'mild infection!' I sometimes wonder if it was that tourist...

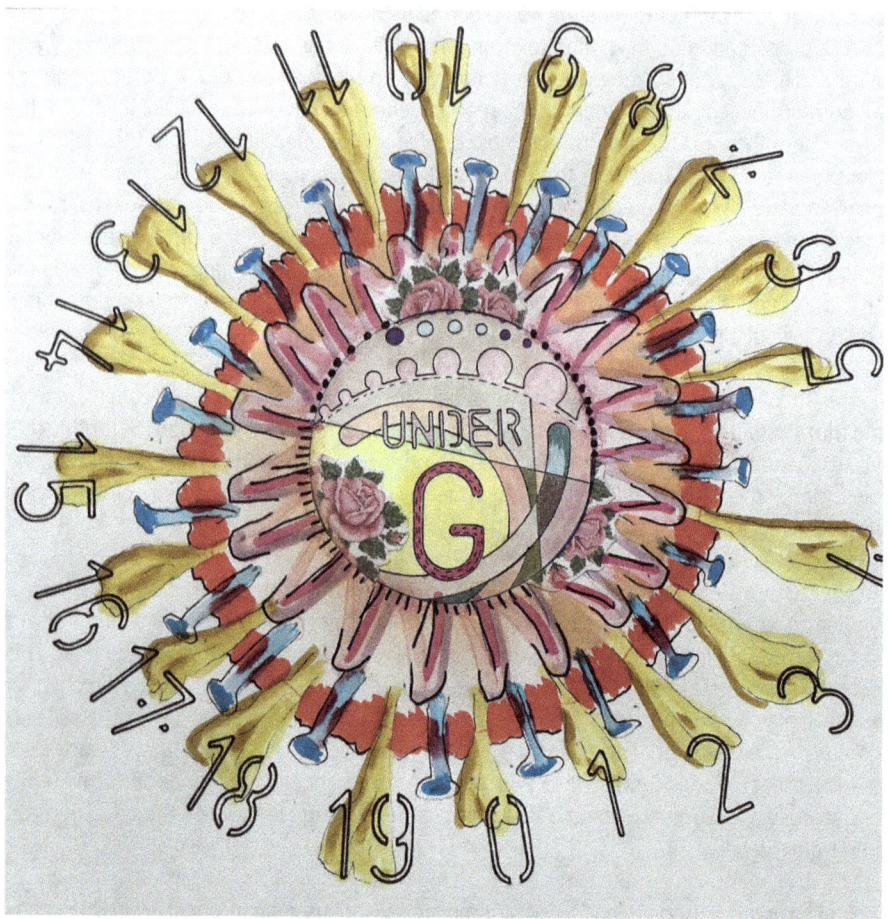

Figure 21: Jennifer Kanary, Drawing of the COVID-19 virus.

My husband had fewer symptoms and recovered faster, while our daughter didn't seem to be affected by it at all. Fortunately, we did not infect anyone as far as we know. We had plenty of food stock, and we were already in a self-imposed 'lockdown.'

My husband and I are both artists. We earn(ed) our money by giving workshops with one of my projects: *Labyrinth Psychotica*, a VR environment through which people learn to understand how someone with psychosis might experience the world. On the 11th of March, hubby gave the last workshop with one of our teams at the Zaans Justice Center. After that everything was canceled/shifted. We are a non-profit, so lost income equals no food on the table. That was a stressful idea. Fortunately, on the 4th of March, I had already made agreements with our clients that if the Netherlands also went into lockdown, they would give a 50% downpayment. Almost everyone agreed. With that money, we could stay afloat, although it was not ideal to live on borrowed money from the future. The worst part was that many of the freelancers who worked for us, most of them artists, suddenly had a drop in income, and the colleague who was just about to start had no more work (we hire self-employed people). It was also sad for our intern master student from the Vrije Universiteit, who had just started. She had to adapt her research to the new situation and also had to graduate from home.

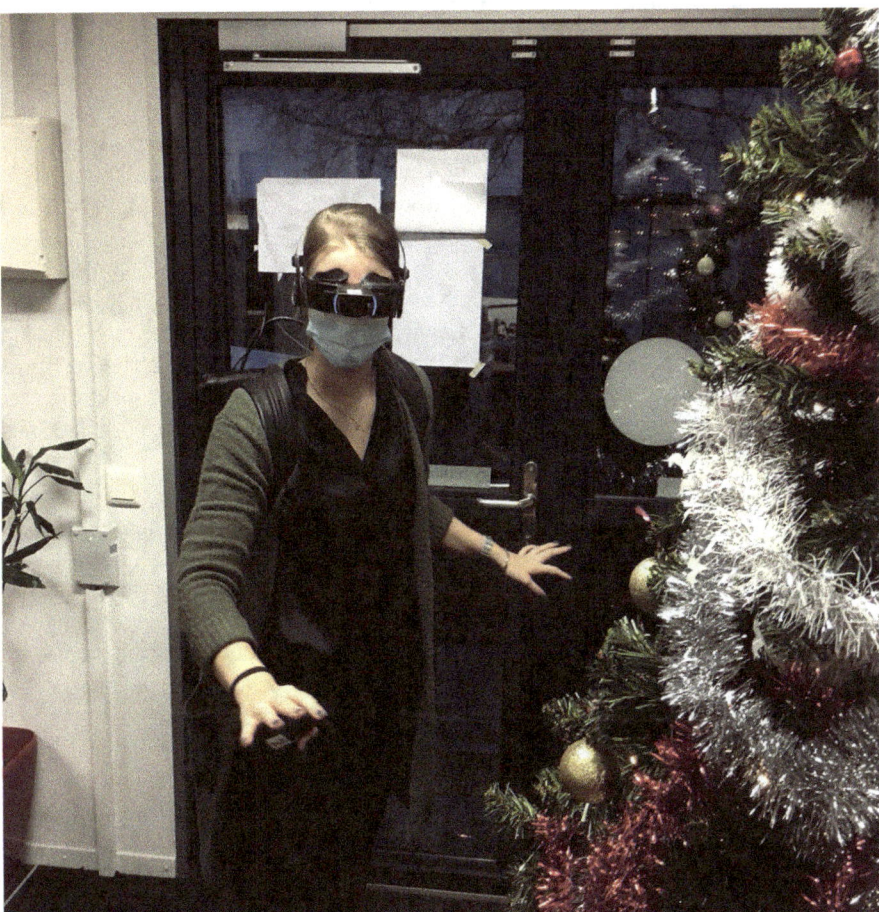

Figure 22: Labyrinth Psychotica VR workshop at a GGZ (mental care facility) just before the second lock-down.

I was mostly dealing with all the cancellations/shifts. Combined with the red tape, homeschooling, and uncertainty, it was not an easy time. I was also working on setting up a foundation. Stichting Doen promised us money, but we would only actually receive it if we had our own foundation. We succeeded in creating a foundation on the 1st of April 2020. After overcoming several other challenges, a new project could begin, giving us income for three months. Things started to look up again. My husband got a well-paid job. After a small setback, I was almost myself again in July, just in time to enjoy a camping vacation in France.

Unfortunately, my husband's job was unexpectedly terminated when we returned. Because of COVID-19, there were fewer assignments. He had joined the company as a self-employed worker but was no longer needed. I had a major relapse in the fall; ten days of temperature and fever, four weeks of metal taste. Fatigue and shortness of breath were back. I also developed palpitations. However, the COVID-19 test came back negative. Now, in April 2021, I have almost recovered from the shortness of breath. Long-haul, or 'long Covid,' they call it. The virus is present in your body and regularly disrupts your immune system if you push yourself too much. You get symptoms again, such as inflammation, or the headache suddenly comes back (feels like a very bad hangover). Not knowing what your body will do next makes you feel insecure. I had and still have a lot of reassurance from the support group on Facebook. It is nice to know that you are not alone with this unpredictable virus. Other than that, it's doable for us and we should count ourselves lucky. Other 'long-haulers' still can't walk 100 meters after a year.

'Brain fog' is strange; memory loss and saying weird words. When my markers fall, I say the tape fell. Or I find myself in the bathroom to warm up my coffee in the microwave or telling my daughter to put toothpaste on her toilet brush and that I'll come and brush her teeth in a minute. Oh, and, for example, putting my daughter's vitamin in my husband's mouth and not understanding why he looks at me puzzled... We have a good laugh about it, but sometimes it's scary too.

Walked too long? In that case, I might get a fever that afternoon, which can subside after an hour. In the evening you can feel fine again. Because I can't get much exercise, I have gained 10 kilos. That makes you feel even worse. But it's going reasonably well now. On and off, you have to find your balance again. Being a self-employed person brings a lot of uncertainty with it, but also a lot of flexibility. You can work when you can and take a break when you need it. And so life just ripples on. The work we continue to do has a social impact. It helps people deliver better support in care positions. I have been thinking about how we could offer our valuable service in a different way. When I was suspected to have COVID-19, and I was glued to the couch because of fatigue and shortness of breath, I finally had time to elaborate on a theory I had been working on for a while, but which I had not yet developed into an article. My body was weak with corona, but my mind (if not for the headache) was sharp. I felt so much uncertainty because my breathing became more and more difficult. In retrospect quite silly perhaps, but I felt the urge to leave something behind, just in case... With about ten people as co-readers and advisors, a path from the past to the future unfolded.

My theory is inspired by a traumatic personal event. After the death of my sister-in-law in a state of psychosis, I began to explore her subjective experiences. I learned that little research existed on such experiences and that I was not the only one who wanted to know more about them. Through close study of several subjective experience stories, I discovered a pattern, a common thread that potentially connects these at times conflicting stories. An awareness of this pattern might support early recognition and prevention of psychosis, and thus it could also prevent much suffering and expense.

The article I wrote about it was well-received, and it even got translated into Hebrew. As a result, I was allowed to submit a professional publication to the ISPS, the International Society for Psychological and Social Approaches to Psychosis.

I was also invited to apply the theory in an educational project for third-year care students (Minor Misunderstood Behavior) and art students (Minor Art and Interaction) in collaboration with care professional and educator Xiomara Vado Soto. It was exciting to teach in this strange time. I have great respect and admiration for all students who have to study under the current conditions of the pandemic. The results of the collaboration between the art and care students of Hogeschool van Amsterdam and Avans St Joost were impressive. Xiomara and I were allowed to develop a new project for second-year HvA healthcare students based on this same theory. It is an honor to see a hypothesis that arose from autoethnographic artistic research tested in practice with student cases. Following this, a lasting collaboration has now developed between us, and we are working on a new educational pitch involving imagination, connection, and empathy in healthcare. This project would not have happened without COVID-19.

Through a combination of teaching, a bit of funding, an occasional workshop assignment, a new temporary job for my husband in construction in November, and being frugal, we have managed. As an artist, you already live in uncertainty, but usually, it is 3-6 months ahead. Now we often do not know where the money will be coming from in 2-3 weeks. That causes a lot of stress.

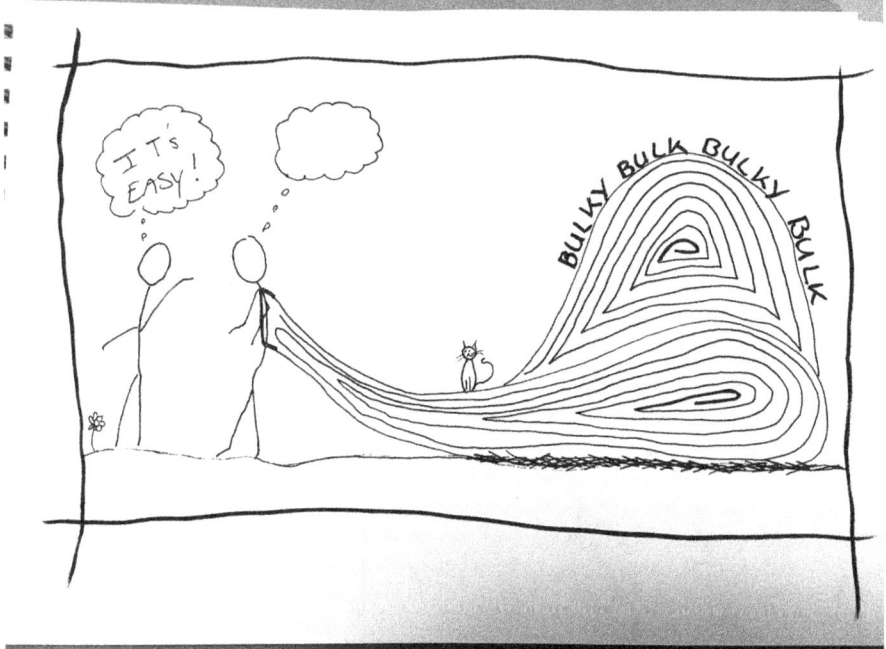

Figure 23: Jennifer Kanary drawing made for INKTOBER 2020; Trying to be normal.

We were not eligible for government schemes such as the TOZO support measure because our customers paid a deposit and a subsidy had been received (which counts as profit from business). You could receive a TOZO only if you had no turnover. Apart from that, you received a maximum of €1,500 per family. That is half of what we need as a family and as a business to make ends meet. A third measure, TVL (compensation for fixed costs) was used for people who had lost turnover in the past year. Thanks to our membership of a contemporary artist alliance called platform BK, we found out this existed, and fortunately, we received the money. It was not much, but it gave us a month to go. In retrospect, sometimes I don't even remember how we made ends meet.

Because our normal activities came to a standstill, there was time to pick up other precious projects. For this, we submitted a corona-support application to the Mondriaan Fund, twenty minutes before the deadline in 2020. Fingers crossed that we receive Mondriaan support! It is still precarious for us. My husband has been out of work for two weeks now (construction has stopped), and income taxes are coming. Health care premiums have to be paid and more, but it will be alright. Our work is picking up – bookings for after the summer are coming in again. We assume that thanks to the vaccinations, these can now go ahead. Almost everyone faces challenges in these times. Fortunately, support comes in many forms.

Although there were times when I felt I would collapse, there were also very nice moments. I must say that I had a lot of support from my THNK School of Creative Leadership network. They were an inspiration in how to translate the magic of human interaction into an online experience when they had lost all patronage themselves. At the same time, they organized and facilitated meetings where we could support each other. Stichting Doen also gave a lot of support in the form of a coaching budget for artists who are also social entrepreneurs and who had previously received a grant from them. With that, I also felt privilege and deep gratitude. It helped me deal with stress.

Further, it was very memorable, even though we have been together for twenty-three years, to be so intimately together as a family. To witness our daughter learning to read and write was impressive during homeschooling. I won't forget that easily. So there was a lot of happiness too, while so many others had to go on without human touch and deal with much more uncertainty or insecurity.

SACHIKO HAYASHI

I was accused of being a right-wing populist by a couple of my oldest Swedish friends when I criticized Sweden's COVID-19 policy on Facebook. As a person of color with a political view definitely toward the left, I found this incident to be not only outrageous but also unfathomably absurd.

Figure 24: Sachiko Hayashi performing her motion controlled audio-visual work 'Still Untitled' (2018) Photo: Emanuel Schütt.

Sweden, my country of residence, went for natural herd immunity. The choice was made quite early, and whereas the other two countries that made similar decisions in Europe, the Netherlands and the UK, later reversed their strategies, Sweden did not. With a loose recommendation for social distancing, we continued with the strategy to spread the virus naturally, while our government and other institutions in charge presupposed a certain amount of death tolls.

A notable characteristic of the Swedish strategy was also the denial of scientific findings of the novel coronavirus and its disease. In a much similar manner to Trump supporters, they accepted neither WHO's nor other international institutions' medical consensuses. The only, nonetheless considerable, difference from the U.S. was that the Swedish counterparts didn't come from the right but the left of the political spectrum. This was probably because we currently have a center-left government, but it also made the Swedish circumstance even more unique.

The Swedish COVID-19 strategy has resulted in two disastrous consequences:

1. Once the virus spread to the homes of the elderly, the residents there who fell ill during this period were given palliative care by administering morphine instead of proper COVID-19 treatments. This was carried out without consent from the patients or their relatives, some even without any real-life consultations with their doctors. Various decision-making bodies involved in the process all claim that they were following the guidelines from the Ministry of Health and Social Affairs to prevent intensive care units from overcrowding. However, there was no shortage of ICU beds in Sweden at the time this was going on. In fact, the extra facility set up in Stockholm to cope with the demand for more hospital beds and equipment was never used. We simply prioritized other age groups. In my eyes, this was euthanasia of the elderly administered by our society.

2. As much of the rest of the world condemned natural herd immunity as a COVID-19 strategy and watched the Swedish experiment with horror, it brought out a detestable nationalism in many Swedes, especially in the left, who felt obliged to defend the decision of their public authorities. With a nasty display of national chauvinism, those who supported the Swedish strategy launched verbal attacks on us others who didn't, bullying some in public by way of ridicule and mockery, and dismissing the opposing opinions simply by labeling the individuals as 'traitors' to a certain political ideology or even to the country itself. The issue grew exceedingly politicized and ultimately transformed into a question of social identity and loyalty. The way the Swedish authorities handled this pandemic became a highly inflammatory and extremely divisive social issue.

Although the pandemic inarguably brought certain inconveniences in my daily life, my feeling of isolation didn't derive from public regulations such as social distancing (we never had any lockdowns). Instead, it originated from the undeniable feeling that because the Swedish condition was so unique, people outside of Sweden won't be able to relate to what we were going through here. That was, and still is, my isolation during the pandemic.

Currently, the political game around the issue of this pandemic continues. As late as the 9th of February this year, the state-funded public broadcaster Sveriges Radio (Sweden's Radio) reported on a certain private Facebook group whose intention was to challenge the 'unscientif-icness' of the Swedish coronavirus pandemic response. Many of its ca. 200 members are academics, scientists, and concerned parents (i.e., far from the militant and conspiracy-driven Trump supporters). However, the report vilified them as destructionists of Sweden's interests and reputation, whose inclination to secrecy, i.e., their closed Facebook group, as well as their proneness to conducting discussions in English instead of Swedish – an indication there are many foreigners in the group – are worrying tendencies according to our society. The founder of the group, a journalist of Irish origin who has worked for human rights organizations for ten years, had to flee Sweden with the help from the Irish embassy, as he feared for his safety due to the escalation of threats fueled by the report. The openness to discuss the topic seems to be still some distance away in this country.

Sadly, the above-mentioned journalist is not the only one to flee Sweden. Several cases have been reported of people who, ostracized at their workplace by their co-workers because of their opinions on the Swedish pandemic strategy, felt they had no choice but to move to another country. These include medical doctors and other medical specialists.

I was accused of being a right-wing populist by a couple of my oldest Swedish friends when I criticized Sweden's COVID-19 policy on Facebook. As a person of color with a political view definitely toward the left, I found this incident to be not only outrageous but also unfathomably absurd. In the end, I unfriended them on Facebook as well as in real life. Needless to say, my story is not an exception.

Total Deaths as of 10.03.2021 (population: 2019):

- Sweden 13,042 (10,23 million)

- Denmark 2,381 (5,806 million)

- Finland 776 (5,518 million)

- Norway 632 (5,328 million)

- Iceland 29 (356,991)[1]

For the last 5-6 years, I've had to cut down the amount of work due to a series of health problems from which I have been suffering. So the pandemic didn't affect me too much in that sense. The change in my life came several years before the pandemic and has continued through it.

In terms of work, I had to cancel three audio-visual performances that would have taken place in Stockholm last year. Regarding other commitments I had, I could either postpone them or have them done over other communication methods such as web meetings, emails, or phone conversations.

---

1   Source for deaths: COVID-19 Dashboard by CSSE at John Hopkins University, https://coronavirus.jhu.edu/map.html, Accessed March 2021. Source for population size: Google.

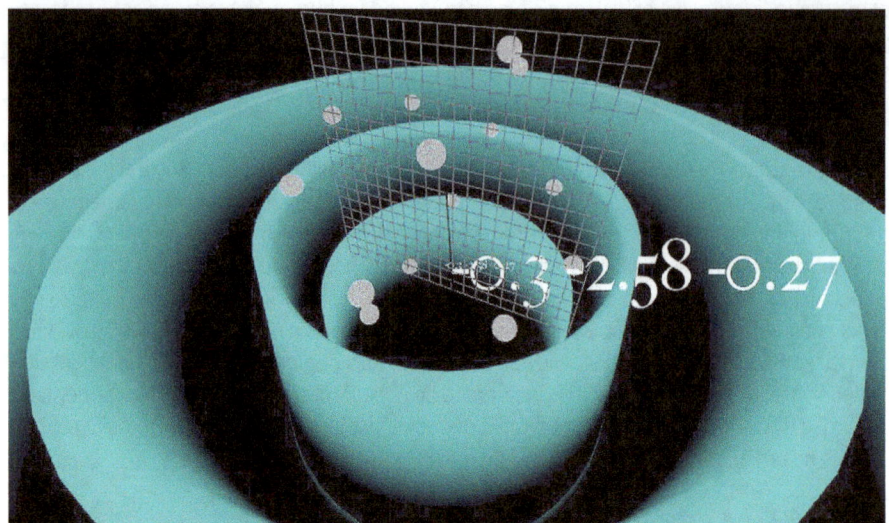

Figure 25: A still from motion controlled audio-visual work 'Still Untitled' using Leap Motion, programmed in Max Jitter (2017-2018).

I've grown to be closely involved with the artist-run not-for-profit art organization in Stockholm I joined with several other members three years ago. For the past two years, I have been one of its internal auditors. Restructuring the organization has taken much of my time. Because of that and my health issues, I have refrained from throwing myself into a new demanding creative project during this pandemic. Instead, I've been focusing on updating my knowledge in various areas, like:

- 2D skills and video editing skills using various mobile/iPad apps instead of relying solely on desktop applications,

- discovering new possibilities of apps that employ the use of machine learning,

- exploring VR using Oculus Quest and Unity, acquiring another MYO armband to equip both arms for interactive audio-visual performance in RL using Max Jitter,

- studies of Kabuki costumes on YouTube for various combinations of colors and forms in movement.

It has also been an incubation time for ideas and thoughts for a new project, which is now in the process of being percolated and distilled.

As I have some underlying conditions, I belong to the group of people vulnerable to COVID-19. However, since I live in the countryside and my partner does our grocery shopping, I did not have too many reasons to worry about the spread of the virus.

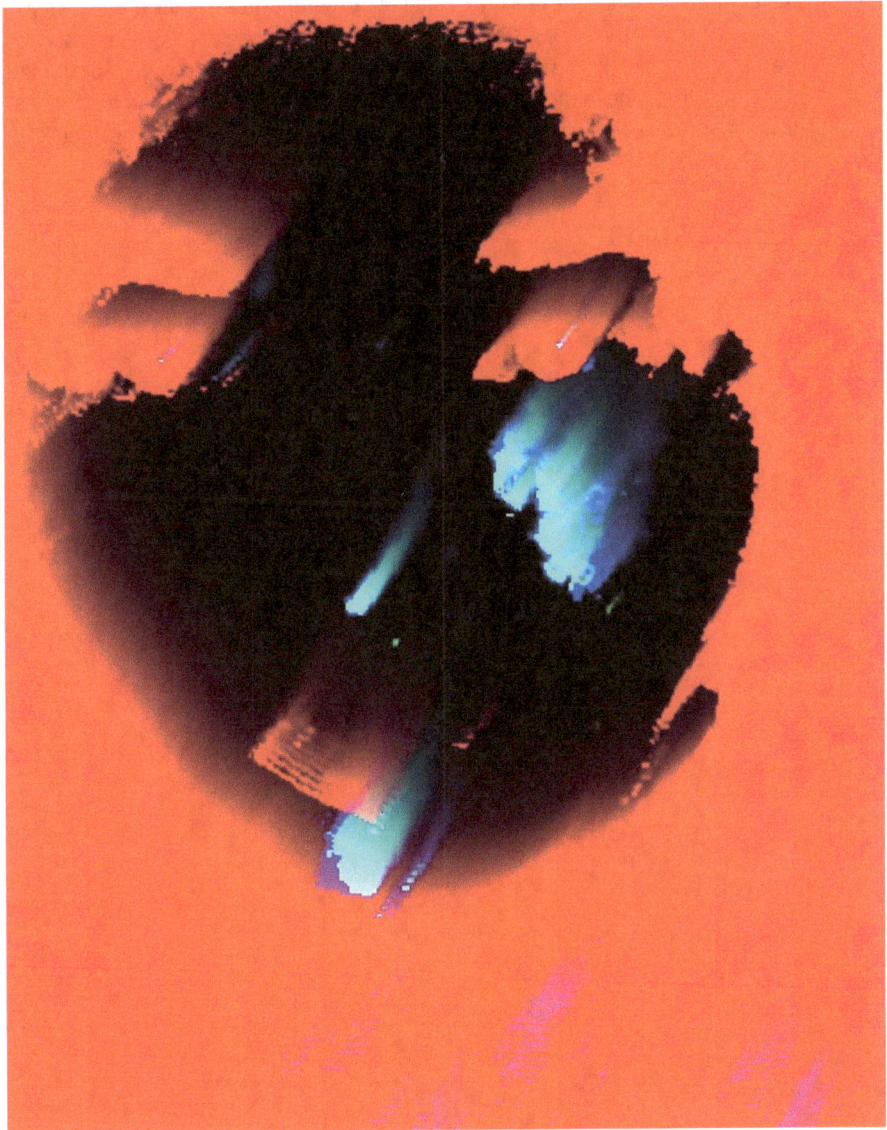

Figure 26: A still from from gesture controlled audio-visual work 'Hard Candy,' using Myo armband, pro-grammed in Max Jitter (2019).

Or so I thought. Then, about a week ago, we received an email from my niece-in-law explaining my brother-in-law had come down with COVID-19 and become hospitalized. He had already spent a week in the hospital with a ventilator.

I know several people who had COVID-19 and got better without any hospitalization. I also know people suffering from lingering symptoms from the virus. But having someone of close

kin suffer severely from it made me feel the danger of the coronavirus as real and more fright-
ening. Despite the arrival of vaccines, I fear the threat is getting closer, and with the new and
more dangerous variants of the virus, no one seems to be certain of their safety. Fortunately,
after another week in the hospital, the brother-in-law got better. He is now in the process
of being dismissed. But as I wait for my turn to get vaccinated, my fear of the virus persists.

GARNET HERTZ

The pandemic has exacerbated inequalities, with the tech sector winning and the arts sector way behind.

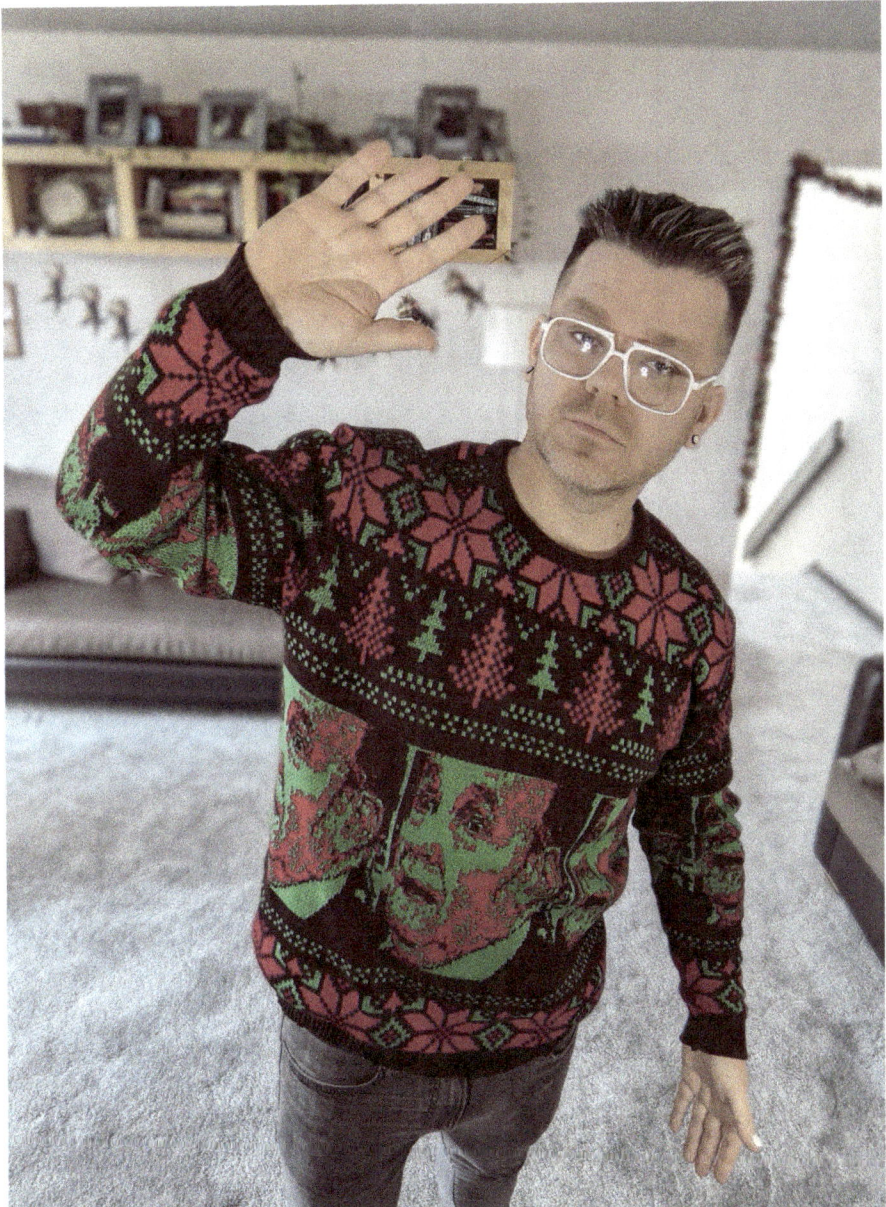

Figure 27: Garnet Hertz showing custom Ugly Rudy Giuliani Christmas Sweater made December 2020.

I live in Vancouver, Canada, and the situation has been relatively calm during the pandemic. Vancouver was the first place in Canada to have COVID-19, and as a result, it has been locked down longer than other places – although breakouts have been relatively small compared to our population density. This has created a kind of quiet monotony of lockdown, with everything in holding mode.

The university system in general has been experiencing a massive rollercoaster of stress. Many professors were completely unprepared for online teaching: there is a vast difference between good in-person teaching and good online teaching.

I teach at university and I am paid to produce research. Each of these things was impacted differently. In other words, the two core tasks of my employment were influenced in different ways by COVID-19. Although many of these changes were negative, several important positive changes took place: I learned better ways to connect with my students, I learned more about the function of art as a psychological aid, and I learned how my physical health impacts my artistic and academic practice. In addition, I gained insight into the disparity of employment practices between the arts sector and fields affiliated with computer science.

In terms of in-person teaching, COVID-19 has turned it upside-down. The start of the pandemic was mentally difficult and disorienting for teachers across the board. At the start, I desperately wanted to go to the university and my studio space there. Part of this was because I was teaching a course that needed access to fabrication and electronic prototyping equipment, plus we needed a Risograph machine to complete the course capstone project and this hardware was not available to us. I managed to gain access to the campus and tore out a lot of equipment from my studio and dumped it into my garage but finishing a semester capstone publication with the students was still incredibly difficult.

Some of the class had family in Wuhan, and others were uncertain about whether they had COVID-19. We had planned to publish a book of student projects, and this had to be scrapped because the students were not really in the headspace of wanting to do something extra like this. For context, this was in the 'toilet paper era' of the pandemic when lockdowns were starting and there was more uncertainty about the disease.

I participated as a speaker in several online forums and conferences that were interesting, but for the most part, I felt a sense of disillusionment in that most of the art world felt like a useless waste of time. I sensed that my little academic art panel wasn't helping the larger world all that much. What I mean is that at the start of the pandemic I felt a bit like the art scene's gyrations were a novel frivolity. It was an extra, nice thing that had little to do with survival. In hindsight, it felt like humanity as a whole was thrown to the bottom of Maslow's hierarchy of needs, where the luxury of self-actualization quickly had come to a stop as we started to face physiological jeopardy.

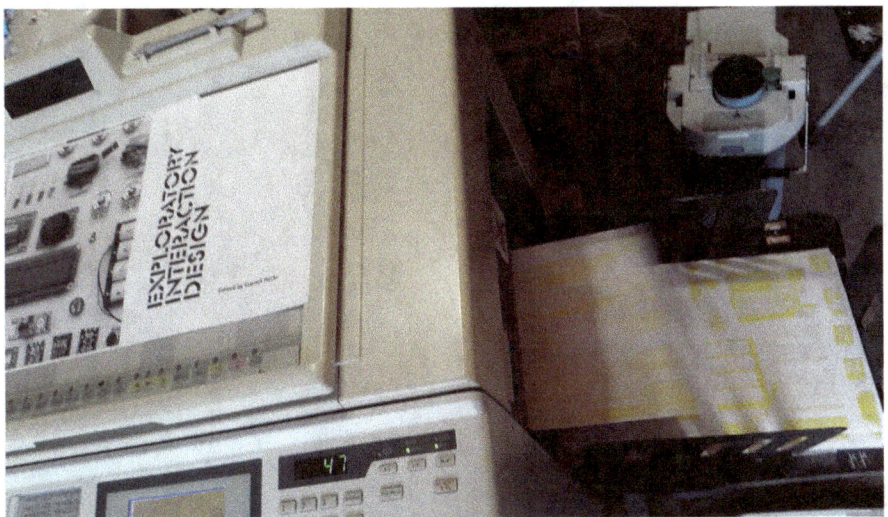

Figure 28: I had brought an old Risograph machine into his garage and started producing a capstone project booklet titled 'Exploratory Interaction Design' with students. This project was abandoned.

After feeling disillusioned about art for about a month – and after feebly trying my hand at figuring out epidemiology via Facebook – I started my studio production just to improve my mood. I had been posting one good-ish quality clip to Snapchat per day, primarily for myself, but an important shift took place soon after posting the work. People started responding to my quick sketches in ways that I hadn't anticipated.

The most shocking surprise happened when a family member who works as a public nurse in the Toronto region became a fan of this quick-and-dirty and generally nonconceptual work. This development was notable to me because she is currently a high-ranking supervisor of vaccines for over 1,3 million people. She is under an unbelievable amount of stress. Despite all of this, she was one of the most active viewers of my quick and dirty studio experimentations. It was perplexing. I was a bit surprised by her uptake. It's not as if I felt like my artwork was helping with the pandemic, but I had a clearer view of art that I hadn't seriously considered for a while. Simply making beautiful or curious things to make people happy or engaged was something that had sort of slipped into the margins of my work as conceptual critique took the center stage back in the 90s.

As a result, I felt a renewed focus in the arts – but this was considerably different than my 'critical' or 'hacker' stance from the past. The power of art at that point seemed quite basic: there is considerable value in making things to cheer people up and inspire them to get out of bed. It's basic. People needed it, my sister-in-law needed it, and I needed it. It's important to be critical of stuff that deserves it, but it is just as important to not forget the nurturing, beautiful, and heartwarming aspects of artmaking.

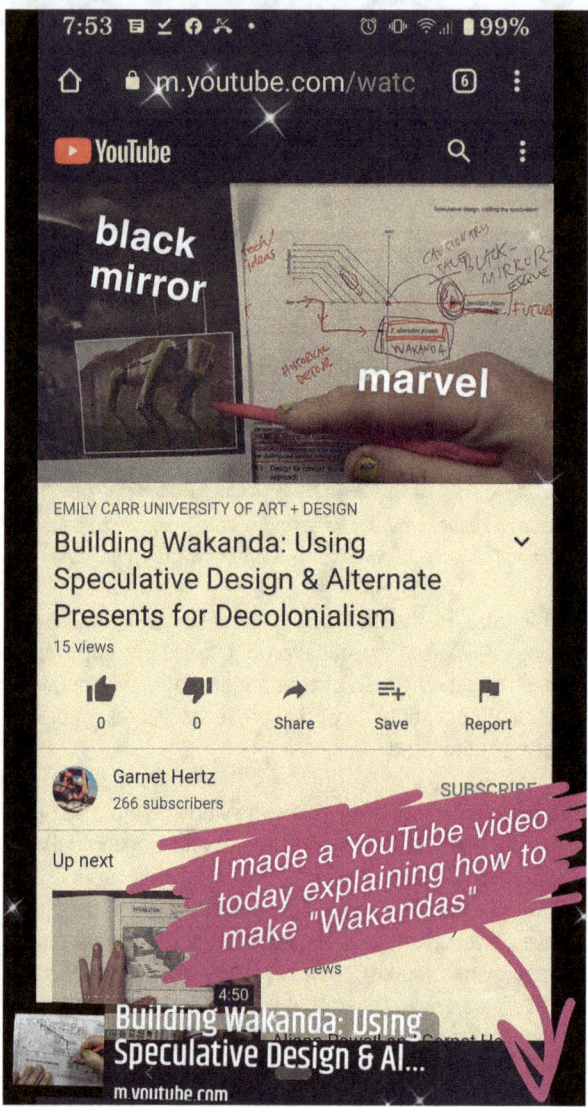

Figure 29: Screenshot of a Snapchat from October 2020 talking about a YouTube video Garnet had made about speculative design and decolonization.

At this point, the dynamics of my job as a professor were also getting strange — a lot of uncertainty and stress percolated through universities in the summer of 2020. Some smaller campuses were afraid of going bankrupt, and no one really knew what fall 2020 was going to be like. The dynamics of working at a university had become considerably worse. Arguably the dynamics of working anywhere had become considerably worse as well, but it posed many unique problems to hands-on skill education. For example, it was difficult to envision exactly how to teach something like welding, soldering circuit boards, or aluminum casting over

Zoom. Related to this, it's my perception that fall 2020 saw an excess of senior professors retiring – and this makes good sense because many professors have little interest or skill in being an on-screen 'YouTubey' personality.

The pandemic affected my research work too. Research currently occupies 80% of my time and involves producing studio and written work. I've been working on an academic monograph for a long time on the topic of do-it-yourself approaches to technology in media art and critical design practice, and the top item on my to-do list is this beast of a book.

I found writing incredibly difficult. It was like I couldn't focus.

I found that my writing brain went to hell. It was challenging to have the mindset required for smooth, clear thought on metalevel topics. In normal times I tend to work in between writing and the studio and fluctuate between the two. Instead, during the pandemic, I started to find it incredibly difficult to focus, and this resulted in almost exclusively going into doing studio work. I spent more time on producing short sketches. I found that when I had the energy, my work was relatively sudden and erratic. I tried capitalizing on this by working with mechanisms, stencils, booklets, zines, and other forms of tactile media.

The comradery of my campus workplace had absolutely vanished. I draw a lot of energy from the tactility of experience and from the serendipity of interacting with diverse individuals from many backgrounds. Everyone was desperately trying to just keep their heads above water. Morale tanked for many reasons, but at the core was the stress over giving students a sub-par education experience.

In hindsight, I see that I was missing the social interaction of the university so much that I started seeking out different forms of distanced socialization with different groups. At the same time as I committed to making one sketch per day, I also decided to go skateboarding every day on a halfpipe. Skateboarding in many ways has been there in life when I'm at my lowest – I regularly return to it as a practice (with lots of faceplants) when I hit adversity. It gets me out of my head, basically, and provides a healthy casual social interaction that I see clearly missing from many middle-aged men's lives.

Through the pandemic, I have reconnected my understanding of how physical health impacts my artistic output. In other words, I knew all along that exercise was important in a general health sense, but I hadn't linked it to my artistic and writing abilities until the harshest parts of the pandemic. Skateboarding substantially helped me on this front. Days that I skateboarded were also days that I got a lot of writing or design work done.

Most of these pieces were more therapeutic than great portfolio additions, but they were important because they got me active and re-inspired to make great work. It's one thing to be a great artist when you're 25. It's a different story to kindle that spark of inspiration while being 35, 45, 55, and 65 years old.

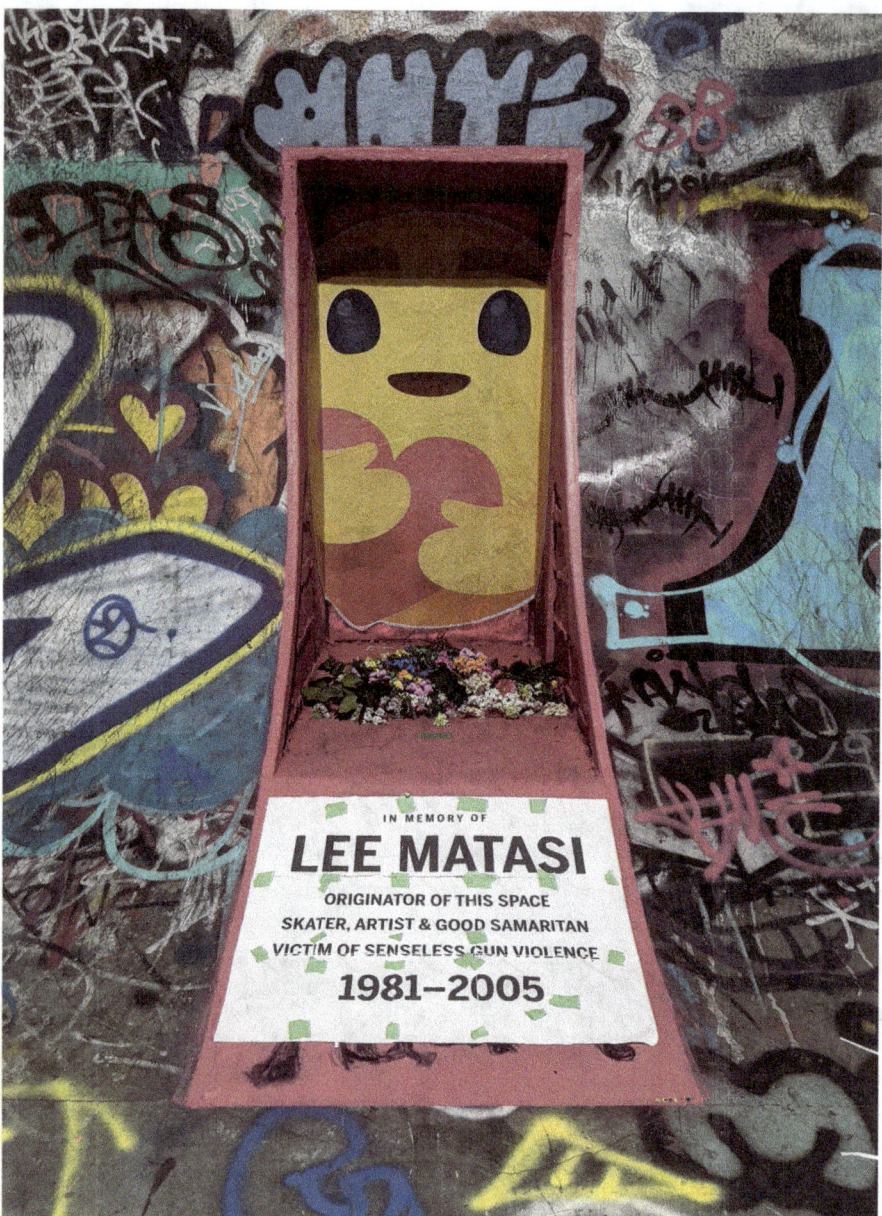

Figure 30: I printed a six-foot tall inkjet Facebook 'care' emoji poster and stuck it in the dirty nook where I liked putting my backpack while skateboarding at Leeside Skatepark in Vancouver.

Many folks run out of ideas after making it big once, and the 'second album problem' that many musicians feel is similar for artists. Ideas and inspiration take hard work and different techniques. For me, the pandemic forced me to rethink my practice in a real way, and oddly enough, skateboarding played a role in that.

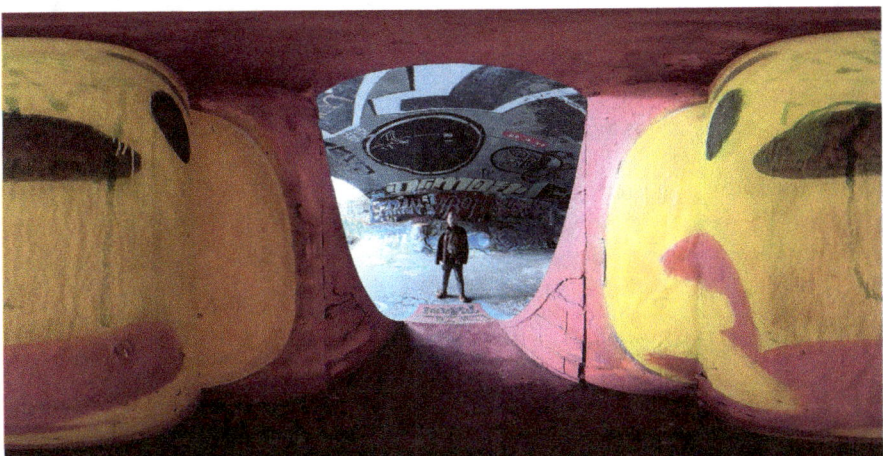

Figure 31: Alternate view of installed Facebook 'care' emoji poster at Leeside skatepark. This site ended up becoming used as a memorial for Lee Matasi, a skater, artist, and originator of the DIY skatepark in Vancouver. Matasi was killed by senseless gun violence in 2005.

In the summer of 2020, I sort of hit rock bottom after needing to quarantine in my own house away from my family when I thought I had COVID-19. There was also considerable turmoil at the university. The George Floyd protests in May, June, and July also occupied a lot of my focus. I had also become continually more unproductive as I was researching epidemiology and pandemic issues.

To get rolling again, I decided to create something small every day. I had a Snapchat account, and I started just shooting a short clip every day and posting it there. I had entered the platform when three of my children were teenagers. I used it to communicate with them, but I ended up staying longer, using it as an 'off grid' social media platform for experimentation purposes with relatively random audiences.

I started by posting at least one decent video clip per day and experimenting with some new format styles including tabletop, short loop, visual eye candy pieces, and tutorial shoots.

This was a generative and productive time, but my focus was quite scattered: I'd paint a canvas for a bit, then work on a motorized sketch of a device, then do some paste-up graffiti. I worked on simply making things with my hands and tried to give myself the leeway to experiment and try new things without fear of failure or being way outside of my established areas of expertise. This process helped me remember that I work like a materials-led fine artist (as opposed to a more problem-oriented design approach). It was also an opportunity to get back more into the studio art component that has always been a part of my background and work.

To be honest, I also found myself questioning the structure of a university and the university as an institution of learning. I still have a lot of difficulty coping with how universities use people in exploitative ways. This is especially the case in financially underprivileged disciplines like the arts. I've worked in different areas — in business, in computer science, in humanities, and at art schools – and my opinion is that artists have a hard time promoting themselves and see-ing their value within society. Society also regularly scoffs at the ideas of art being important, real work, or real knowledge. Because of a lack of self-esteem in the discipline and a lack of general respect, the arts as a whole is a difficult sector to work in if you want to pay your bills.

Universities don't have a monopoly on handing out crappy jobs, but many art schools leverage the double desperation (of being a struggling artist and struggling academic) and exhibit morally disgusting employment practices. Those that have only worked in the arts know little else: it's a scene built on desperately trying to be seen and to get a big break for something that most of the culture doesn't consider financially valuable. According to most, art is a fun curiosity, but it isn't real work. It's correspondingly funded like a curiosity, not real work.

The net result is that artists and arts organizations are often treated like children: they're not listened to, trusted with lots of money, or even given a real job. They receive scraps. I've worked in computer science departments, and the entire landscape of that employment scene bears little resemblance to the arts sector. Many tech companies can indeed treat their software users like impersonal piles of big data, but on the employment front, they operate with vastly more personal leeway and budget to treat people like people. The pandemic has exacerbated inequalities, with the tech sector winning and the arts sector way behind.

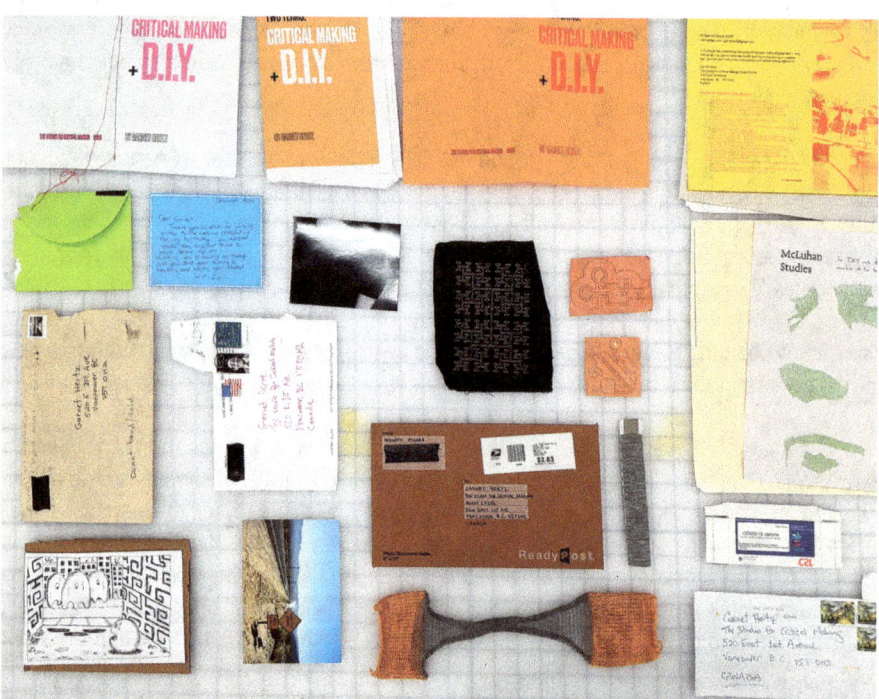

Figure 32: During the pandemic, I also produced a risographed zine titled 'Two Terms: Critical Making + D.I.Y' that I gave away to anyone that mailed me a physical item. These are some of the things people sent to me.

Another thing that I changed in terms of my teaching as a result of the pandemic was that I started giving my phone number to my graduate students relatively freely, inviting them to just call me whenever they had a question or problem. I have found that this is actually much more preferable to scheduling, and it suits me better in terms of forming a stronger relationship with my graduate students. I tell people that if I cannot talk, I simply won't pick up and will call them back as soon as I can.

I found a renewed sense of focus by just thinking about how I could help my graduate students as individuals, not primarily as graduate students. With that said, it has taken about 150% effort compared to other years. This shift has worked out quite well, with students generally respecting my time, and I have had much better relationships with my graduate students because of the pandemic. Go figure. I'll definitely continue giving out my phone number after the pandemic subsides. Wandering phone conversations have renewed my understanding of graduate studies being a transformative personal journey that is best served in a personal way.

S()FIA BRAGA

We are witnessing a trivialization of the internet as an artistic medium.

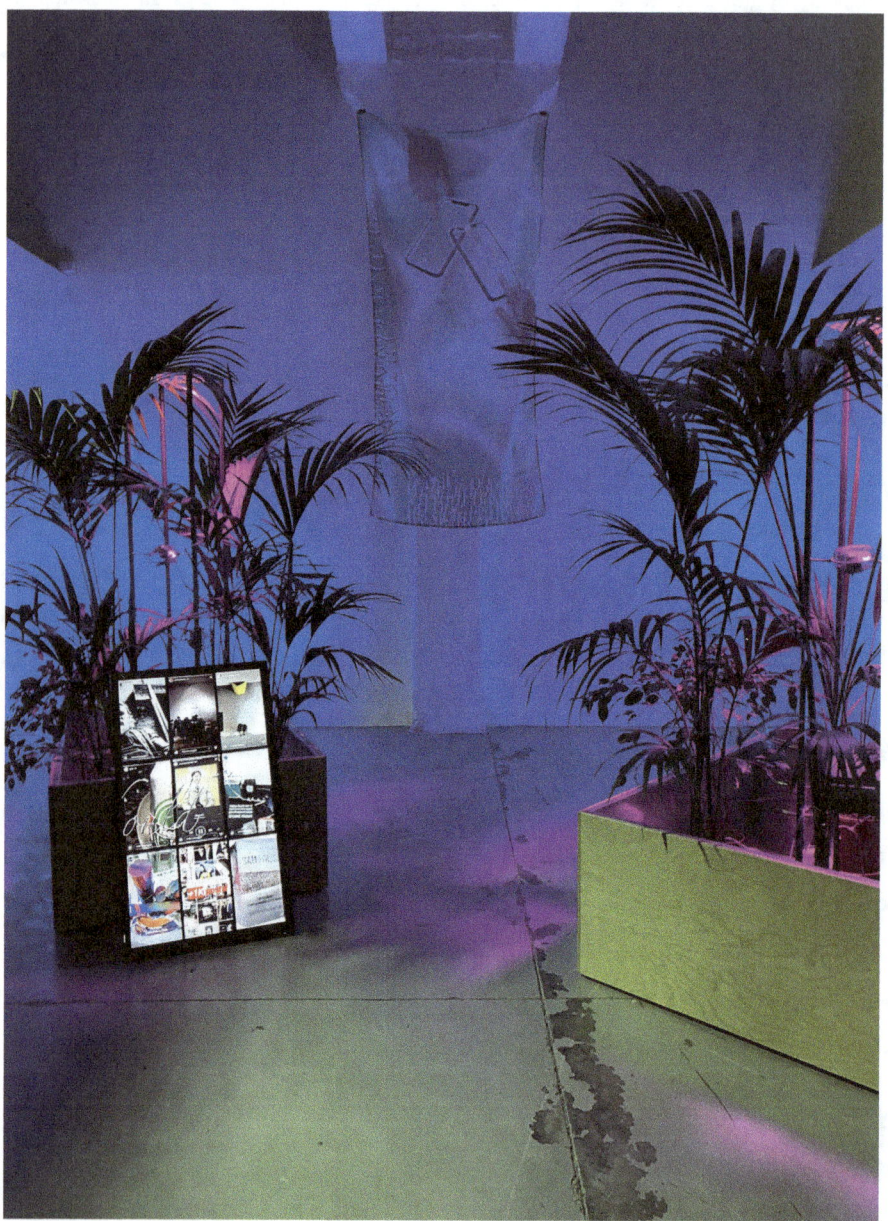

Figure 33: S()fia Braga, 'I Stalk Myself More Than I Should,' installation, SHARE Festival, 2020.

In February 2020, life in Linz was quite pleasant. At the time I don't think we really understood the seriousness of the situation. At the beginning of March, the university announced the closure of all buildings. I was angry. I was not used to spending time at home and I hated the idea of working in my tiny room in the shared flat I was living in.

During my days at home, I would wander from room to room hoping to find comfort within those walls from which I had been fleeing for two years. That flat, which was an almost unknown place to me, tried to penetrate, under the guise of a silent observer, the most intimate aspects of my daily life. There were times when the bed remained untouched for days, if not weeks, the refrigerator empty and dust accumulated under the desk. During the isolation, every little crack, scaling, and everything else I had ignored until then, became unbearably visible and tried to get my attention.

I kept myself busy all the time to not think. I became more productive than ever until I even began to believe that the social activities I was used to doing before the pandemic were a waste of time. The house I had rejected for years had completely absorbed me.

I couldn't understand how people around me felt unmotivated and lazy. I was convinced I somehow managed to detach myself from what was happening in a very healthy way. After a while, I realized my attitude wasn't normal and the lockdown affected me as much as everybody else.

Right now, it's still hard for me to stop working and go out without feeling I am wasting my time.

Paradoxically, 2020 was the year in which I gained the most through my artistic practice. I guess this is because many institutions, even the 'classical ones,' realized they would have to rely on digital art and the internet to continue their activities during the pandemic.

Since my artistic practice focuses on the social impact of web interfaces and the subversion of centralized social media platforms through online-based projects and videos, I found myself fitting in every kind of situation. Almost every project I created last year was commissioned; definitely a new thing for me. During the summer I could finally be a part of some physical exhibitions and I have never been so happy to create an installation in my life before. For the first time in years, I was almost bored of working digitally.

I'm aware that the pandemic made digital artists 'shine' more than ever, but on the other hand, I am not enthusiastic about this art world migration to the online space. I believe many artists, curators, galleries, and so on, are ignoring years of internet art history and we are witnessing a trivialization of the internet as an artistic medium.

The pandemic definitely influenced my work, conceptually and aesthetically. The new projects I created have a sort of dark aura, which does not seem to be present in my older works. I'm honestly intrigued by this twist, it was something quite uexpected and unintentional, but I believe I was looking for this change for a while.

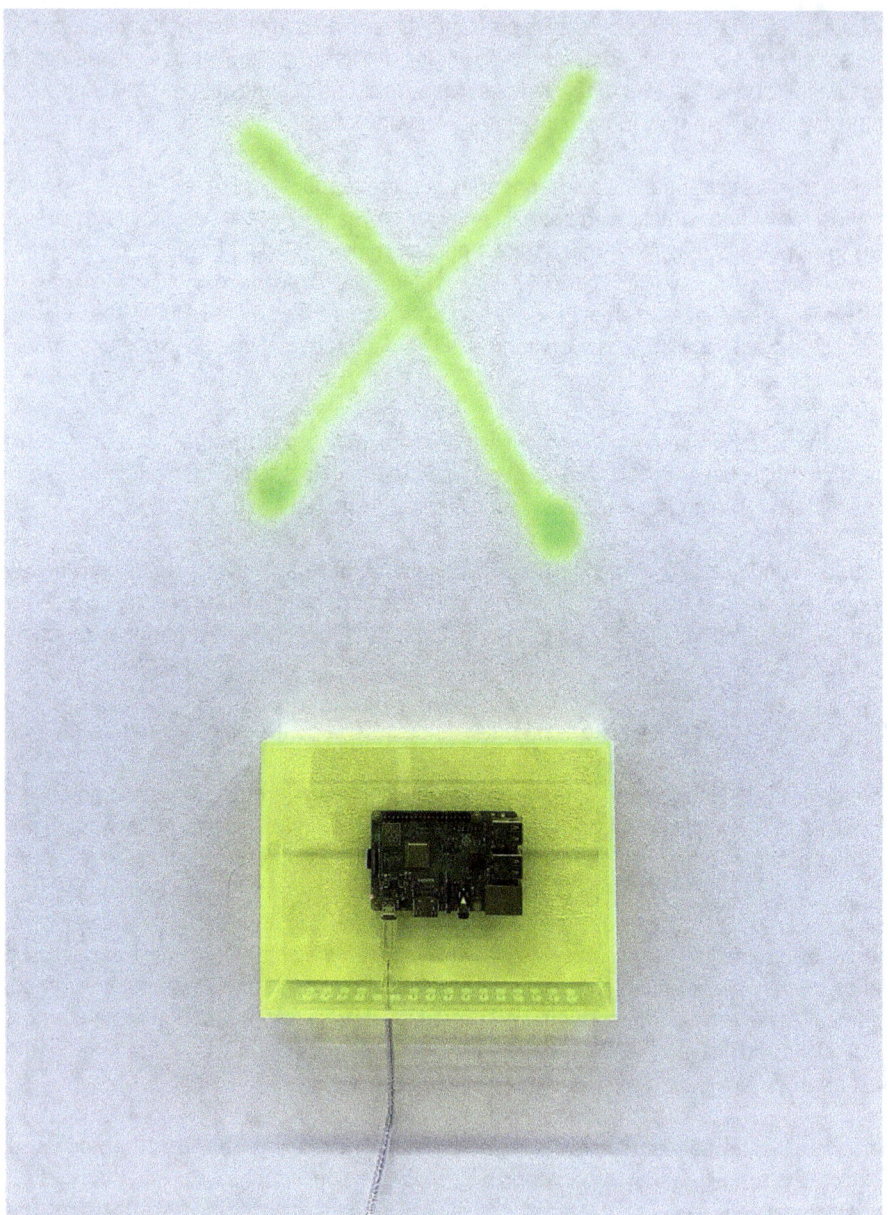

Figure 34: SSID: @tagme

During the first quarantine, I created *Die Verwandlung*, a short movie for Instagram (IG) Stories developed for the Ultra-Event of TBD Ultramagazine, in which a disturbing everyday life is narrated through an atmospheric mix typical of the psychological horror genre and inspired by the found footage sub-genre.

The short movie is permeated with a continuous feeling of alienation towards the domestic environment and the body. The latter falls victim to a slow process of mutation that makes it alien and an undesirable element. The title is inspired by Franz Kafka's 'The Metamorphosis' where the transformation of the main character into a monstrous verminous bug makes him acutely aware of certain social behaviors he never consciously suffered from, but that he had to perform daily. Unfortunately, the impossibility of living a 'normal' life, because of his socially unacceptable transformation, leads him to a very drastic decision.

In my project, I depicted metamorphosis as something scary and momentarily undesirable, but in the end, this transition doesn't have negative connotations. It is a necessary step to personal growth and acceptance. I enforced this idea in the project *ENTER PROMOCODE*, which I made a few months later. In this commission by OÖ Landes-Kultur for their IG account, the main character from *Die Verwandlung* fearlessly shows herself and her body in a series of pictures and short videos.

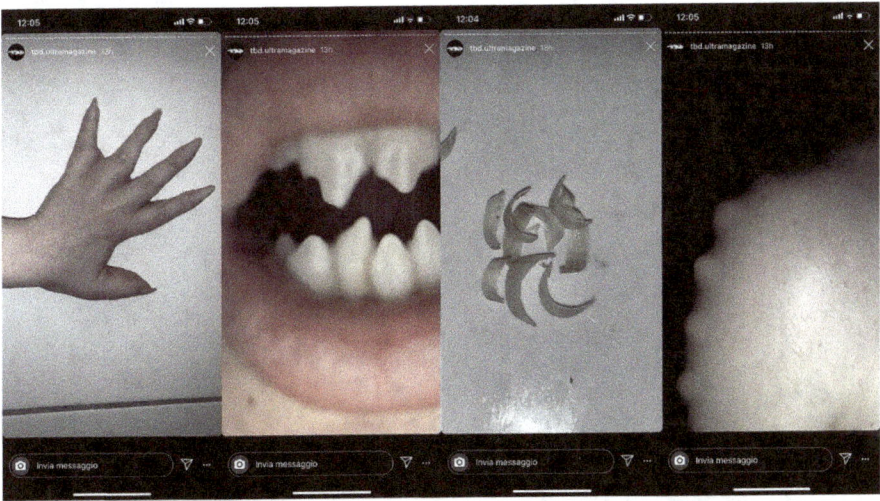

Figure 35: Screenshots from 'Die Verwandlung,' short movie for Instagram Stories, 2020.

I wanted to combine a fictional narrative with a medium that was specifically created to share videos or photos of daily life routines such as IG Stories. Here, the inclusion of a surrealistic horror narrative produces a sense of estrangement and disquiet in the user, the audience. It can make people question reality and its representation within social media platforms.

Die Verwandlung marked the beginning of a new 'era' in my artistic production that I ironically like to call my 'black period,' contrasted with the 'pink-kawaii period' of my pre-corona times.

BEN GROSSER

It's hard to describe the panic that sets in when you realize that the federal govern-ment not only refuses to help citizens during an uncontrolled pandemic but actively works to mislead them about the virus. It does not just thwart state-based efforts to manage the crisis, but practically ignores the needs of states based on their ideologi-cal alignment.

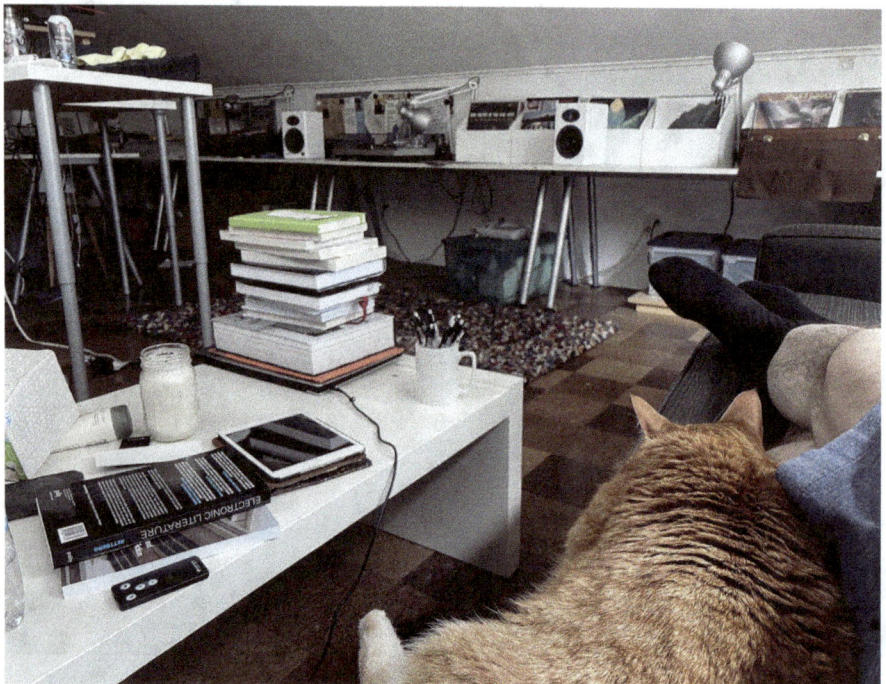

Figure 36: Ben Grosser's home studio, March 2020.

As someone who reads Reddit pretty regularly, I was watching the COVID-19 situation soon after its emergence in China, worried about the virus's potential to spread. I think the moment that really gave me pause was when I read that Wuhan was going to build a 10,000-bed hos-pital in a week. Not only did that suggest an overwhelming and scary severity, but I also knew that my country, the U.S., would never (be able to) do anything like that if need be.

I was getting wary of the virus coming here during February 2020 and had started making preparations in case of lockdown: buying extra food at the grocery store, for example. I took a mask with me during plane travel that month. But so many around me here were unconcerned. Once early March hit, our federal CDC (Center for Disease Control) finally announced that it was a problem for the U.S., and it was going to get worse. I finally relaxed a bit because I thought *now* the country will take it seriously.

But since we were living under Trump at that time, it was just a mess from then on. It's hard to describe the panic that sets in when you realize that the federal government not only refuses to help citizens during an uncontrolled pandemic but actively works to mislead them about the virus. It does not just thwart state-based efforts to manage the crisis but also practically ignores the needs of states based on their ideological alignment. Thankfully my state, Illinois, has a proactive governor who took the virus seriously, so we did go into a 'shelter-in-place.' Regardless, we had almost no testing available for many months, so the spread that was happening wasn't well-understood.

Because of the non-existent testing situation, my university (a large state school with around 50,000 students) designed its own saliva-based COVID-19 test and brought students back to campus in the fall with a testing requirement every four days. Even with that rigorous and unusually proactive testing plan – and with most classes conducted online – we averaged about 40 COVID-19 cases per day on campus, saw nearly 4,000 cases in fall, and are now at 5,800 campus cases since last summer. That amounts to about 18% of our undergrads. In our county, we have about 1 death per day from the virus.

For family reasons, I've been more cautious than many people I know around here. Since March 2020, I've only been inside other buildings for absolute essentials (e.g., doctor's visits), have only visited with friends outside with masks, and have not traveled apart from car trips to state and county parks.

Thankfully, Trump was finally ousted from power last month, and so we now have a national strategy for managing the pandemic, about a year after our first case in the U.S. Vaccinations are ramping up. A relief bill is in progress. We may be stuck inside with winter (this past weekend saw temperatures around -20°C), but there's a bit of hope on the horizon with spring coming. Though people are on edge regarding the new virus variants.

As an artist whose work is mostly net-based, I had less disruption with exhibitions than many. A percentage of shows I was scheduled to participate in was planned as online already, pre-pandemic, so those were unaffected. A summer 2020 group show at arebyte Gallery in London was reimagined and released as a browser extension-based exhibition, which suits my work well. I ended up giving more artist talks than usual, as I didn't have to travel to each festival or show to present.

In addition to working as an artist, I also work as a professor. Over spring break, we transitioned to online classes. So, as for many, all of a sudden everything was happening over Zoom. I was thankful to be able to keep working, but it was definitely a massive disruption for me and the students. I also lost access to my campus studio, so everything (teaching, studio, etc.) was and still is happening at home. I don't teach in the summer, but much of it was spent preparing to teach online in the fall: rewriting syllabi, assembling tech, etc.

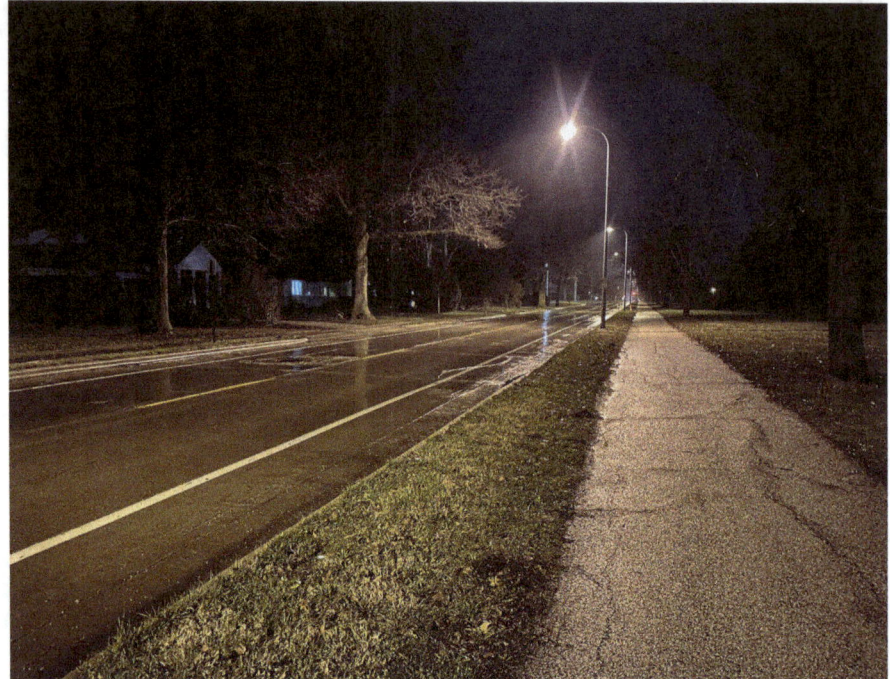

Figure 37: A usually busy street at 9pm on Friday from March 2020 in Illinois, U.S.

Fall was all online. I've spent years developing techniques to teach humans in front of me, learning to interpret their reactions to what I say and to use what I perceive as a guide for what to say next. Teaching over Zoom required new techniques and broke many old ones. Because most students wouldn't turn their cameras on, I could no longer gauge how they received what I said. Few students contributed to the discussion. Collective media-based activities (e.g., listening to a sound artwork) became independent; we all listened separately and then talked online after each listening session. Overall, I would say the semester went okay, and that many students made fabulous work. But it was exhausting. And slower. And some students had a very difficult semester.

Overall, as an introvert, losing direct proximity to other humans (except my spouse) was not as hard for me as it has been for some. But it was, and still is, a strange, surreal experience. I don't miss some of the loud, crowded spaces I would find myself in as a part of regular life. I don't miss airports or airplanes. But I really miss getting to see friends, students, colleagues. I miss getting to visit other places. I miss coffee shops, where I was always able to reset whenever I felt stuck. I miss live performances of music and theater and dance.

My imagination was pretty active right from the start of the pandemic, thinking of ideas for new works that had some relation to it. For example, one of my first ideas was to create a VR headset app that would function as a sort of public space re-integrator. Basically, you'd walk around an extremely crowded area in VR, with everyone trying to lick you as you moved through the crowd. But I found it hard to focus. It was difficult to concentrate enough to get started on anything. At least at first.

Eventually, in April, I broke out of that by committing myself to build the tiniest thing, a website called *amialive.today*. I was thinking about how much we were all loading up software-based pandemic trackers, or reading feed-based bad news headlines, or other online activities driven by our new personal and collective anxieties. *amialive.today* was a small alternative or perhaps an antidote to these activities.

A key interaction also began that month, with media theorist Geert Lovink. He and I started trading a text document back and forth via email for a while, using it to write about platform capitalism, online video, net art, social media, and more. This text was eventually published online at the Institute of Network Cultures blog, and a revised version will be published in a book this year. Geert's enthusiasm and ability to crank out complex thought-provoking ideas so quickly kept me focused and inspired me to keep thinking and writing. Our efforts weren't just useful for me as a method for developing new ideas, but that his desire to move quickly also kept me from obsessing about the pandemic (more than I would have otherwise).

I also spent much of the spring working on a video piece about romantic comedies and social distancing. This idea came out of watching TV and movies in the early days of the pandemic, finding myself shouting at the television every time humans were getting too close to each other. I would apply the new rules of social distancing to the unaware people on the pre-pandemic shows. I extracted key romantic couple scenes from well-known romcoms and then manipulated the video so that the actors were never closer than 6 feet. This led to some funny videos where the couples that had been walking hand-in-hand in the park or having a fight in the front seat of a car or even engaging in happy talk after sex in bed were now pushed apart and cropped into separate areas of the screen with black space between them, often leaving them smushed up against the far left and right edges of the frame. I didn't finish it and haven't released it. Maybe someday I will.

In the summer, I began creating and posting (on social media) periodic visualizations of the U.S. COVID-19 death toll. These images take as their starting point satellite photos of the 9/11 Memorial in New York City, a site built where the World Trade Center towers used to stand, and which commemorates about 3,000 deaths. Using that memorial's death-to-land ratio, I started copying and pasting its footprint and overwriting additional equal-sized parcels of land in lower Manhattan with it. In other words, for every additional 3,000 COVID-19 deaths in the U.S., I would copy and paste the Memorial site onto an adjacent spot.

My first image, posted on the 6th of July 2020, shows the lower tip of the island covered in 50 Memorial parcels representing 150,000 deaths. This project is ongoing; the latest from the 22nd of February 2021 shows 167 parcels representing 501,000 deaths. At this point, almost the entire map of lower Manhattan is covered.

When this project started, I was trying to grapple with the scale of the death and to think through the dramatically different national response we've seen in this country towards casualties from 9/11 (3,000) and the often dismissive, cavalier, and/or numbing response to 150,000, 300,000, 500,000 deaths from COVID-19. I don't know how long I'll continue to make these.

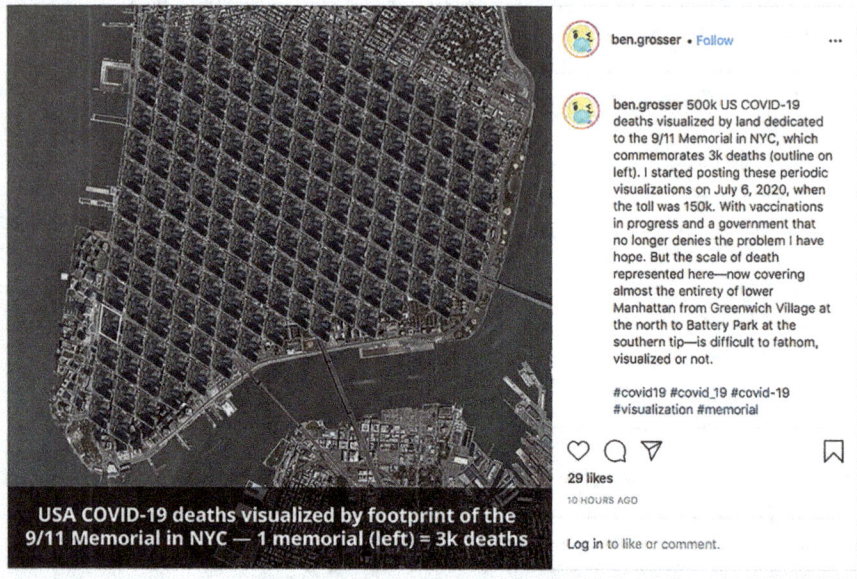

Figure 38: U.S. COVID-19 death count visualization, Ben Grosser, 2020-ongoing.

During the first few months of the pandemic, like many of us, I found myself in bed late at night scrolling the day's (increasingly) bad news on my phone. I'd often stay up way too late doing this, and then get up in the morning and go right back to my phone before even getting out of bed. As summer approached, I started thinking about why I found it hard to stop scrolling, especially given that I wasn't really learning much with each additional headline.

A relatively new word (from 2018 I believe) was gaining increasing attention around that time to describe this common activity: 'doomscrolling.' As an artist who focuses on the cultural effects of software, I thought about how this behavior wasn't just a natural reaction to the news of the day. Instead, it was the result of a perfect yet evil marriage between a populace stuck online, social media interfaces designed to game and hold our attention, and the realities of an existential global crisis. Sure, it may be hard to look away from bad news in any format, but it's nearly impossible to avert our eyes when that news is endlessly presented via social media interfaces that are designed to be addictive and know just what to show us next to keep us 'engaged.'

So, I built an alternative interface called *The Endless Doomscroller*. It's a website that presents a list of bad news headlines in the style of a simplified social media feed. The headlines I wrote, and continue to write, were generalized abstractions of those we were seeing every day, e.g.: 'Bans Are in Effect,' 'Shortage Looms,' or 'Further Devastation Likely,' and the scrolling list existed as a feed that literally never ends. You can scroll the site as fast or as slow as you like, but you'll never get to the bottom.

For me, it was a way of thinking about the mechanism behind our scroll-induced anxiety: interfaces and corporations that always want more. More doom (bad news headlines) compels more engagement (via continued liking/sharing/posting), which produces more personal data, making possible ever more profit. I thought of it as an aesthetic opportunity for mindfulness about how we spend our time online and about who most benefits from our late-night scroll sessions. Or maybe even as a form of exposure or substitution therapy, a way to escape or replace what these interfaces do to us and want from us. When I released it in mid-summer 2020, it had a strong response, especially on Twitter where people reacted by saying things like 'most trusted source of news,' or 'ha ha ha sob,' or 'this is your brain on news' or 'I FEEL SEEN.' Perhaps the only way out of too much doomscrolling is endless doomscrolling.

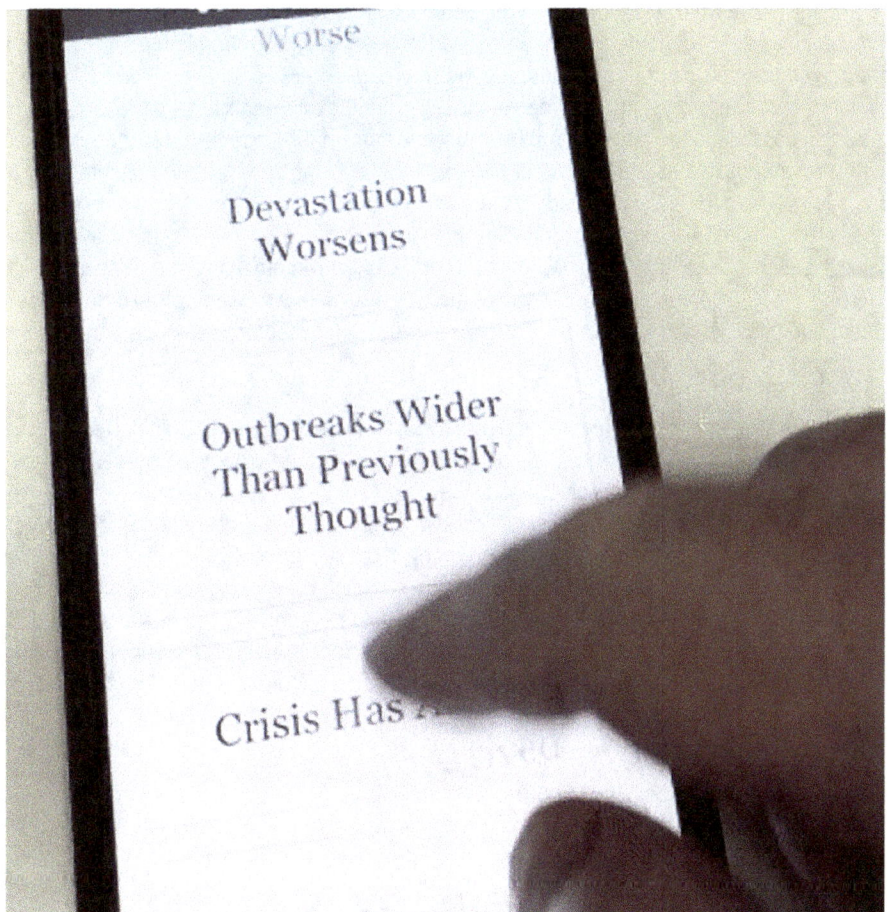

Figure 39: Ben Grosser, 'The Endless Doomscroller,' 2020.

An app that got an increasing share of my time in 2020 was the video-based social media platform TikTok. It is renowned for its AI-driven feed called the 'For You' page, an interface that presents a never-ending stream of videos and that tries to learn from how you look and scroll and like so it can supposedly give you more of what you want. I did indeed find that I would often spend way more time scrolling the feed than intended. But I also found that the videos it showed me pretty quickly consolidated into a set where many (most?) just weren't that interesting to me. Regardless, I'd often keep scrolling because the interface design made it so easy to just flick my thumb and try another one. I was also thinking a lot around that time about algorithmic social media feeds and disinformation. In the U.S., we were seeing an alarming number of individuals disregarding pandemic medical advice (e.g. ignoring masking and social distancing guidelines). We were also in the final months of the presidential election that would either allow us to escape the pandemic-dismissing Trump or be stuck with him another four years.

I'd already made work post-Trump, aimed at disrupting algorithmic profiling and other user manipulations on Facebook, and so this new addictive-feeling algorithmic feed from TikTok had me concerned. That background led me to create a new work called *Not For You*, an 'algorithmic confusion system' designed to mislead TikTok's video recommendation algorithm, making it possible to see how the app feels when it's no longer made 'for you.' It's a browser extension that navigates the site without intervention, clicking on videos and hashtags, and users to pollute a TikTok profile with noise. I wanted to see if such a change would surface videos I wasn't otherwise seeing, and to find out if it would make my feed less addictive. From using it, I learned it could show me whole sides of TikTok I never otherwise see. For example, I saw many foreign language videos, strange memes I was unaware of and often didn't under-stand, and piles of videos that didn't conform to the star-focused pretty person and opulent interior vids that usually crowd my feed.

This spring I'm spending my time developing several new works for a solo exhibition at arebyte Gallery this summer. With a working title of 'Software for Less,' the show will present these new works alongside some recent projects, all of them examining how so much of the software we use every day is designed to activate what I call our 'desire for more.' From viral misinformation to the climate crisis to wealth inequality, so many of today's most vexing societal problems can be linked to capitalism's need for endless growth — and the ways this need embeds itself into so many of us across the globe. I think it's time to start rethinking the role of software in this equation, to examine its roles in the perpetuation of acceleration and accumulation, and to begin building alternatives that intentionally generate a culture of less.

TINY DOMINGOS

Many artists are disoriented by the cancellation of fairs and exhibitions and by the impossibility of planning trips. I, too, have been affected.

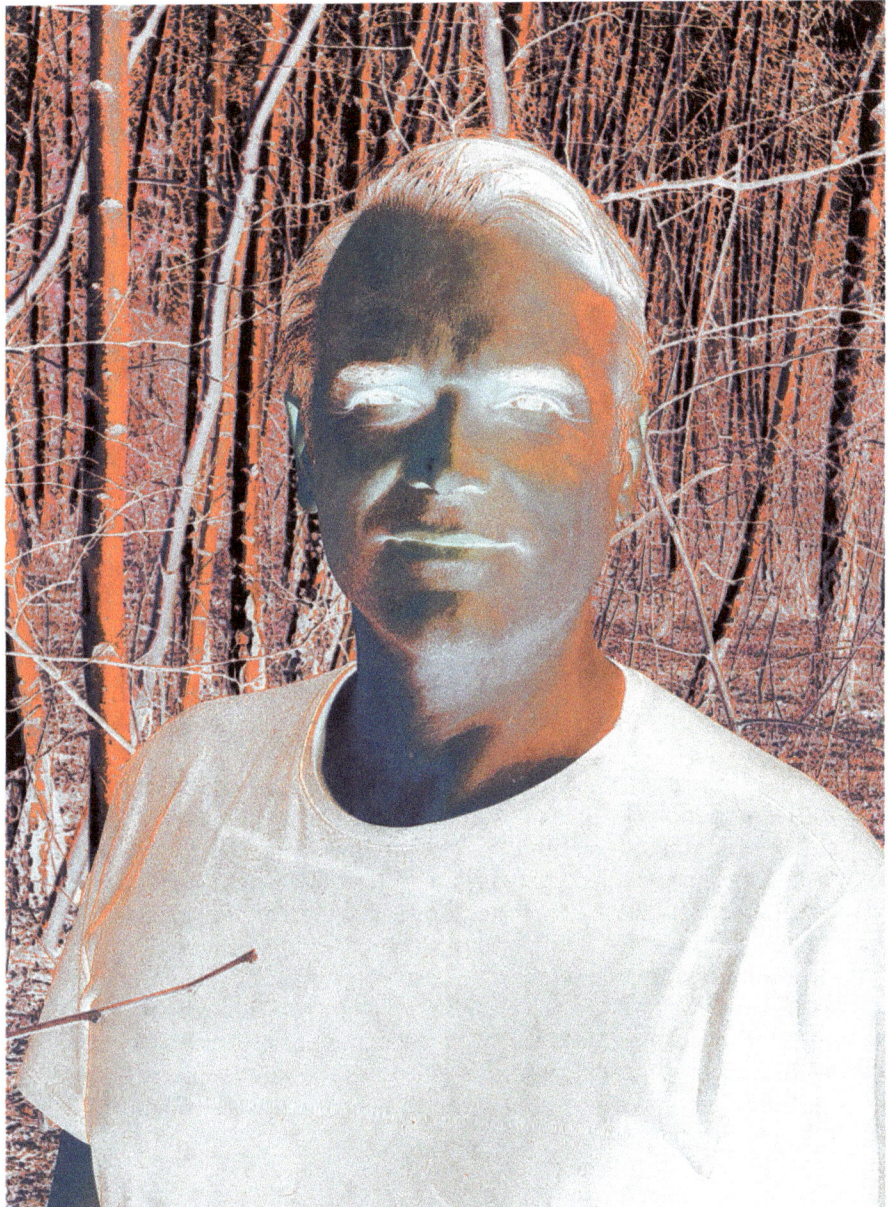

Figure 40: Tiny Domingos, Portrait in rot, digital edition, 2021.

Since January 2020, German scientists have been proactively dealing with this new virus. This resulted in the first test for the detection of COVID-19. The German authorities have been well-advised by scientists. The confinement measures were the subject of much deliberation. This is understandable, as the individual rights enshrined in the German Basic Law are a highly sensitive issue. History shows that rights are taken away in a matter of days but that restoring them takes much longer and is much more difficult. One cannot be too careful. German officials act with velvet gloves on these issues. Despite the existence of minority movements that refute the seriousness of the pandemic and try to stop the measures, there is a broad consensus regarding the decisions that were taken.

However, a group of anti-corona demonstrators almost succeeded in breaking through the front door of the famous Reichstag on the 8th of August 2020, an anticipation of the occupation of the Capitol by North American citizens moved by the same conspiracy theories. Imagine the effect an intrusion into the house of German democracy would have had...

German hospitals are very well-equipped with intensive care beds, but a lack of nurses means that some units are not working. A *sui generis* situation: unlike in most other countries, there are beds and equipment available, but manpower is missing. Meanwhile, and despite the reasonable management of the pandemic crisis, vaccination numbers are very slow, and the rapid progression of the new variants acts like a Damocles' sword, preventing the much-desired relaxation of anti-pandemic measures.

In Berlin, the confinements allow a certain freedom of movement. Designed in the 18th and 19th centuries, the city's airy urbanism – which reserves one-fifth of its total surface area for parks and forests – has revealed its full potential at a time when people cannot travel. One of the ideas behind this urbanism was to combat contagious diseases such as tuberculosis. Today, thousands of Berliners in forced confinement benefit from this concern for public health, enjoying the delights of the numerous green areas dotted around the city. Let's hope the urban planning of the 21st century maintains its functionality in the centuries to come.

The city is unrecognizable: no tourists, openings, or parties. Concert halls, theaters, museums, bars, and restaurants are closed. In the first half of 2020, the Berlin Senate allocated aid simply and effectively to the self-employed, which opened a window of hope. Other measures by the Federal Government followed, mainly benefiting companies and their current expenditure. The Federal Minister of Culture is committed to defending the sector, but the aid goes primarily to institutions and artists on the institutional scene. This is to the detriment of independent artists, who are advised to enroll in social aid programs (a shock for some successful music professionals and a common situation for many visual artists). The Neustart (anti-corona) program for the visual arts rewarded about 10% of applicants. Another program which goes by the same name but dedicated to galleries rewarded about 86% of the applicants. As is often the case, the trial and error method followed by the authorities left most of the independents out. There is room for improvement.

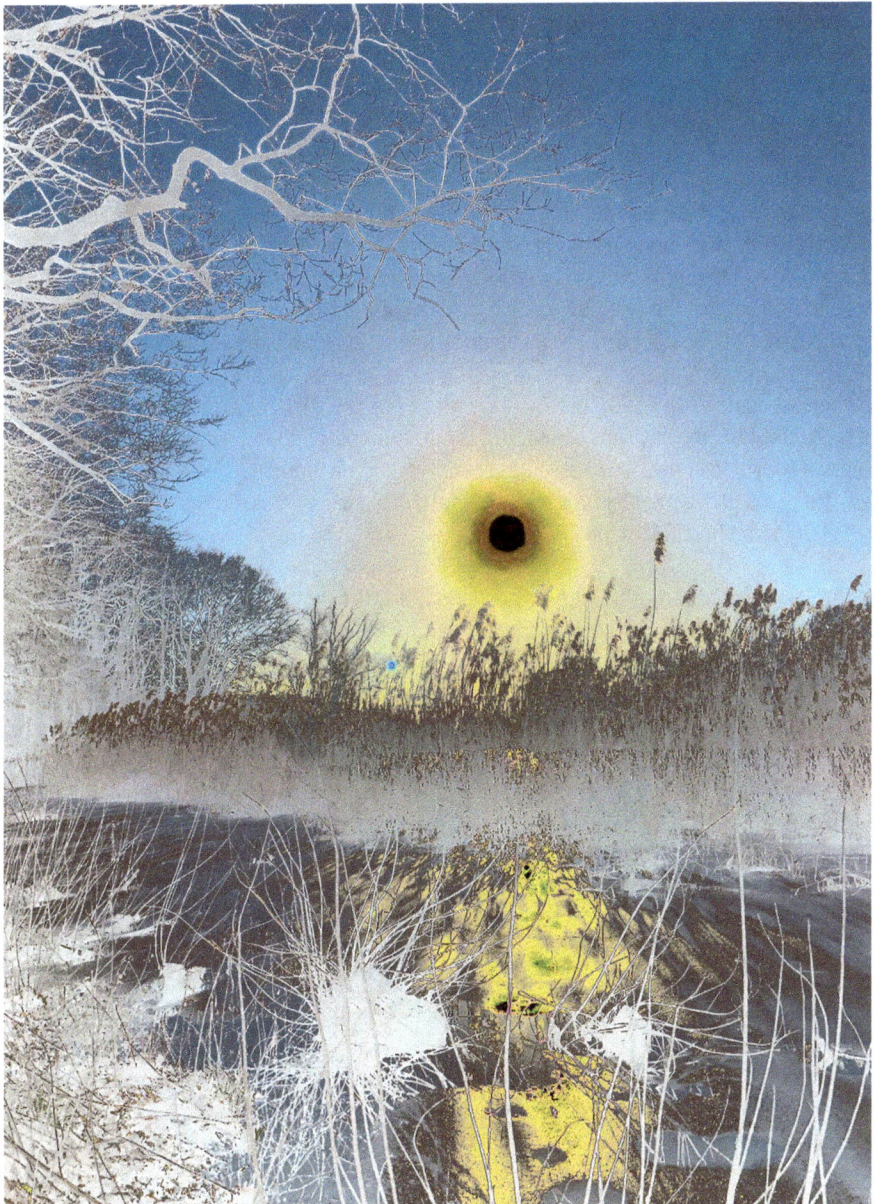

Figure 41: Tiny Domingos, 'Sonnenuntergang am Tegeler See,' digital edition, 2021.

In this second confinement, the measures are more restrictive. The world seems to be turned upside down; to influence the rate of homeworking, companies now justify why employees have to work in offices rather than from home.

After a year of the pandemic, a general increase in fatigue and existential anguish is percep-
tible, despite the German Minister of Finance assuring that the country's financial health is
strong and able to cope with a prolongation of the crisis.

Many artists are disoriented by the cancellation of fairs and exhibitions and by the impossibility
of planning trips. I, too, have been affected. Before the pandemic crisis happened, I frequent-
ly traveled to residencies and exhibitions in various countries. Last year, several important
projects were canceled or postponed a few times. One of them was a solo exhibition in the
U.S. for which I had obtained support. This year, I still have a lot of things on standby. Due to
the situation, organizers are slow to set dates for planned events. I run a small project space
and I have had to postpone its programming myself. I still don't know when we can reopen.

It's not all bad news. In 2020, I received a grant from a special program that the Berlin Senate
organized to help the local arts scene. I think that extending support for artistic creation is the
right way out of the crisis. Several voices are calling for the promotion of art and research as a
way out of the pandemic's slump. I believe that the measures taken in Berlin in this direction
will bear interesting fruit in the near future.

In terms of personal routine, the biggest change is the fact that I cannot organize or visit
exhibitions in Berlin (in this second confinement). I work a lot at home. In a writer's way, I am
used to solitary work and so my daily life has not been disturbed much. However, there are
some important changes. My teenage children are at home and interactions are therefore
more frequent. It feels like we are on a boat trip, each in their cabin and with frequent encounters on deck. It is like a journey through pandemic time in which they increasingly resemble
university students, busy meeting their deadlines and perfecting their laptop presentations.

Since 2018, I started working on the notion of resilience and risk management. My project
LANDSLIDE (Resilience in Unstable Times), presented to the public in 2019, drew a parallel
between natural cataclysms and financial crises and pointed to the dialogue between art
and science as a way out of a crisis. The presented works were inspired by graphics and
statistics used by scientists and policymakers. The pandemic has reinforced the ubiquity
of data visualization. Since its inception, we are confronted daily with graphs, statistics, and
3D representations. The word 'resilience' has been battered to the point of becoming almost
unbearable. But the near future of our family, social and professional lives, the reopening of
schools, borders, and airline connections depend on the evolution of the upward and down-
ward curves of contagions, deaths, and vaccinations expressed through graphic language.
The symbolism and implications of these digital images are fascinating.

LANDSLIDE allowed me to understand the importance of monitoring and interpreting data to
avoid or at least mitigate the next crisis. I was fascinated by the interrelation between practice
and theory and the interconnection between areas as distinct as mathematics and geophysics
with art history, cultural heritage, economy, and civil protection. The COVID-19 pandemic
further widened the range of interconnections between disciplines. Almost everything is inter-
connected, from the tiniest subatomic particles to the furthest celestial bodies in our galaxy,
from the urbanization of forest areas in remote regions of China to Portuguese hospitals.

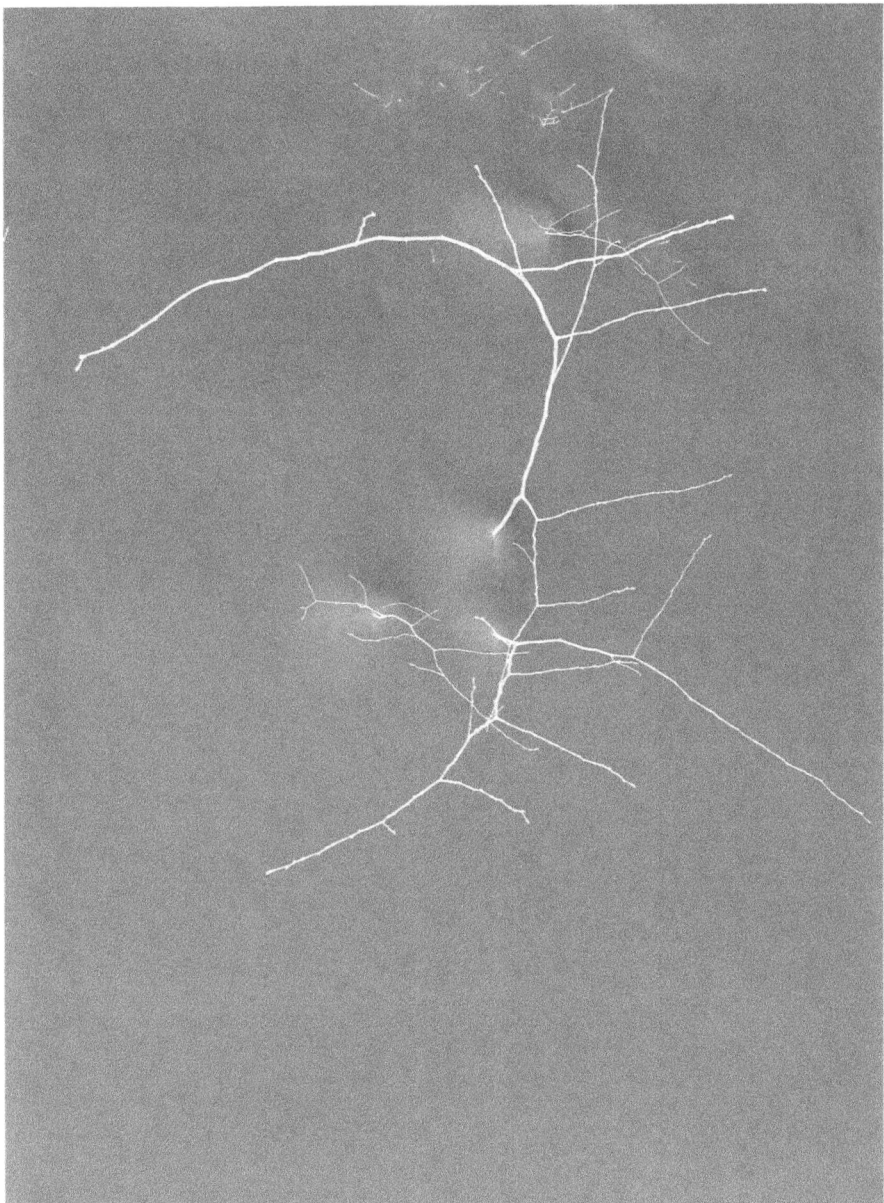

Figure 42: Tiny Domingos, Spross, digital edition 2021.

I took advantage of 2020 to intensify my interdisciplinary research. I was privileged enough to immerse my body and soul in the maelstrom of thoughts, reflections, workshops, and reading groups on the internet. The result is an extremely enriching drift.

There are several recurring themes: deep time, the fragility of the living conditions on our planet, the need to change the way we inhabit it, recreate a new sense of belonging and community with the living and mineral world with the help of fiction, AI, and technology.

I think I am living in one of the most inspiring periods of my life. It fits perfectly: a paradigm shift is urgent. My new challenges are the translation and presentation of my reflections into an artistic language. Low tide corresponds to a period of retreat and recollection. High tide will be the moment of advance, of transporting new elements to the shore.

The photos included with this interview are part of a completely new series I did locally during the lockdown. They are inspired by the lockdown's mobility restriction and local landscape rediscovery. Before that, I was working on digital chart imagery that has now become the very visual language of the pandemic's evolution.

DANIELA DE PAULIS

Having spent most of my past few years traveling for work, conferences, exhibitions, and so on, this suddenly extended time of settlement and focus felt almost like a retreat for my whole being.

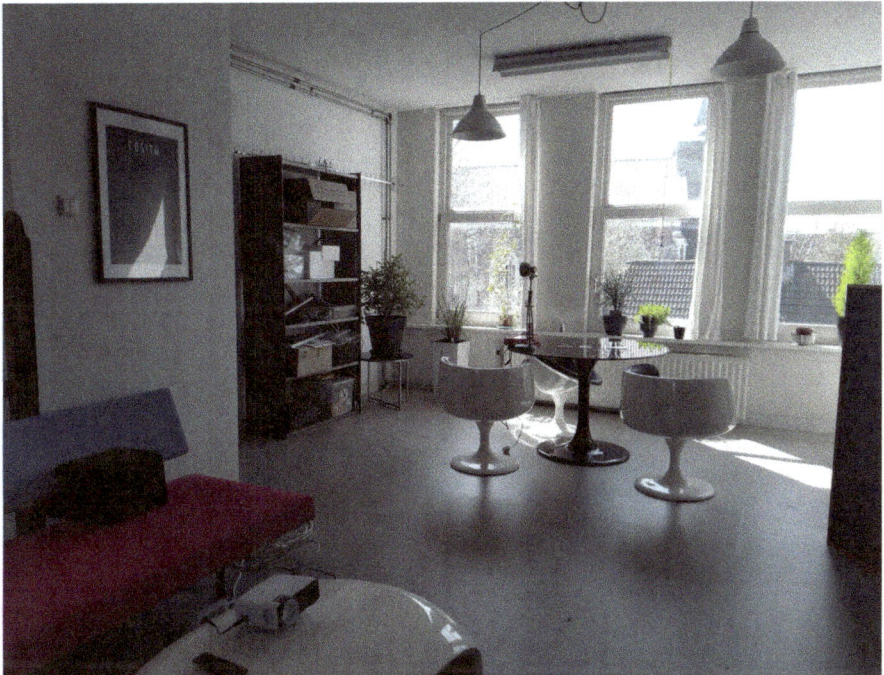

Figure 43: Daniela de Paulis' new home studio.

I live in Charlois, in the south of Rotterdam. In late January last year, I had just returned from Rome where I was working on a project at the Ancient Appian Way. Just as I left Italy, the pandemic was declared in the country. It wasn't clear how and if that would affect me in the Netherlands. However, it soon became clear that the pandemic was spreading everywhere and, although cautiously, the Netherlands eventually took some measures to contain the spread. At first, it seemed as if the restrictions would last only for a few weeks.

It was interesting to witness how different countries tackled the emergency of the pandemic. During the first wave, for example, the use of masks was compulsory in Italy but discouraged in the Netherlands due to their shortage in hospitals. My parents, in a helpless attempt to be close from a long distance, thought of sending me some masks by post. Knowing they are elderly and they had to queue at the post office with all the restrictions in place made this a special gift for me. Speaking with my relatives and friends in Italy, it was clear they were enjoying very little freedom or none. Trivial actions such as walking the dog or buying food were regarded as major outings and social events.

Eventually, spontaneous forms of interaction such as singing in balconies and solidarity amongst people made the headlines in international media. At the same time my life here in Rotterdam, and especially in Charlois, felt very dissimilar. After an initial reaction of surprise to the sudden changes in habits, people seemed to maintain some degree of optimism and a skeptical approach towards social distancing and using masks. At times, going to the local shops and supermarket, it felt as if my area was shielded by the pandemic and that the international news somehow didn't reach here; wearing a mask was a reason for being observed with suspicion in the shops. Hiding my face behind the mask was probably not well received by some people proudly breathing the shared air of denial.

Weeks and months went by and gradually the pandemic shed some critical light upon established Western values such as 'freedom.' It was interesting to observe how differently such a fundamental concept was understood and claimed by people from around the world, concerning pandemic-related restrictions. In Italy, where the culture could be superficially perceived as rule-adverse, people were keen to obey the very strict regulations, almost feeling united by them. In the Netherlands on the other hand, it felt as if each step of the containment was received with some resistance, perhaps in the name of personal and commercial freedom.

Still, I was pleased to be here. I simply limited myself to seeing very few people and spending most of the time in my house and my studio. This provided me with a safe zone. Having spent most of the past few years traveling for work, conferences, exhibitions, and so on, this suddenly extended time of settlement and focus felt almost like a retreat for my whole being. Being for approximately four months mostly confined in my studio allowed me to work on projects I had left behind for years. This period became an opportunity to gather energy and sharpen ideas. When the rules were eventually relieved across Europe during the summer of 2020, nobody perhaps expected that the confinement was going to become normality for the year to come.

During the summer, I had the opportunity to briefly visit my family in Italy. When I left them again, we greeted the feeling of not knowing when we would see each other next. I was pleased to hear that my father, who turned 93 this April, got vaccinated last month and that my mother will follow in May. In the Netherlands, vaccinations started in January but I am not fully aware of its extent yet and if vulnerable people, such as the elderly, are being made a priority, like in some other countries. Especially now I regret not being fluent in Dutch, as I don't fully grasp the current situation here. Another puzzling aspect for me has been making sense of how daily deaths are counted in every country. The criteria and parameters seem to vary. I am left with the feeling that the overall numbers worldwide are underestimated and that we are suffering a much greater loss, especially in large countries where it is even harder to monitor the spread of the virus.

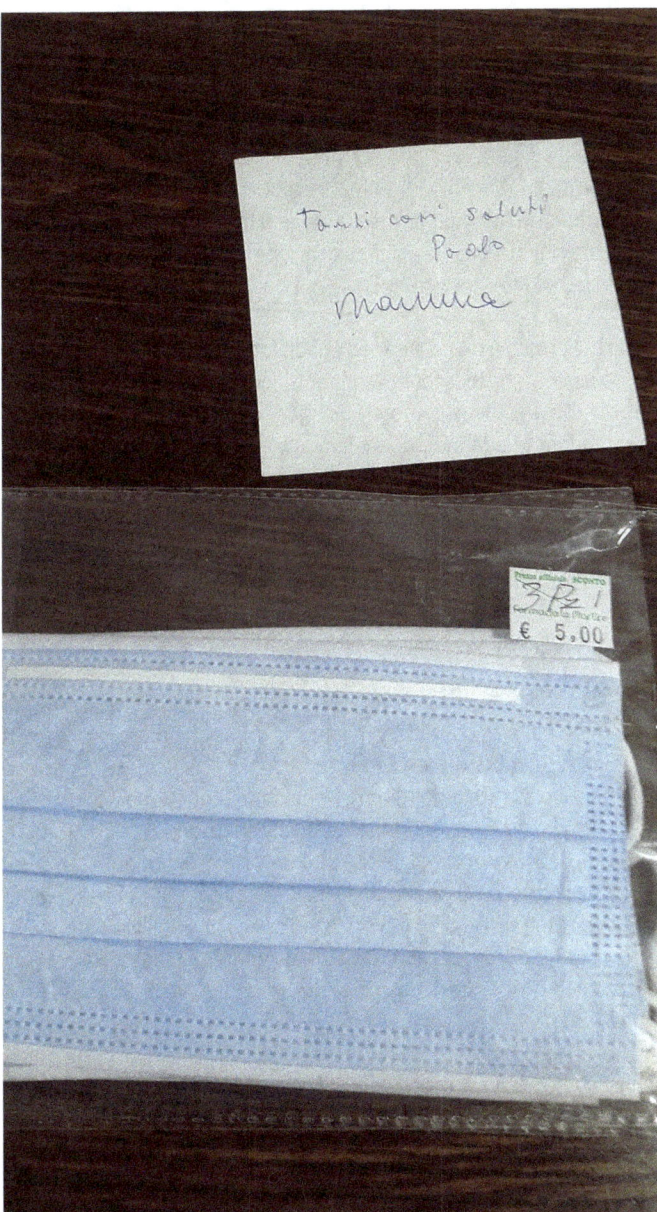

Figure 44: Facemasks, a gift from Daniela's parents.

The virus has affected some of the people I know. A dear friend is still recovering from 'long Covid' and the father of another dear friend has been hospitalized with a 50/50 chance to survive. This man is currently recovering from being on a ventilator for a week. His family thought they were going to lose him when he entered intensive care. Having him back felt like regaining a loved one from a place of despair for them. Knowing these and other personal stories from people who are close to me, made me think of the countless untold personal stories of people who suffered directly or indirectly from the virus. After more than a year since the start of the pandemic, it feels as if a sense of vulnerability is encroaching. For now, the psychological and social consequences of the pandemic have not been properly outlined yet, but I think this historic event will generate an enormous cultural, scientific, and social response in the years to come. With time, we might better understand how people's lives have been affected in different countries. In the meantime, for me and the people around me, the social restrictions feel necessary but increasingly difficult to cope with. At times, a feeling of hopelessness prevails; a feeling that life as we knew it will not be restored.

At first, the pandemic helped me create a much-needed space for reflection. I used this time to work on ideas, research topics, and logistics for new projects, looking for collaborators, and applying for funding. I could do all these things remotely using my computer. I even fully developed a new project and I wrote four academic papers in a few months, an absolute record for me. Online talks and teaching helped me financially, as I saw several of my exhibitions and other plans being canceled. This was perhaps the part that affected my work the most, as these exhibitions would have been hosted at prominent art spaces internationally and were the result of months of planning. Governmental support – additional funding schemes especially released for artists during the emergency – has been very helpful and has allowed me to continue working for the past year.

During the first wave of the pandemic, it has been very supportive to connect with new collaborators, and with the international art community in general, through online meetings. It was great to see new possibilities arise from these conversations. It has been very positive for me to share concerns and struggles with other practitioners from around the world during this time, while it seemed things would improve in the relatively short run. It felt as if some art communities were blooming in this period of crisis, and several new initiatives started taking place. I felt especially connected with the Leonardo Network that organized regular meetings, which helped to keep some sense of direction. Also, a regular weekly meeting with space philosopher Frank White and other space professionals and enthusiasts helped me keep a window open towards society at large, focusing on topics that have been relevant in my artistic practice for many years.

During these meetings, sharing the struggle of social isolation with people from around the world provided some solace. We shared a sense of connection and genuine empathy in each of these virtual gatherings through electronic screens and small digital windows. Now, after more than a year, with restrictions becoming alternatively more severe and loosening down, a profound sense of uncertainty is settling in though.

Whereas most events have moved online by now, it is very hard to implement plans made for projects during the first wave. Plans keep being shifted. On the other hand, as an artist, I am exploring new ways of working, without physically moving. At the same time, I am revisiting my past work as a movement artist, for which I have mostly mental recollection and very little visual documentation. I started to realize how my training and my work as a dancer have been informing all my projects, even those I now develop remotely. During this lockdown, I started reading about the Extended Mind Thesis and I drew intersections with the kind of mindset I have been adopting during the pandemic. The entire world seems to be operating in this extended mind mode through technology while physical distancing remains mandatory.

Watching *No Home Movie* by Chantal Akerman, amongst the many other films I had the opportunity to see over the last year, partly inspired my renewed interest in movement and dance. The film focuses on the daily life of the director's elderly mother. Watching this particular movie during a time of constricted mobility allowed me to experience the film as a touching reflection upon the daily life of many people around the world in this particular time in history. The film records the daily movements of an elderly person in and around her home in a very meticulous way. Her movements are shown as if belonging to the house, merging with the furniture and every single space of her home, leaving invisible traces of her presence on pieces of furniture and the spaces between them. These signs become visible once the mother is not alive anymore; every part of the house seems to project back her movements, making her absence even more vivid. In the film, the home becomes a sanctuary of her presence and her physicality.

The spaces and temporal cadence in *No Home Movie* are even more poignant and tangible in the current time, when we carry out our lives mostly inside homes, shaping a form of a profound dialogue between our lived spaces and ourselves. Such spaces become for many the main companions, the main reference to confined existences.

After spending several months of the pandemic on my own in a small house which has been doubling as a studio, I was pleased to acquire a larger studio at the end of 2020. While my house in a 'normal' situation would have been big enough, during the pandemic it started to feel like a cage, filled with the moods that had been accompanying me. I felt quite relieved once I could use the new studio that provided me with a revived environment. New plants started filling the space and since then I became fascinated with observing their subtle daily changes.

During the pandemic, I gathered enough energy to work on several projects at the same time and to turn disappointment into new opportunities. One of the 2020 highlights for me was the invitation to join the Leonardo/OLATS Space Art-Science Workshop «All Women Crew» in Paris, an international meeting of prominent women artists, with the plan of sharing experiences and getting to know each other. As the workshop was eventually canceled, Annick Bureaud, one of the meeting's organizers, suggested traveling to the Moon as a crew thanks to an amateur radio technology I helped develop in 2009 called *Visual Moonbounce*. Teaming up with some radio operators around the world, we sent to the Moon and back images created by French artist Quentin Aurat for the workshop, featuring the portraits of all of us, 'women crew' members. This virtual journey into space through radio waves of an all-women crew remains a key memory of the workshop and our unconventional collaboration. I can imagine us looking at these images in twenty years and thinking of the many memories associated with them and of this time in history

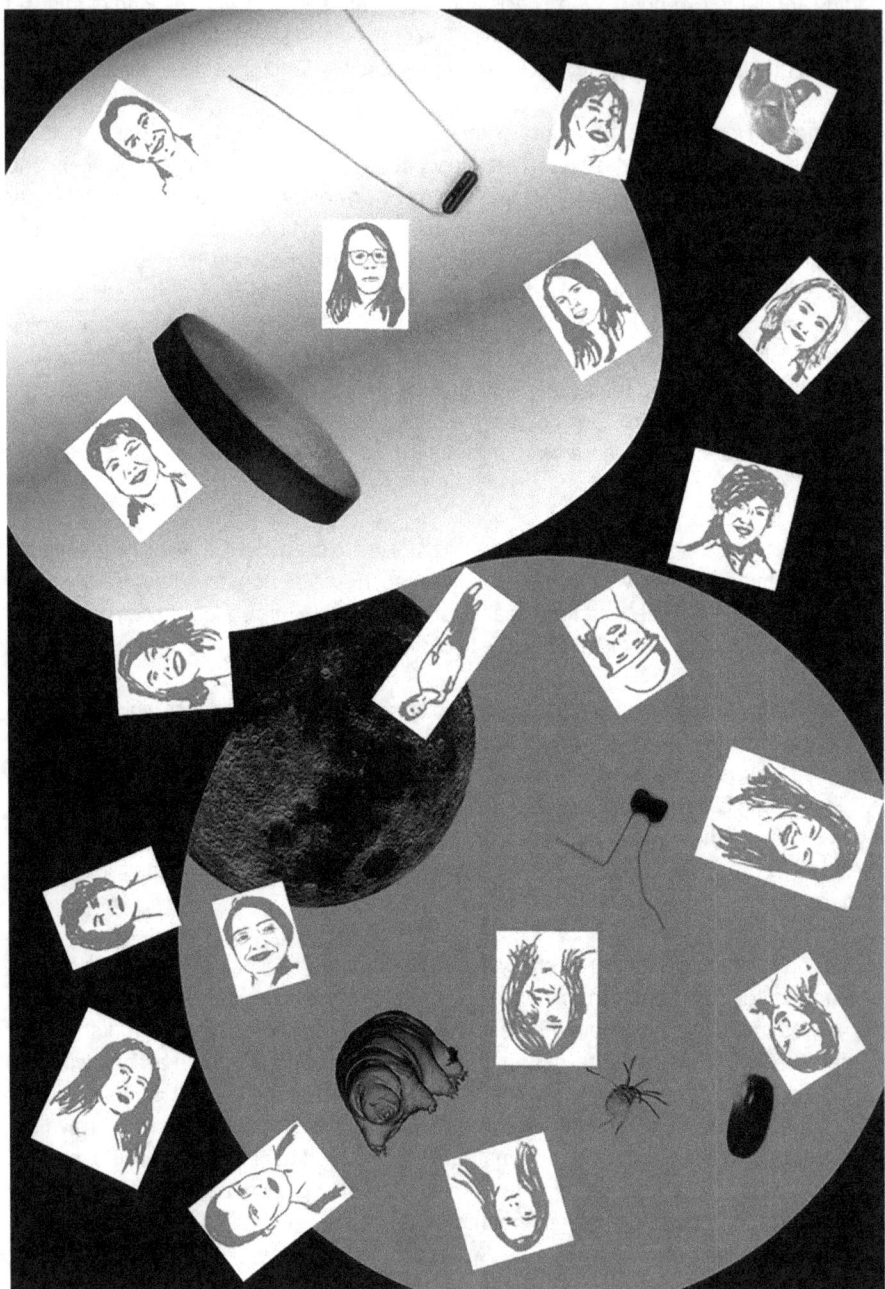

Figure 45: Original image by Quentin Aurat for the 'All Women Crew' workshop, organized by Olats/Leonardo.

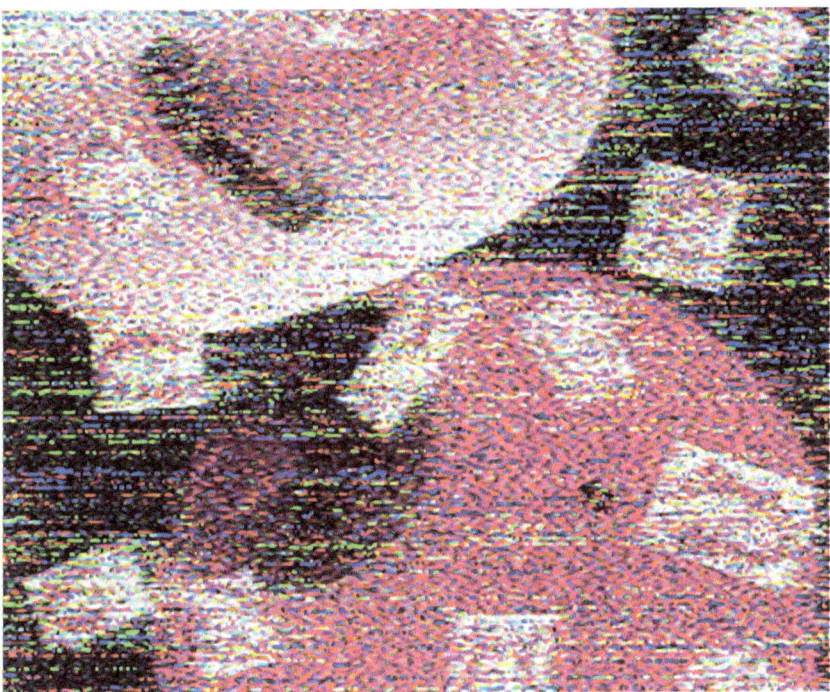

Figure 46: Moon reflected image. Credits: Quentin Aurat, 'All Women Crew' participants and organizers, Daniela de Paulis, Dan Gautchi, Mario Armando Natali, Nando Pellegrini.

As the pandemic gradually eroded all travel plans and physical exhibitions, other projects and ideas left behind for some years started taking shape. More remote collaborations were established.

I resumed a project that I started in 2015, for which I obtained the neural activity of insects, recorded by researchers at the University of Tel Aviv. I called the project 'The Metamorphosis of a Periplaneta Americana' and I transmitted the neural recordings into space remotely, in collaboration with a radio operator in Italy. This project started as an extension of my long-term work *Cogito in Space* into the realm of animals other than humans. It generated an interesting conversation with the scientists involved and a philosopher specialized in animal ethics. The result of these conversations was published in a recent paper for the Leonardo MIT Journal.

In addition to working on 'The Metamorphosis...,' I initiated a new interdisciplinary project that is part of a larger study on how COVID-19 is affecting sleep, in collaboration with a team of neuroscientists at the University of Cambridge. They are researching the effects of the lockdown and pandemic on sleep and dreams as part of an international research project, involving several laboratories. For this, we have been hosting weekly online meetings It is my first time working with collaborators I had never met in person but, interestingly, we are building a positive atmosphere amongst us, thanks to the mutual interest in the ideas we are developing for the project. However, we are working with the ever-present sense of uncertainty that the plan we are developing might not be implemented soon or might have to be postponed or even canceled, depending on how the international travel scenario evolves.

After more than a year of living and working online, with the inability to plan ahead, things are starting to feel unreal. Past, present, and future are becoming one grey area. There is no way to know in advance how you are going to be affected by the virus or how your actions might affect the lives of other people. I am distressed by the possibility of losing loved ones and by the uncertainty of how sustainable my life as an artist can be in the current and future scenario.

IGOR VAMOS

The reduction of travel was a great thing for my time and health — I was on the road far too much.

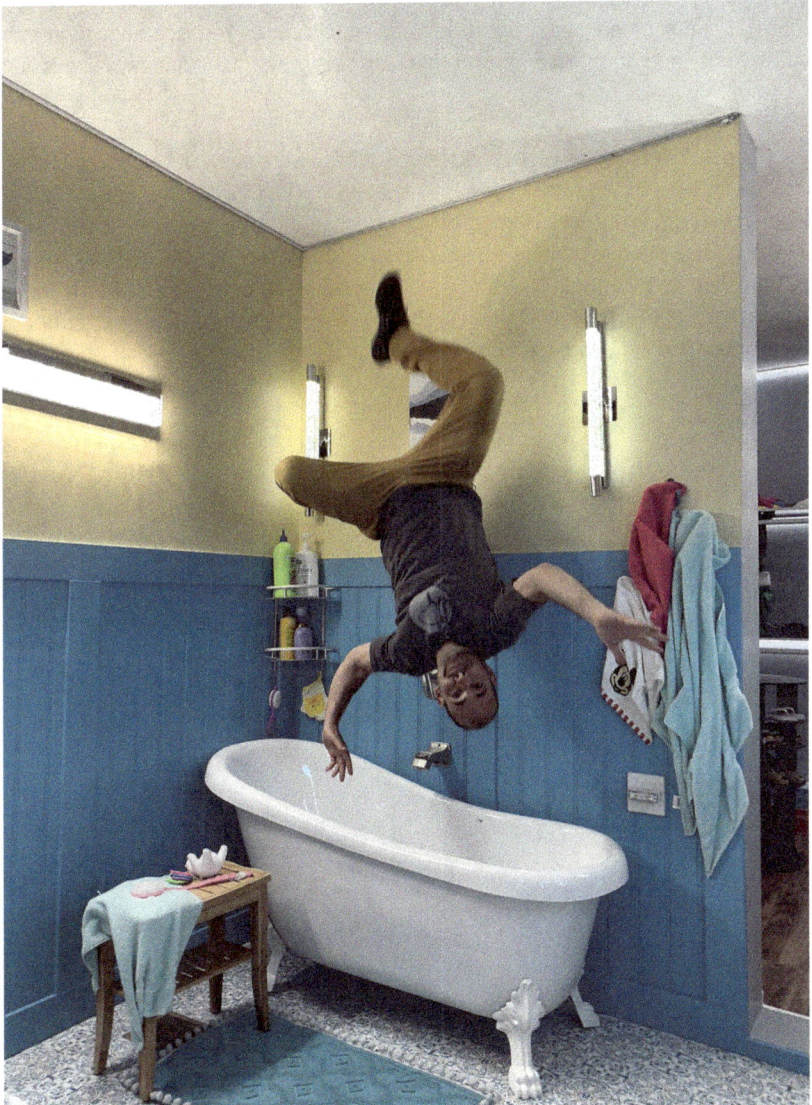

Figure 47: Vamos (or Bonnano, I can't remember which one I am) has found more fulfilling ways to enjoy life without leaving home.

Despite being in two countries that have handled the pandemic very badly (U.S. and UK), I have been fortunate to spend most of my time in smaller cities — Troy in New York, and

Dundee in Scotland. These two regions have somewhat lower rates of COVID-19 compared to other places in the world and have easy access to natural areas for recreation.

I am lucky to have an academic post that has not gone away during the pandemic. The reduction of travel was a great thing for my time and health – I was on the road far too much. I have been enjoying staying put and not being tired all the time. Adapting to these new circumstances has been not too hard. I also have three kids, so when I am spending time with them I am very busy and don't have time for much else anyway. I don't find myself missing much as a result.

For me, the pandemic has been a really good opportunity to write again. It has been good for generating new ideas and new work. I have frankly been in a kind of rut for about a decade – I have been doing largely the same things without much attention to innovation, or at least that's the way I have felt about it. I have been doing things that required lots of travel and I was tired all the time, so this is actually leading to some new ideas for me. I'm excited to move out of the pandemic, but I am very lucky to have been able to have my former life interrupted while maintaining my job and income.

MELINDA RACKHAM

I think as a nation Australia was at a very low ebb when the second wave of the COV-ID-19 pandemic hit, and there is a sadness and a bitterness that the arts sector, which is always supporting our communities when there is a crisis, have been completely ignored in recovery efforts except for instances where, like me, you slip through a crack into the safety of the system.

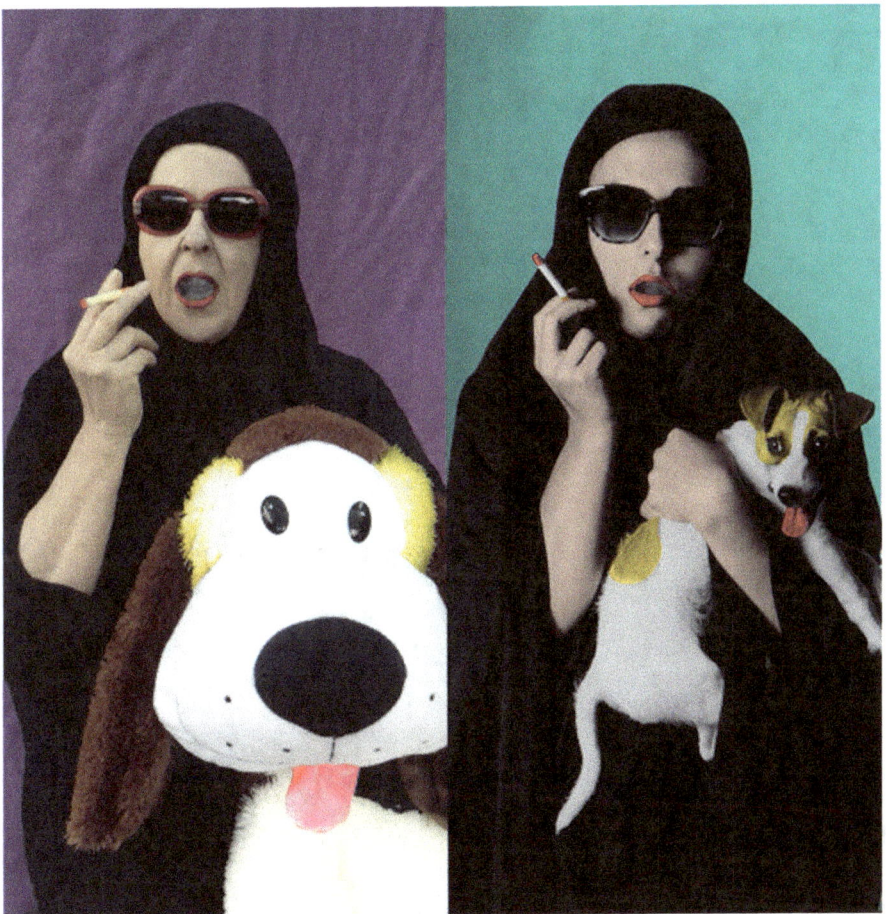

Figure 48: Melinda Rackham, 'Remake Hoda Afshar,' 2020.

I'm fascinated by viruses, having researched, written, and made net art on virial infection, immunophilosophy, and epidemiology to understand my own chronic debilitating Hepatitis C Viral infection and the systemic autoimmune disorders which codeveloped, including losing my thyroid, other malfunctioning glands, joint inflammation, and fatigue. The ability of a virus to shimmy past immune defenses, nestle into our human body's cellular core, using us to replicate itself and infect others while leaving the host/ess permanently damaged or dead, is the ultimate colonization by stealth.

So, when the Wuhan wet market story broke, I followed it closely. Just as interesting as the zoonosis were the packaged responses, denials, propaganda, and conspiracy theories coming from political and market interests, making a global pandemic into a divisive crisis of faith. Geographically, Australia is an island, and it is theoretically easy to shut down air and seaports quickly. But swiftly mutating news, opinions and theories infected us all. The world began to feel medieval.

Border control wasn't as simple as it could have been, as each of Australia's eight states can operate independently. The Ruby Princess cruise liner docked in Sydney with COVID-19-infected tourists allowed to disembark and mingle with the general population in a city of five or so million people. That was when it hit home and national borders were shut down, except for returning citizens and those with special entry permits doing two-week quarantines in large city hotels. Meanwhile, celebrities got to quarantine in their own palatial estates. All of our Australian outbreak clusters and deaths come from quarantine protocol breaches such as security guards partying with people they were there to secure; medical equipment transmission; hotel cleaners working second jobs making pizzas and driving Ubers.

Australia has had some of the lowest death rates and some of the heaviest lockdowns in the world. Tracing apps are not uniform and regulations can change almost instantly. It might be announced at midday interstate borders will close at midnight and there is chaos at airports and roads with people trying to leave or return. While this has been incredibly effective with only 909 COVID-19 deaths in the past year, there is also a long list of co-morbidities of the infection as well as the collateral damage of job loss, social isolation, a mental health epidemic, suicide, higher drug use, protests, border runners, fines of $1000s for leaving home. Businesses, art galleries, theatres, cinemas, hotels all shut down. However, our billionaires all managed to double their wealth. Women have been hardest hit as the more casual workers in the more vulnerable industries. I've removed people from my life because I couldn't bear to hear any more righteous views that we aren't told the truth by the media and the world is run by an evil cabal. Really!!

I'm in South Australia (only four COVID deaths), which has a coastal Mediterranean climate and inland desert, with a large wine and fruit industry and strict biosecurity on imports and infectious diseases. It's proud to have the last genetically pure population of the Italian Ligurian honeybees on the planet, isolated from the mainland on Kangaroo Island about seventy kilometers across the bay from where I currently live. Just before COVID-19, KI as we call it was ravaged during the 2020 bushfires. 50% of the island was destroyed along with 80% of the farm and native animals like sheep, black cockatoos, lizards, kangaroos, koalas, and the beehives and ecosystems. Across Australia, those fires killed three BILLION animals, with around 450 humans dying directly from burns or later from smoke inhalation illnesses. The daily news cycle of devastation and death was a horrific and traumatic reminder of our human frailty on the planet.

Artists, while mostly not on the physical bush fire frontline, were organizing community fund-raising responses, food, and shelter; performing benefits; donating artworks to help those directly affected. I think that as a nation, Australia was at a very low ebb when the second wave of the COVID-19 pandemic hit. There is a sadness and a bitterness that the arts sector, which is always supporting our communities when there is a crisis, has been completely ignored in recovery efforts except for instances where, like me, you slip through a crack into the safety of the system.

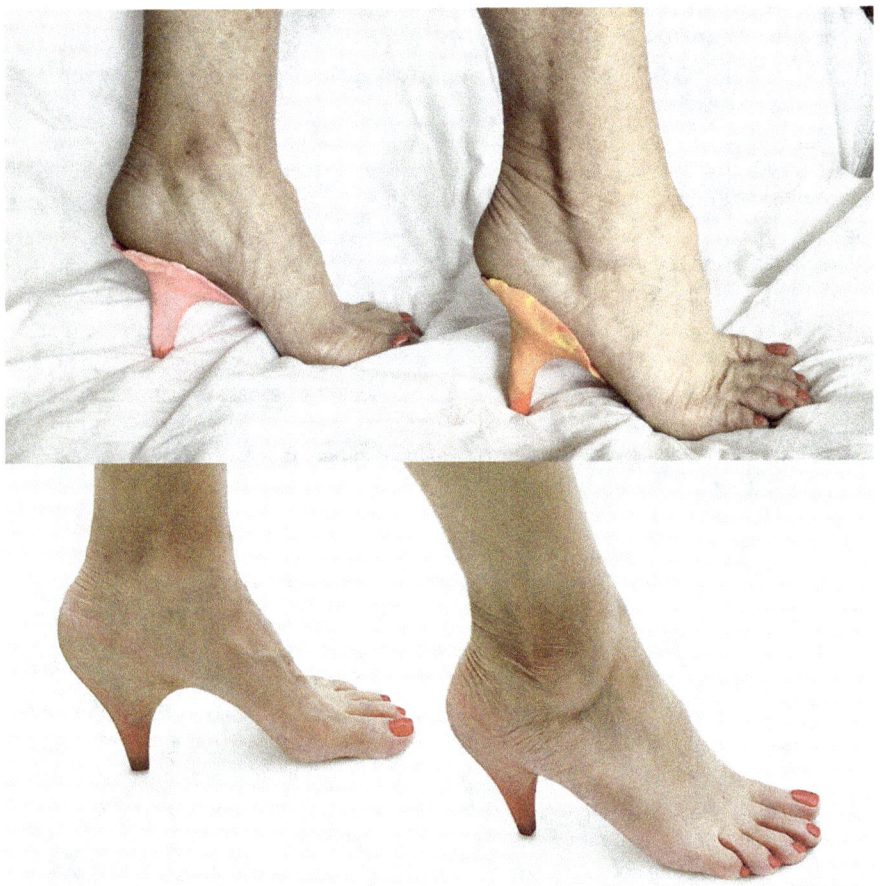

Figure 49: Melinda Rackham, 'Remake Julie Rrap,' 2020.

I consider myself very lucky to have flourished, partially from being eligible for the Australian government's frantically enacted financial support measures. Everyone from small businesses, major corporations, and religious orders, received the same amount per employee. My long-term creative practice qualified me as a small business with a significant downturn in income with travel, articles, shows, talks, and contracts canceled. So I've had a 'JobKeeper' income supplement from April 2020 – originally at $AU1,500 (€975) per fortnight, decreasing over a year to end in March 2021 at $AU650 (€422) per fortnight. At any time it's incredible to have a consistent income as an artist, but this ongoing support was bittersweet proof that national economies are flexible systems, budgets never have to be balanced, and every government in every country could enact a Universal Basic Income today if they wanted to.

There was lots of talk of financial stimulus, but the arts were only ever mentioned in terms of trade skills such as set builders for the opera. A dated pop singer occasionally stood behind our Prime Minister at press conferences to weakly signal diversity. The plethora of individual and collective artists, writers, dancers, musicians, all creatives who question, challenge, celebrate both everyday life and overarching issues – the very people who hold our cultural space in times of trouble with beauty, insight, and meaning – were rendered invisible and superfluous to society under the guise of the pandemic emergency.

I am in a high-risk category for severe COVID-19 illness, and my partner works in front-line health with vulnerable communities, so I moved to her house on the Fleurieu Peninsula while she stayed in the city to work, visiting for a day a week. 25 years ago, when I started working online, I lived by myself in a small seaside village and the situation felt a bit like coming full circle. I'd been avoiding social media for most of the past decade. The Web 2.0 Suicide Machine helped me to sign off Facebook and meet my neighbors again, but I picked up its almost as questionable sibling Instagram to search out reassuring niches. I'd found an Adelaide jeweler's 'lovely things I have seen today;' a Londoner's delicately illustrated lockdown diary; storm damage, shopping lists, and squirrels from Iowa. Reconnecting with artists and writers from Sao Paulo, Berlin, Hong Kong, Beijing, and comparing COVID-19 experiences always left me feeling incredibly grateful for my island home.

The vaccines are being rolled out here now and I'm having more of a hard time adjusting back into the local community. I don't want to see groups of people and I get tired quickly when I am out. Last year I couldn't see a very close and very loved family member before she died or attend her small funeral, but I traveled interstate a few weeks ago to her belated memorial service. It's the end of a sense of family for me and there is a lot of sadness. My interstate re-entry permit was approved after I outlined my travel plans included visiting the graves of my mother and son. Thankfully, when my flight home landed, the border rules had changed in the previous 12 hours and I didn't have to self-isolate again. After passing through banks of technology and security, the final checkpoint person gave me a retro ADMIT ONE cinema ticket. I stared in a sort of detached way at the small piece of paper I was crumpling in my hand and couldn't quite comprehend its meaning and purpose. Was it a COVID-19 souvenir or a surreal joke?

I feel almost guilty saying this as elsewhere in the world so many were struggling under very different circumstances and difficult conditions, but it's been a very creatively fruitful time for me. I had financial and housing security – a room of one's own to loosely quote Virginia Woolf. I pretty much self-isolated for the past year in a seaside town with our very protective camp dog for company. I had contactless home-delivered groceries and ordered and ate way too much ice cream... all very normal.

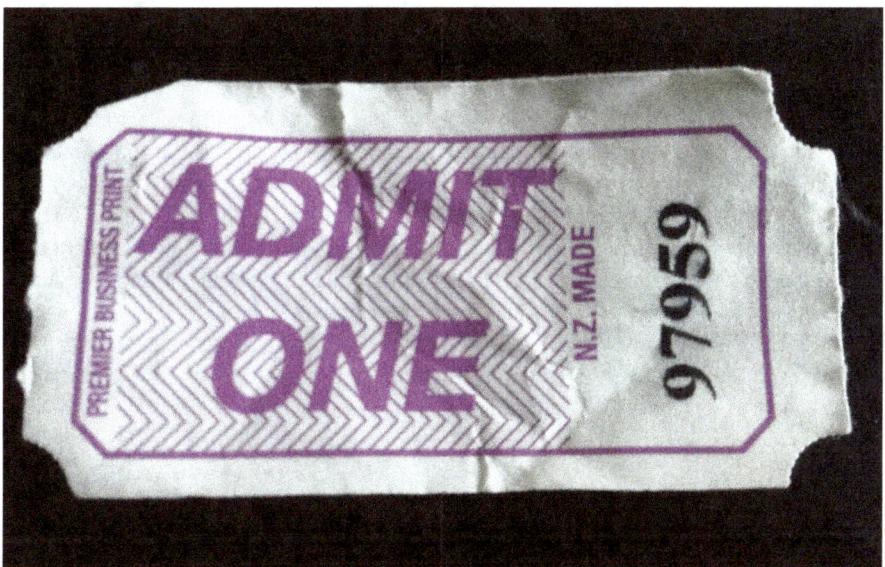

Figure 50: Ticket to cross the border between different Australian states.

It gave me the time and focus to finish *CoUNTess: Spoiling Illusions since 2008,* a book on gender asymmetry, unconscious bias, systemic prejudice, and blatant discrimination against women in the arts, which I am co-authoring with CoUNTess founder Elvis Richardson. And, as I don't think of myself as a maker of visual art, I made some very unexpected and playful works on Instagram.

Elvis (a dear friend I met at art school in the late 80s) and I had been traveling backward and forward between Adelaide and Melbourne, where she lives, for intensive writing residency periods pre-COVID. Then, when Melbourne had the hardest longest lockdowns, Elvis, her husband, and her adult son couldn't leave their house. We video called every day or every second day; we had our lunch together; worked away saying nothing or muttering to the computer; found a theme song which we fangirls screamed thru the screen at each other and danced in our respective studios and on our chairs. Of course, there were frustrations, but the memories are tinged in glowing light. I think I've spent more time in the past year with my co-author than my life partner. Yesterday, the ban on public dancing was lifted and Australians can legally dance near their chair or in a designated space with 50 people.

But back to social media. When seriously funny (or hilariously serious) remakes of the Edvard Munch's *The Scream*, monobrowed portraits of Frieda Kahlo and Vermeer's *Girl with a Pearl Earring* started appearing in my feeds, I tracked the source to @tussenkunstenquarantaine's *Stay at Home Challenge!* Following their lead, the Rijksmuseum in Amsterdam, the Getty in Los Angeles, the National Gallery of Australia (NGA), and others rushed online to engage their now stay-at-home audiences in the century's old pastime of recreating famous paintings or *tableau vivants*. Because my head was full of statistics of the poverty of women's representation in the art world, I knew women composed a mere 25% of the works in Australia's national collection and much less in many other countries. This call to create shared cultural moments from art collections of 'old masters' was asking for an intervention.

So, I decided to remake contemporary Australian women artists instead. I am actually quite a shy person but give me a sequined frock and a wig, and a diva appears. Using only materials I already had, I began to compose myself into works by 'modern mistresses;' not necessarily the best-known artists, but powerful works of self-portraiture across multiple media. All have a tinge of sexiness, humor, and intelligence, and use parody and irony playfully and critically. I wanted my remake and the originals to both speak to each other and to stand as discrete images, to encourage viewers to discover the context of the artist and their original work to add a deeper level of viewing and thinking pleasure. They were shot on an iPad mostly by my partner on her one-day visits, minimally edited, and posted to Instagram and Facebook (which I had to re-join briefly) under #remakemistresses.

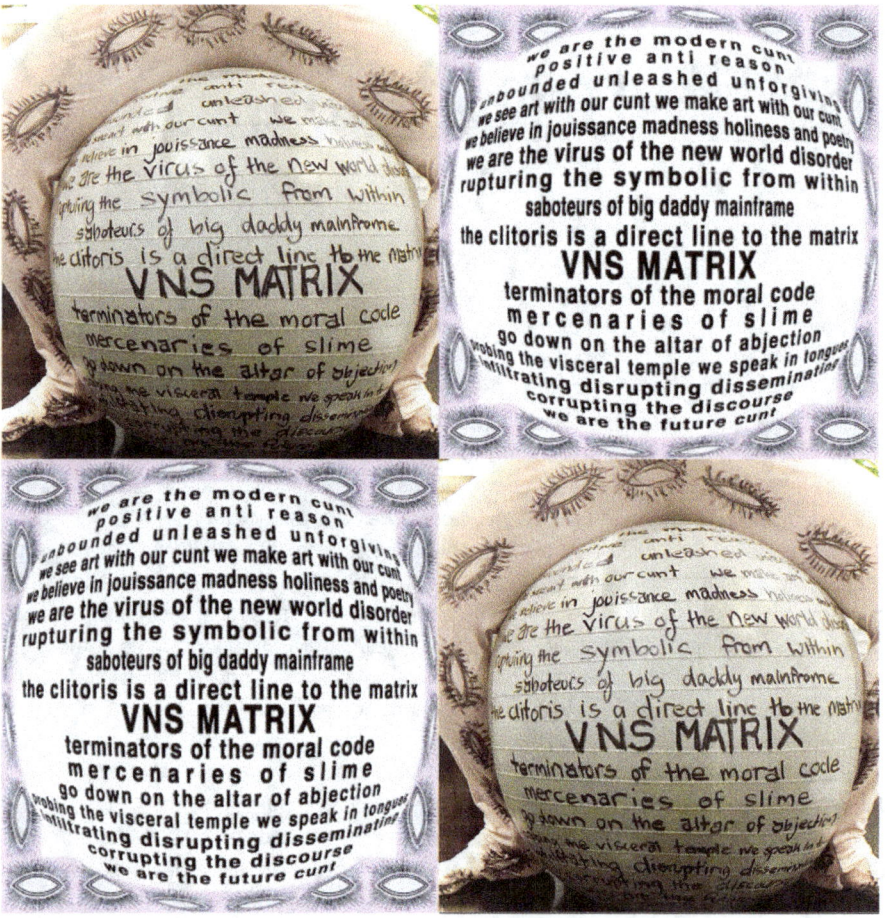

Figure 51: Melinda Rackham, 'Remake VNS Matrix,' 2020.

And the work has manifested back into the material – #remakemistresses was exhibited as a very lo-res video and printed as postcards. The hot pink Shining Cunt leggings I made for the VNS Matrix Cyberfeminist Manifesto shoot are now spandexy and spangly, made sustainably on-demand in California with 80% of profits going to anti-racist and Aboriginal Deaths in Custody organizations and funds. It's also brought unforeseen immaterial gifts; one remake reconnected me after 30 years with the woman with whom I had my first art exhibition within the gallery we co-ran in 1988; another incorporated tangible artifacts of the artist's generosity in regularly repositioning her practice to raise money for refugees. The remakes reverberated and returned, each having a story of goodwill, perseverance, and hope that goes way beyond the glittery facade and air-kissing of the art world.

So much more than smart or funny Instagram pics, they extended me in ways I couldn't have imagined. I'm in my 60s now. It was amazing to have a sense of freedom to creatively and unselfconsciously platform and celebrate the aging female body. Social media comments revealed strong webs of connection between women artists and writers who champion and encourage each other. Some interesting dialogues began with First Nations women artists regarding the ethics of remaking their works that are already critiquing and reappropriating culture. I have wanted to take this further and had quite a few works in progress, but I sort of ran out of steam after thirty works. Perhaps it was a project that could thrive only under specific conditions, and they now no longer exist?

And the book needed attention again; it will drop in July! Our co-designer Maria Smit finally got to fly back to Australia from the Netherlands and was overjoyed to be allocated a quarantine room with a balcony. Over this COVID-19 year, I missed my old routines, like the yoga class where I don't know anyone personally but have felt so familiar with their bodies. There is a subtle shift in what is important. I've valued the collaborative process in ways I never have done before. I have an urgent need to write on my own identity and loss. I've really enjoyed hard physical work in the garden and would like to grow better vegetables. A dip in the ocean is like a week's holiday and I don't know if I will ever make visual art again. And there is a sense that none of this really matters.

IVAR VEERMÄE

We are facing a cleverly mediated and lobbied system, which aims to keep a status quo that in the end is destructive.

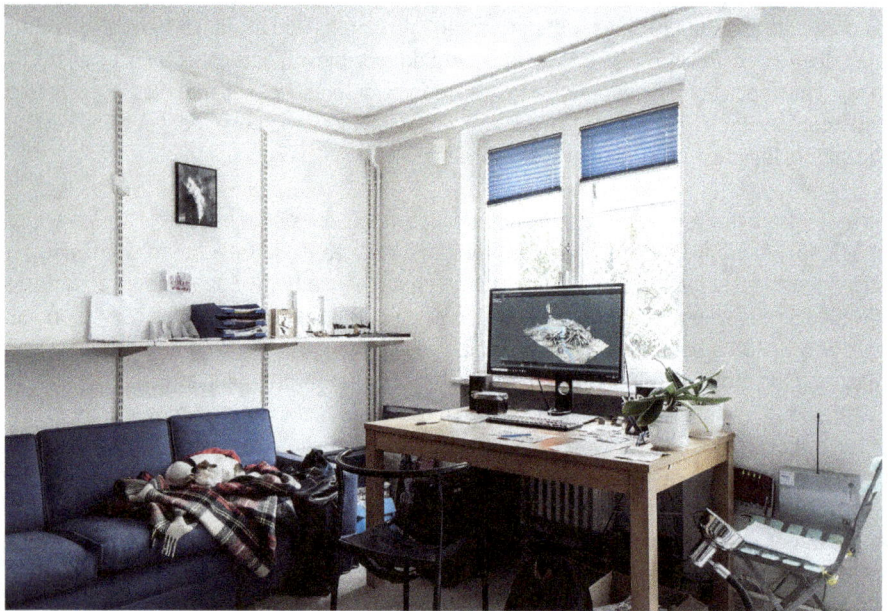

Figure 52: Ivar Veermäe, Studio (with Lily), 16.04.2021.

I live in Berlin, and Germany is now around three and half months under lockdown. I think that it seems reasonable when I compare it with Estonia, where I am from. Most of the places were open there during the last few months, and the partial lockdown started just now when the number of cases went up enormously.

Last year, at the beginning of the pandemic, the whole situation seemed weird. It seemed as if it was something temporary. Because I went through big personal changes in my life – by becoming a father in September 2019 – the loss of work opportunities meant more time to spend with my family. In the spring of 2020, my daughter was still very small and happy to be driven around in the *kinderwagen* [eng. baby carriage]. I went on so many walks with her, more than ever before. I tried to pick a different route almost every day. This approach drew my attention to Berlin's very diverse and weird architectural mixture. Additionally, I acknowledged the whole environment much more consciously. At the beginning of summer, galleries were open again, and I started making trips that included one or two exhibition visits.

Now, in March 2021, some openings are happening, like museums or smaller shops. Openings correspond to the number of COVID-19 cases: when these go up, places will close again. If they stay on a low level or go down, some more access will be possible. I think this dynamic could be quite a good way to find some balance. COVID-19 infection numbers vary across different places in Germany, which creates a bit of confusion. But I think it's okay. Why search for uniformity in complex matters?

In general, I noticed many more people being outside. At one point, I thought that maybe people were now more DIY in their actions because the (consumerist) offer was just not there. But these are just guesses. Similarly, I guess that many people had and are having a really hard time.

At the beginning of the pandemic last year, I stopped visiting my studio for two months. It is a room in a private house where other residents are elderly. I had time to read a lot, analyze my work and rethink it. I gathered thoughts and prepared for some projects, but I did not directly work on them; not really filming, photographing, editing, or doing 3D work.

Financially it has been a very difficult time, with no photography jobs and no exhibitions. In the beginning, financial aid for the self-employed from the German government of 5000 euro helped me get by until the end of the summer. After that, it was really difficult. I spent a lot of time applying for art grants. The flow of 'unfortunately your project was not selected' responses created a somewhat hopeless feeling, but not too hopeless to stop trying. Fortunately, I got one grant a few weeks ago that will help me until mid-summer 2021. This crisis created a massive push in competition in an already extremely competitive art field.

In my practice, I started working again in autumn last year. I would say that I was rather blocked throughout 2019, the year before the pandemic hit. In 2018, I had a very busy year doing new projects, participating in several solo and group exhibitions. After that things slowed down, apart from doing some paid photography work. Weirdly, for me, the pandemic was timely, in the sense that it didn't felt like a rupture. The situation, and most certainly in combination with the birth of my daughter, directed me towards new ways of thinking and acting.

I started thinking about what is important in life. Art practice is one possible human action among many. I think about human actions in general — how to reduce their importance but at the same time increase their weight? I mean humans are a force that penetrates quite a lot, but we are much more penetrated by the environment and things in it, other beings. Think about how a human is not just a human, but a collective organism; there are more nonhuman cells in humans than human ones.

Well, all these thoughts lead me to think about the climate crisis. How the pandemic makes the global crisis, which is mostly invisible and imperceptible in my geographical location, suddenly evident. The virus is not a separate alien entity that disturbs the normal, but a kind of relational planetary reaction. And 'things-as-they-were' had been quite CO_2 expensive. This is not just a personal moral issue.

We are facing a cleverly mediated and lobbied system, which aims to keep a status quo that in the end is destructive. I have been thinking about how to deal with it not so loudly. I mean activist groups like Extinction Rebellion and Greenpeace exist and are working well, but what can I do as an artist? I also think that (most of) the art audience is relatively well-informed about such issues. An important concern for me now is how to also act outside the art world.

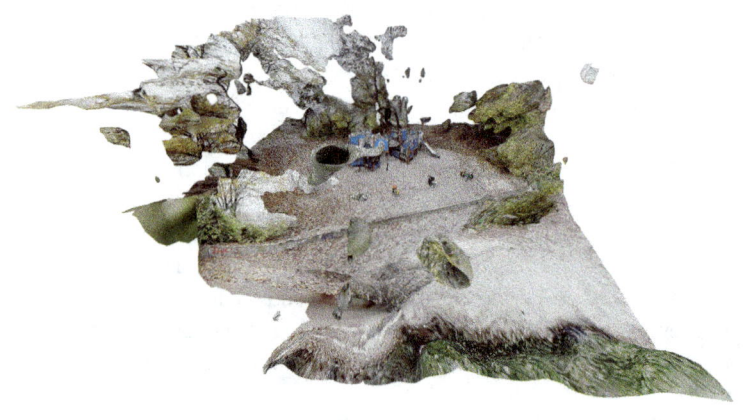

Figure 53: Ivar Veermäe, 'Spielplätze' (work in progress), 2021.

I am now preparing a project that will take shape through discussions with people in different locations across our planet Earth. I want to discuss possible futures and workable solutions for the climate crisis. We will also talk about misunderstandings that might occur: what seems like a good topic or question here might be quite alien somewhere else. My goal with the project is to create connections between very different disciplines and diverse audiences. The shape of the project will depend on the type of collaborations we will have. I aim to make it widely accessible, both on the web but also in specific physical locations. There will for example be public screenings and (digitally mediated) workshops and talks.

Additionally, I started a more modest work. It revolves around a strange question: would it be possible to reduce or relativize anthropocentric thinking to some extent, by manipulating images representing basic human emotions, behaviors, or processes in the brain? I will make digitally and physically altered prints, through experimentation with microorganisms for example. Maybe the idea is a bit far-fetched, but could these images blend the self and the environment, and make these distinctions less clear?

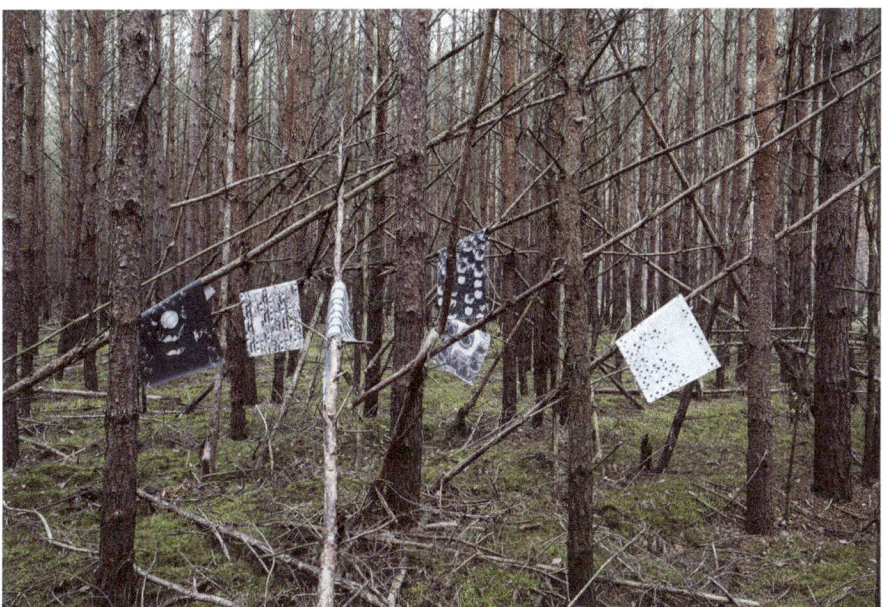

Figure 54: Ivar Veermäe, 'Backgrounds' (Test), Grünheide, 2020.

Somehow, I take the overall situation quite calmly. This does not mean that I am not careful or not protecting others and myself. Things are really bad, but my worrying does not improve the situation.

ARCÁNGELO CONSTANTINI

There are forces that are against social unity, that want to see us as competitive entities, consumers, predators of ecosystems, a social Darwinism that has the planet in jeopardy in its social, economic, and ecological processes. I think we should think of life and society as based on mutualism instead.

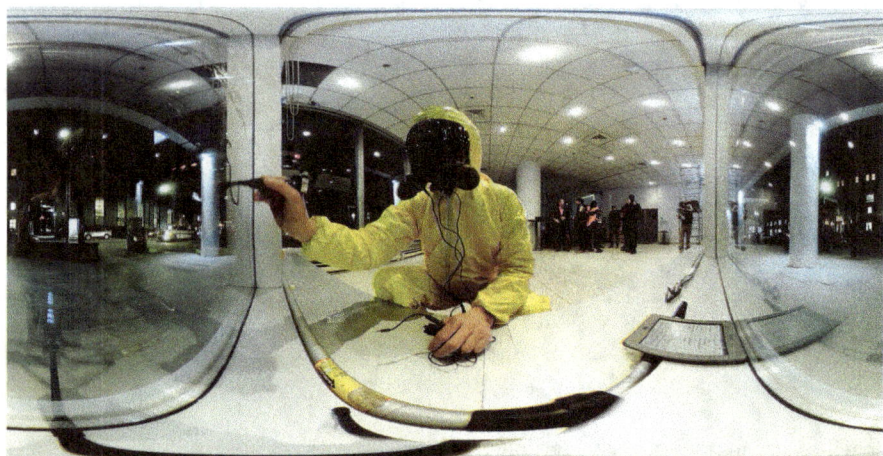

Figure 55: Arcangel Constantini, VitriNa SuBjeTiVa, Espacio Mexico Montréal, 2017.

The Mexican government took its time to implement security measures, and when it finally did, they were thinking more of the economy than of health. We already went through the H1N1 pandemic in 2009, which was the first time we lived a similar experience, globally, and Mexico was the epicenter of it. It was a kind of training, a way to understand how a pandemic would impact the current times we live in, and the government was not prepared to act effectively or correctly. In Mexico, two economies prevail, the informal and the formal: the former is outside the tax system and the latter is formalized. The rules are stricter for the formal economy and that is where the restrictions were applied. Movie theaters, restaurants, shopping malls, etc. were closed, while the informal economy continued with its activities in expanded form. A twilight zone economy developed: in front of the closed shops were now informal traders that would act as an intermediary between the closed shops and its customers. 'Tell me what you need, and I get it for you.'

In Mexico, we have a big problem of obesity and health issues related to poor nutrition. It is only now, during the third wave, that greater regulation of processed junk food products is beginning. The state is becoming more aware that it must invest political resources to improve the health of the people. However, when the second wave hit, they knew that the number of cases would increase exponentially, as entering the fall and winter influenza cases always increase. They knew that the hospital system would collapse and did not take action on the matter. They did not invest in preparing new hospitals, and now we are in fourth place on the list of countries with the highest number of corona-related deaths. There is a lack of social awareness, which is the legacy of previous governments that were not interested in improving public health, only in supporting big corporations. Mexico now has the first left-wing government in decades.

My last job with a fixed schedule was in 1999. Since 2000, I have been an independent artist. I am used to working from home, but even so, the lack of contact with people in the art world during the pandemic was problematic. Exhibitions, concerts, festivals were canceled. I was a tutor of FONCA, a grant program in Mexico for young creators in various disciplines of artistic production. There are more than 250 grant holders, and a fundamental and central part of this program is the face-to-face meetings. Artists and tutors travel to different states of the republic to hold meetings by discipline, where the artists make friends and contacts and share their processes and hypotheses. For this new generation, it is an important experience. Due to the pandemic, they had to cancel the meetings, and hold them telematically. Fortunately, the pandemic happened now, when we have these communication technologies. Ten years ago, things would have been very complicated.

As for myself, part of my work is online. For more than 20 years I have been developing a body of work related to the hypotheses of the hologenome and the microbiota. Scientific research in the last 10 years gave us a substantial increase in the understanding of human health. The pandemic caused a growing interest in understanding microbiotic processes, in the scientific community and beyond. Bacteria form the biggest and therefore most relevant ecosystem in the world.

Mybakteria.org is a ludic project in which through a generative drawing of a neuroalgorithm I have been developing thousands of microorganisms. This generative drawing algorithm is of the mind, not just the brain. It sprouts from the symbiotic interrelations within the eco-system that we are, a meditative process to free the subconscious. It is a form of automatic drawing and writing, like in the Dadaist tradition. Each drawing I make is unique and arises in the moment of the stroke, a process I call 'spontaneous morphogenesis.' It is a project of expanded drawing that uses the internet as a means of propagation and 'infection' through interaction. I began to publish experiments in 1997 and developed interactive visual sound pieces, installations, and concerts as part of the Bakteria project. Part of the performative imaginary is the use of personal protective equipment: yellow Tyvek suits and masks.

Now we live through a pandemic and due to its ensuing social isolation, we see the development of a fear of 'the other;' the microorganism that can affect us. Many factual powers take advantage of this to try to isolate us as a society and as individuals. These are forces that are against social unity, that want to see us as competitive entities, consumers, predators of ecosystems, a social Darwinism that has the planet in jeopardy in its social, economic, and ecological processes. I think we should think of life and society as based on mutualism instead. Mutualism is a theory of evolution of collaborators, in which the most important condition for the emergence of all multicellular species was their collaboration. My work of the past years is inspired by mutualism. We should think of the expanded microbiome: the human body is an ecosystem; it is the home to millions of non-human species!

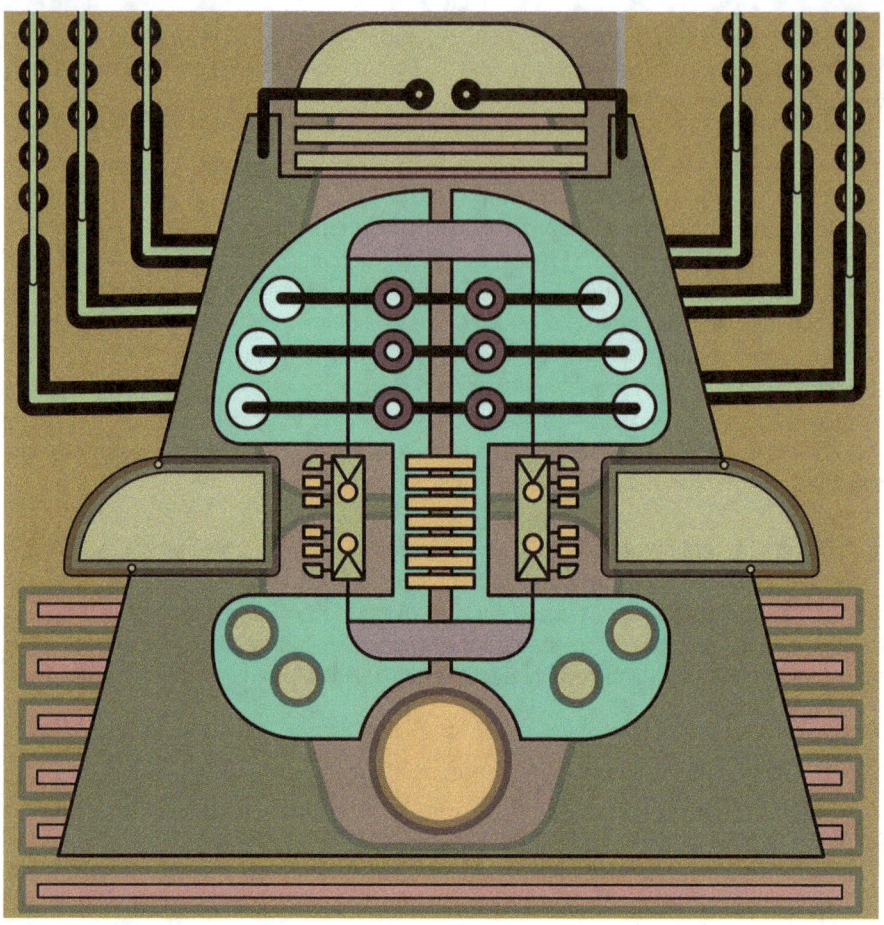

Figure 56: 3sTu:DiøZō ACe_LeRaDø, #biom3k4niko series, 2021.

More recently I discovered the evolutionary hypotheses of Lyn Margulles on endosymbiosis, which helps us understand that collaboration is more important than competition. We have to learn to collaborate with those millions of species, bacteria, and fungi that live inside us and help us process our foods and stay healthy. Some research acknowledges that an important reason for the high mortality rate in the pandemic is the imbalance of the microbiota in the organism, often caused by eating the wrong type of foods. It makes us prone to diseases. Because of the pandemic, eating habits are changing: people are more interested in growing their own food, and many want to stop consuming processed foods.

During the pandemic I have been developing several series of the Bakteria project, publishing them on the Bakteria.org website and Instagram. I had a bit of economic support from PAC to develop experiments in the metaverse, and funding from Sistema de Apoyos a la Creacion y proyectos culturales fonca.

Another project in which I am involved is 'Meditatio Sonus,' a series of performances with sound art and meditation that I co-direct with Marcela Armas. Since the state has been more concerned about the physical health of people than about their mental health, culture is important to help people in this time of anxiety and depression. Because the Mexican government only supports a few institutional projects of messianic proportions, very little investment has been channeled towards other cultural developments.

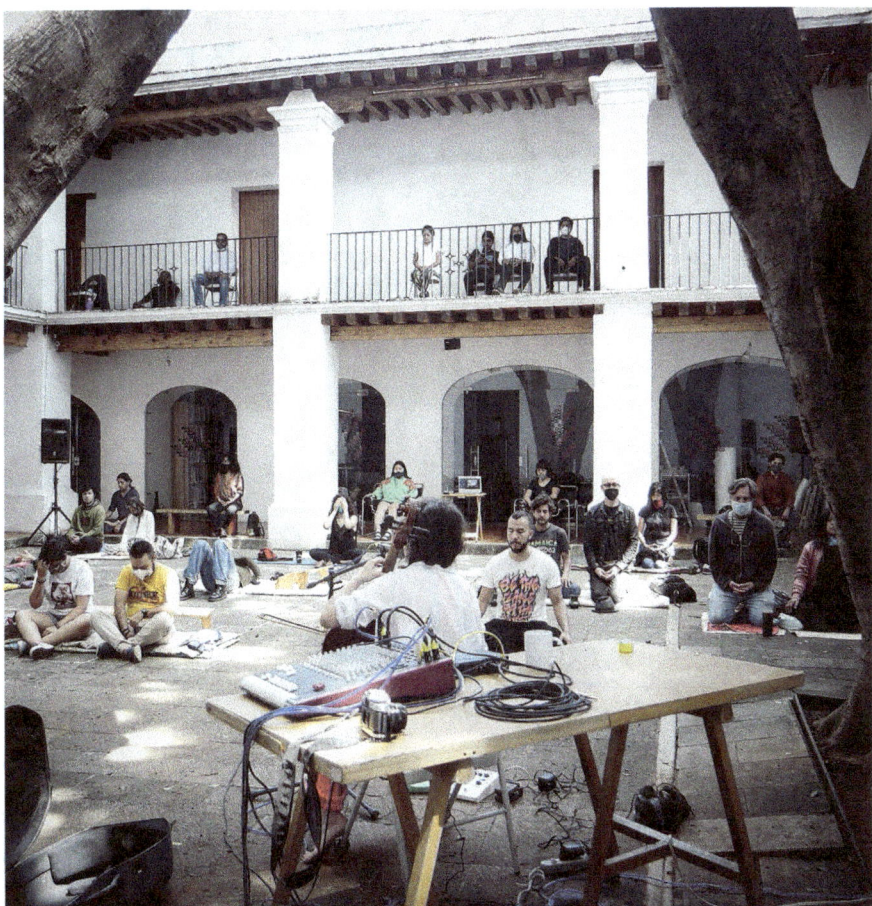

Figure 57: Meditatio Sonus, overview with audience, Muséo Oaxaca, 2020.

We produced the eigth cycle of this performance series in the Museum of Contemporary Art of Oaxaca in September, October, and November 2020. Each cycle consisted of eight Sundays in which we invite artists and experimental musicians to develop work to perform live as a guide for collective meditation, promoting deep listening and mindfulness. We had a public health protocol in place, so the audience felt safe to attend the sessions. The museum itself is going through a very complicated time because the government wants to shut it down.

The workers, including the director, have been without pay for months and yet they keep working to maintain an active program for the public, the artists, and their welfare. The museum staff even sleeps on the premises to protect the museum from eviction! Because of this we first tried to develop the 2020 edition of 'Meditatio Sonus' in Mexico City, but this got complicated due to the lack of art funding. Here, collective cultural events are not developed by institutions yet.

MICHELLE TERAN

We're tired of hearing stories about the virus and the crisis that only feature govern-ments and corporations, and we only appear clapping or as corpses.

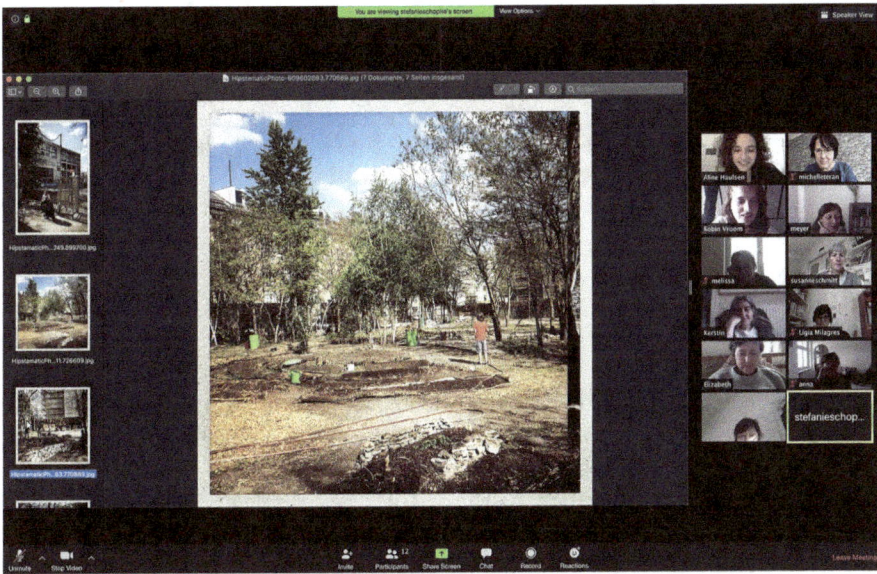

Figure 58: Screenshot 2020-04-27 18.47.14.

Things started going askew at the end of February 2020. It was hard to keep up with all the upheavals that were suddenly happening in my life. This story begins in Berlin and then travels to Rotterdam.

In Berlin, I attended an annual member's meeting of an association that oversees a commu-nity garden project. This meeting was a particularly tumultuous one, and it dragged on for hours. It began relatively subdued but quickly spiraled out of control. One of the association's members was accused of having too dominant a voice in an association supposedly working collectively. There was even talk of emotional abuse. The group leading the allegations had been meeting in secret without informing the other members. Let's say it wasn't on the agenda. The accused member left the meeting, disappearing into the night. The evening ended up in complete disarray: a part of the group was exuberant, while the rest were shell-shocked by what had transpired.

Three days later, a friend, sitting in my neighbor's kitchen, made the solemn announcement that a pandemic was about to sweep over Europe and the entire world. We laughed it off, attributing his sudden proclamation to what he had just been smoking.

I repeated the story to another colleague, making the joke about the impending zombie apocalypse and that soon we would be fighting over tins of tuna. (I watch a lot of "The Walking Dead"). He told me that my comment gave him a stomachache.

On Sunday, the next day, I took the train to Rotterdam, where I have a research position at the Willem de Kooning Academy. The following week was set aside for meetings, when all the teaching, research, and management staff came together for curriculum feedback, future planning, and educational workshops. There was a sense of unease and foreboding in the academy. Many of us commented that we shouldn't be having these meetings and that perhaps having a room full of people together was not such a good idea. I opened email after email, announcing canceled business trips planned for Budapest, Trondheim, and Stockholm. Suddenly, I wasn't going anywhere.

'But isn't it just a bad flu?' said one of my colleagues during a meeting, speaking in a low voice into my left ear.

I could feel her breath.

I decided to start working from (what I called) 'home.' I gathered a few books, some papers and headed to an apartment where I was temporarily living in the north of Rotterdam. The 3-room apartment was in a building zoned for demolition, and I was supposed to be moving to another place, in Rotterdam South, beginning April. The apartment was sparsely furnished. It contained a double bed, a table, chair, table lamp, hot plate, rice cooker, refrigerator, but little else. I cleaned it thoroughly and tried to make my living conditions as comfortable as possible. I bought fresh sheets, new pajamas, two weeks of groceries, and waited.

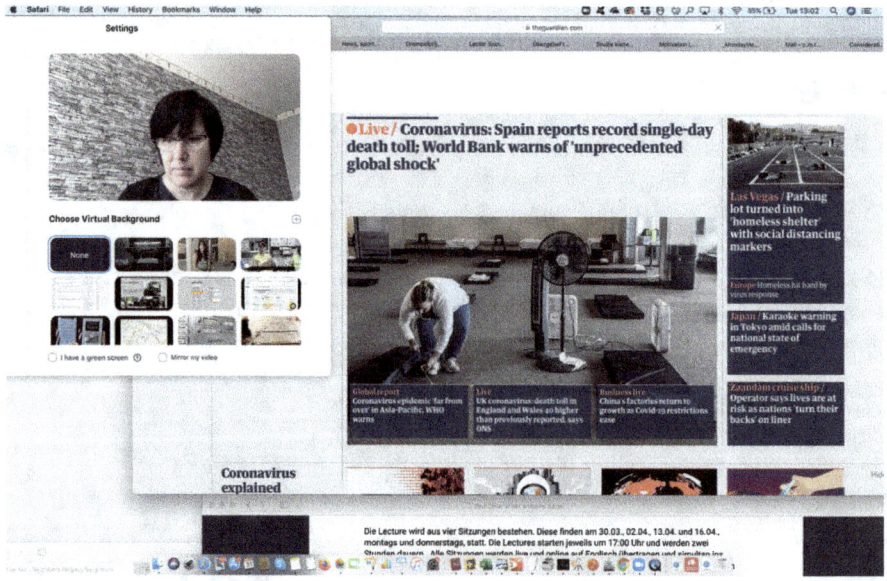

Figure 59: Screenshot 2020-03-31 13.02.26.

My neighbors, and recent arrivals to the Netherlands, were already receiving news of lock-down from their home countries. Our building went into pre-emptive lockdown and waited for the Dutch to catch up.

Over the following weeks, many scenes unfolded from my balcony.

A community café turned into a solidarity kitchen. Volunteers wore rubber gloves and masks, handing steaming bowls of soup to passersby. Someone sprayed chalk lines on the sidewalk. A row of people stood on the balcony, clapping. My next-door neighbor wore a blanket, smoking a cigarette, staring out blankly. Somebody from the sidewalk threw a roll of toilet paper to a pair of willing hands, one floor above. A couple lugged a burdensome shopping cart filled with groceries. A young girl living in the building threw three big suitcases into a taxi, giving all of us a quick, nervous wave, and then dashed to the airport for her flight to Australia before the borders closed. Another neighbor broadcasted a live DJ set from his living room. A group of three people danced on the street, 1.5 meters apart from each other. A boxing gym filled with sweating men, sounds of grunting and scuffling feet, thuds, and blows fell silent. Planes disappeared. Helicopters flew above. Birds sang. Tiny green buds pushed their way out of bare tree branches. Rain fell, the sun shone, rain fell, snow fell. The sun shone once again. Cars went by. Telephones rang. A street grew quiet.

I delayed my move.

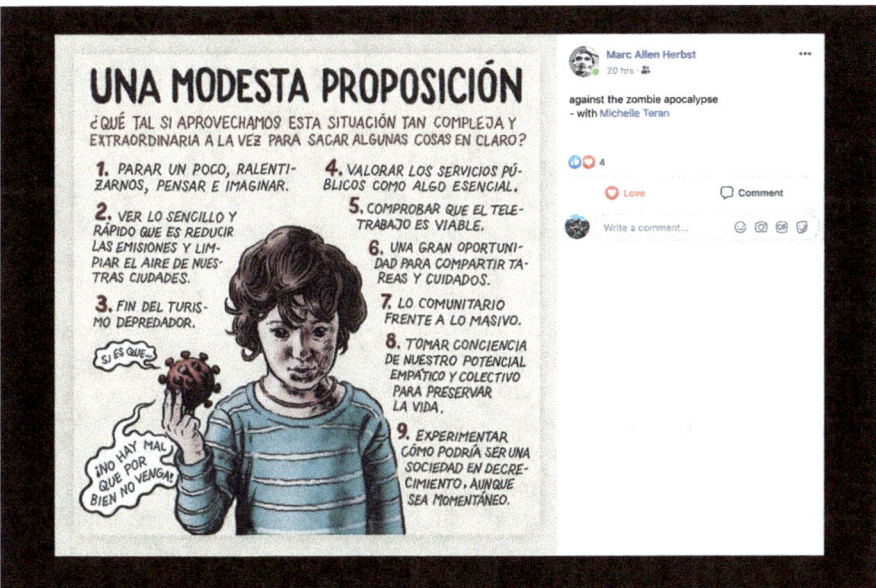

Figure 60: Screenshot 2020-03-13 12.42.48.

I am a researcher with a work contract. Losing my income was luckily not (at least for now) one of my worries. As Research Professor Social Practices, my role and the potential of research I carry out in connection to the academy address a shift in pedagogy both inside and outside of educational institutions to tackle social, economic, and ecological justice issues. Global conditions necessitate a willingness to unlearn and relearn, consider ways of learning otherwise and open up other ways of knowing. These learning spaces call for an ecology of practices, created by making connections between different fields of knowledge, showing the transformative power of collective learning and collective dialogue, based on a paradigm of interdependency.

How do we practice a politics of care and pedagogy of hope in these times of multiple crises? How do we collectively build up learning communities to meet the challenges of our times and for future generations? What might the practices of healing, reparations, and repair look like in our local communities and environments? These questions and concerns have guided me in the past years to community-engaged work and collectivized learning practices. Sometimes I am an active participant (as in the Berlin project). Sometimes I am a guest or an active listener. Sometimes I read about these practices in books or get to know them from afar. But I am always a learner. It is often hard for me to distinguish when I am inhabiting the role of a researcher, an artist or activist, a neighbor, or simply of a person trying to get on with their day without being too much of an asshole.

Sitting in the empty living room of my empty apartment, I spent entire days and weeks online, following the newsfeeds, talking to people, or joining in on some (online) conversation/discussion/webinar/debate. The adrenaline was high. The academy was in chaos. Not surprising, given the circumstances. Management asked teachers to revise their curricula and shift to online education without immediate resources and tools.

Clara (coordinator of Social Practices) created an EtherPad document to gather links for teaching resources. She started with online software. I followed with community-based initiatives and practices. More people working at the academy – teachers, students, researchers – joined in, filling in sections and starting other topics they felt were missing. Renée (Senior Lecturer) proposed a section on mental health and depression, Golnar (Theory Tutor) and Weronika (coordinator Autonomous Practices) assembled a list of films and literature related to self-isolation. Amy (Practice Tutor) suggested an area on safety.

A small group fleshed out the section on open-source and proprietary software for online classrooms, collecting examples of how to meet, chat, map, draw, process diary, file share, transcribe text, stream, and write together. Florian (Research Professor Autonomous Practices) and others built up a section on Rotterdam and Netherlands-based resources, focusing on financial aid and worker's rights, food, housing, and self-organization. I, with others, filled up areas in the pad related to community and communal activities in and outside of the classroom. A few of us gathered examples of mutual-aid networks, care, and solidarity practices developed by crip, feminist, indigenous, BIPOC, and queer individuals, activists, and communities. I became more interested in mutual aid and decided to add another section in the pad focusing on just that topic. Mutual aid is a reciprocal support network, often one in which people exchange care and resources in times of crisis and emergency. It differs from the organizational model typically applied in charity, where an external institutional body distributes unidirectional support. People living within a community or local setting – such as a neighborhood or a residential building – create networks that have people's well-being at heart.[1] I collected examples of actions worldwide: in China, South Africa, the USA, Turkey, France, Guatemala, Vietnam, the UK, the Philippines, Spain, etc.[2] The document took a life of its own. Any time of day, there would be dozens of people in the pad, adding content, editing, or reading through t. Sometime in April, an unknown person decided to vandalize our collective work. We made a public record of the event in the 'Gossip Diary' section:

April 16, 2020:

Pad vandalism. Entire pad erased, history unretrievable for a few minutes, believed at first to be a hack.

Message Log

Written and erased: I don't know how this is going to be useful for my class

Written and left behind:

I am **adding** content here because it is going to be SUPER USEFUL

lol I smell beta male energy

WTF WTF Did the hacker write this?

Lol no I wrote the beta male part.

Was trolling back.

IP Address of vandal: Chicago. Was not a hack, just a rando.

After the vandalism, we migrated our work over to a Wiki. We gave it a name: *The Social Practices COVID-19 Teaching Resources.*[3] This collective document reads like an existential cheat sheet and a blueprint for social transformation. Here is an excerpt:

We stand in solidarity with all workers in these troubling times. A collective response is the only way out of a collective crisis. Go ahead, cancel everything, do what you have to do for the sake of everyone's health, but pay everyone at once. Don't panic but be alert. Do not leave your home if not absolutely necessary. Practice social

---

1. Cramer, Florian, and Michelle Teran. "Letters from Dystopian and Utopian Futures of Arts Education." In *Hoger Beroepsonderwijs in 2030: Toekomstverkenningen En Scenario's Vanuit Hogeschool Rotterdam*, edited by D. P. Gijsbertse, H. A. Van Klink, C. Machielse, and J. H. Timmermans, 427–64. Rotterdam: I logeschool Rotterdam Uitgeverij, 2020.

2   #ClaraBalaguer #RenéeTurner #GolnarAbbasi #Weronika Zielinska #AmySuoWu #FlorianCramer #ManyOthers

3   Social Practices COVID-19 Teaching Resources - Beyond Social, 2020. https://beyond-social.org/wiki/index.php/Social_Practices_COVID-19_Teaching_Resources.

distancing, no hugs or kisses, no handshakes, no high fives. Reduce your amount of travel to a minimum. Do not attend concerts. Stay away from social gatherings. Wash your hands. Don't touch your face. Slowing down is a good thing. Demand recess.

What does it mean to teach artmaking in the 21st century? What can this moment teach about the world that we live in and the fields that we work in? Online learning environments are not built overnight. Curious to learn how you're approaching your Community and Social Practice classes in the age of social distancing. You don't have a flipped classroom. You no longer have a classroom at all! The online experience is as racist and sexist and homophobic as anywhere else. Ask your students if they are having trouble accessing housing, food, water, health care, mental health care, or other necessary resources. Ask about internet connection availability and available technology. Encourage students to check in on each other. What if someone we love has died or is in the ICU, and all we want to do is be distracted? Drawing a difference between toxic productivity and creativity. Just because people are home, doesn't mean they have the same ability to concentrate. This is not design-thinking, how do we solve the 'wicked problems' scenario.

We will not go back to normality, because normality was the problem. We call on everyone who rejects patriarchal, exploitative, colonial, and racist violence. How people fare in the months and years ahead will depend partly on how their countries and, more importantly, their communities respond. Mourning collective loss in the time of COVID-19. Recognize that fear and uncertainty are normal, and these feelings make sense. There appears to be an inflection point where the frustration and hardship of being cooped up inside get suddenly harder to bear. I hope that each of you, and all of us who've experienced the catastrophic COVID-19 will become people who remember; people who derive memories from memory. Archiving, interpretation of information and resources is vital to give us time to figure this out.

If authors have any responsibilities in the face of disaster, the greatest of them is to bear witness. Are you low-paid, over-worked, a freelancer, on a zero-hour contract, an intern, a volunteer, without pension or little job security? How has COVID-19 affected specific struggles for women's liberation and struggles to transform reproductive labor around the world? What are you hoping for? What do you fear? What are you personally interested in or concerned about? What happens after Coronavirus? How realistic is it to keep creating/making/doing business as usual? What are some ways to stay connected? Shouldn't we be putting all our energy/resources/time/effort to design/build/rebuild/demand stronger systems/infrastructures/frameworks? How can we take care of one another and the planet during this unknown pandemic time? What can you share?

Social reproduction is what keeps us alive. The surface that one person touches bears the trace of that person. We are all connected, we have all been there before, and we absolutely understand your fear and suffering at this moment. However, it is clear that the harm caused by COVID-19 has not been equitable. Racial inequalities, poverty, immigration status, culture, and sexual-affective diversity are all intersection-al factors that accumulate and exacerbate gender inequalities in our neighborhoods.

Care in the time of coronavirus. We're tired of hearing stories about the virus and the crisis that only feature governments and corporations, and where we only appear clapping or as corpses. We bring together first-hand accounts and analyses from our communities, including health and service workers and caregivers on the frontlines. Disabled people are leading survival praxis in apocalyptic times. We hope you are all reminded that in times of crisis, community in many ways has always shown up for one another. Embrace ethics of care. Ego conflicts are a liability. Explore solidarity and generous collaboration.

What might the crisis mean for movements and the possibility of a better world? Writing collectively from the relative privilege of our (often precarious) homes, we sketch out a space to reflect on the centrality of housing and home to the COVID-19 crisis. We cannot pay rent in the homes where we live, our businesses, or in offices, where we work. The corona crisis is also a housing crisis.

Assuming that this situation will deteriorate rather than improve in the coming period. We are in the process of setting up democratic coordinating structures and activist working groups. Ensure elderly and vulnerable populations in self-isolation are provided with care packages. Offering free meals and grocery packages for those in Rotterdam North. Affordable food. If wearing a face mask can help protect someone's grandparents, that is your duty. Mutual aid groups are popping up all over Britain. Indigenous innovation in Chad, feminist resilience in Zimbabwe, youth leadership in Peru, and care an antidote to violence in Pakistan and beyond. Socially distanced human chain to protest racism. A network of self-initiated mutual aid groups acting for self-defense by the people for the people. Now is the time to build a solidarity economy. Help me make it through the night. El pueblo unido jamás será vencido.

As the document was coming together in Rotterdam, I continued meeting online with members of the association in Berlin. Some were happy to move on. Now that the expelled member was gone, they could resume the project. Others in the group, myself included, pushed back. Some of us couldn't think about 'moving on' without first addressing the group's allegations of harm to one of the members. We needed more time to process and reflect on the experience of the February meeting. There was also a feeling of deep mistrust within the group.

What were we hoping for? What concerned us? Starting with the intimate realm, amongst ourselves and within the association, if we were to abandon the accountability of our roles in the abuse, in the conflict (victim, perpetrator, 'innocent' bystander), then what we were doing was enhancing the power of the state. The association members were replicating punitive modes of handing out justice while not addressing the systemic (patriarchal, heteronormative, colonial, capitalist) underpinnings that produced trauma and perpetuated harm. Suppose the group could start from the position of radical care and accountability, from the ability to express needs and even to grieve present and past trauma? How might that recalibration affect the socio-political entanglements of the association, the garden, and beyond? Perhaps we would decide, in the end, that the member was toxic and should leave the project. Yet, some of us felt that we needed to at least consider other models of collaborative work.

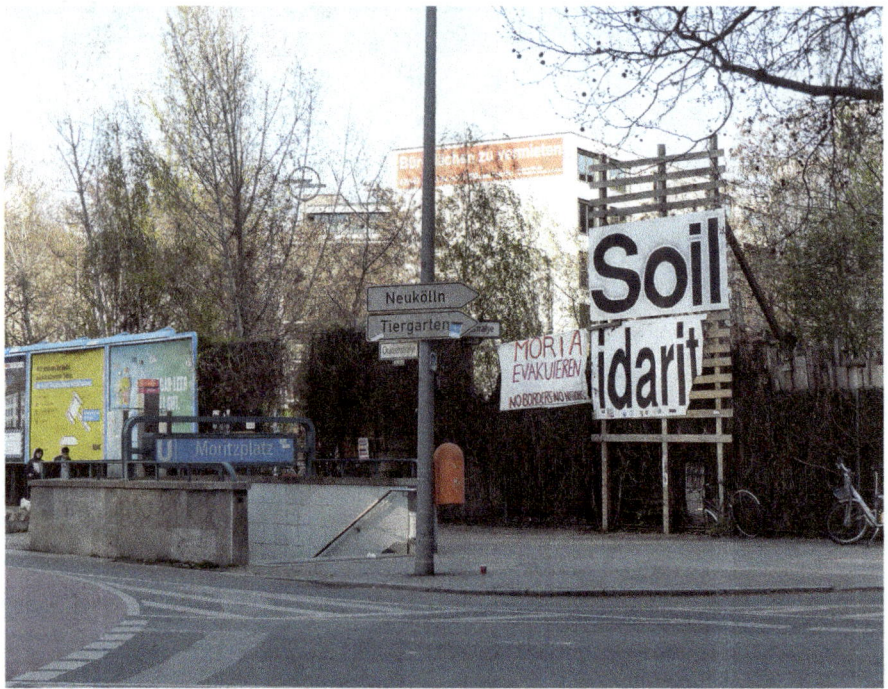

Figure 61: Community garden Prinzessinnengarten as seen from Moritzplatz, Berlin.

Some of us formed a workgroup and we spent the following months researching conflict. We were interested in gathering critical tools to help us think through the calamitous meeting. We studied non-binary methods of conflict resolution, non-violent communication, and transformative justice models. Our research led us into the area of decision-making. We thought about consensus-building and how, in our experiences working in the garden and other projects, it often led to homogenization or conflict (through vetoing and blockage). How non-consensual forms of arriving at decisions, with diverging ideas, opinions, interests, competencies, and literacies, might be a more holistic approach to building a pluralistic group and society. bell hooks' writings on love[4] and Sarah Schulman's work on conflict,[5] Dean Spade's research on mutual aid,[6] adrienne maree brown's emergent strategy,[7] and Alexis Pauline Gumbs's poetic

---

4   bell hooks, *All about Love: New Visions* (New York, NY: William Morrow, an imprint of HarperCollins Publishers, 2018).
5   Sarah Schulman, *Conflict Is Not Abuse: Overstating Harm, Community Responsibility and the Duty of Repair* (Vancouver: Arsenal Pulp Press, 2017).
6   Dean Spade, *Mutual Aid: Building Solidarity during This Crisis (and the next)* (London; Brooklyn, NY: Verso, 2020).
7   Adrienne M. Brown, *Emergent Strategy: Shaping Change, Changing Worlds* (Chico, CA: AK Press, 2017).

ruminations on Black feminist theory and the social lives of marine animals[8] were valuable interlocutors and guides.

We perused through examples of group codes and codes of conduct used by other organizations and community-based projects. One or two of these examples had even been developed (and then seemingly forgotten) in the garden itself. We thought about mutual aid practices, and I turned to some of the examples I had been collecting in the Rotterdam-based *Social Practices COVID-19 Teaching Resources*. In mutual aid, people living within a community or local setting – such as a neighborhood or a residential building – create networks that have people's well-being at heart. Mutual aid suggests horizontal relations, based on reciprocity and care. Some of us in the workgroup tried to imagine a reciprocal exchange network based on the politics of interdependence and community care. How might long-term sustainable care practices, rooted in the places where we live, help build up a community, foster alliances, and act as counterproposals to individuated neoliberal ways of living?

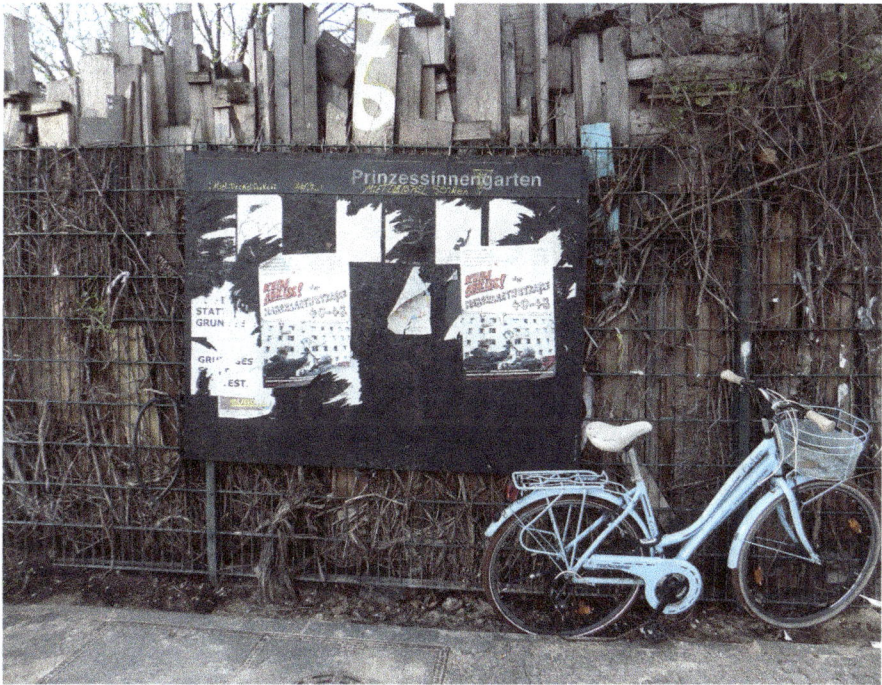

Figure 62: Prinzessinnengarten announcement board.

I wish I could say that we managed to work through all the troubles and move on. We haven't. Yet, there is a growing interest in putting energy, resources, time, and effort to demand more healthy systems, infrastructures, and frameworks. For many members of the association, these are profound questions regarding democratic decision-making structures and responsibilities and accountability. This is what's at stake in the project.

---

8   Alexis Pauline Gumbs, *Undrowned* (AK Press, 2021).

Some of our past year's thoughts and experiences made their way into written reflections. 'Everything Gardens! Working Notes Towards a Solidarity Economy,'[9] co-written with Marc Herbst and illustrated by Lígia Milagres, examines some aspects of the conflict in the garden and proposes an economic model based on community care.

The *Social Practices Covid-19 Teaching Resources* Wiki has become the accompanying volume *Situationer Cookbook* to the 240+ page *Situationer Workbook*. Between two futures – between complete breakdown and metamorphosis into ways of acting together – the *Situationer Workbook* and *Situationer Cookbook*, a book of two volumes, is a meditation on transformative pedagogy and teaching in times of crisis. The book asks: How can times of crisis, or crises, in their many forms, inform and influence the pedagogies needed to situate ourselves in a troubled world? How can one tune in to the conditions, concerns, and difficulties of these complex times, by cultivating new and necessary forms of humility, attentiveness, and recognition toward other knowledges, other value systems, other frameworks of understanding?

Started together with teachers, students, and alumni at the Willem de Kooning Academy and Piet Zwart Institute in 2019, the book will go to print this month, April 2021. While the world is still amid a pandemic, this book reiterates a call for the practices of mending, care, and repair on a damaged planet.

---

9   Herbst, Marc, Michelle Teran, and Lígia Milagres. "Everything Gardens: Working Notes Towards a Solidarity Economy." In *PARK.Reader*, 2021. https://doi.org/https://doi.org/http://park.levart. no/2021/01/19/everything-gardens.

MILTOS MANETAS

Reality is our Non-Fungible Token.

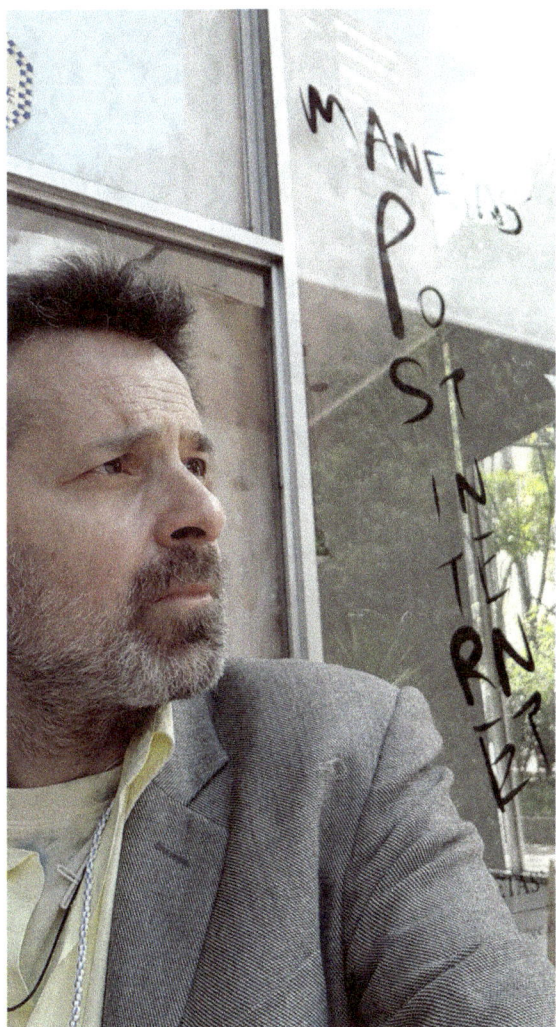

Figure 63: Miltos Manetas.

I live in Colombia, a country with two neatly divided realities: the very few super-privileged and the many underprivileged. The last group also includes an unaccounted number of people who are not at all privileged. Those are a surprise for me because where I came from — the 'Total North,' above and left of the axes of Athens, Rome, Paris, Madrid, Berlin, New York, Los Angeles — similar populations do not exist. Here, everyone I relate with is either highly privileged (Priv++), or, because of being European and socially connected like myself, plus-privileged (Priv+). We are also surrounded by different just-privileged people (Priv), those with stable jobs who can bring at least the minimum monthly wage to their families. Sometimes, we happen to even connect with them somehow: after all, they work for us!

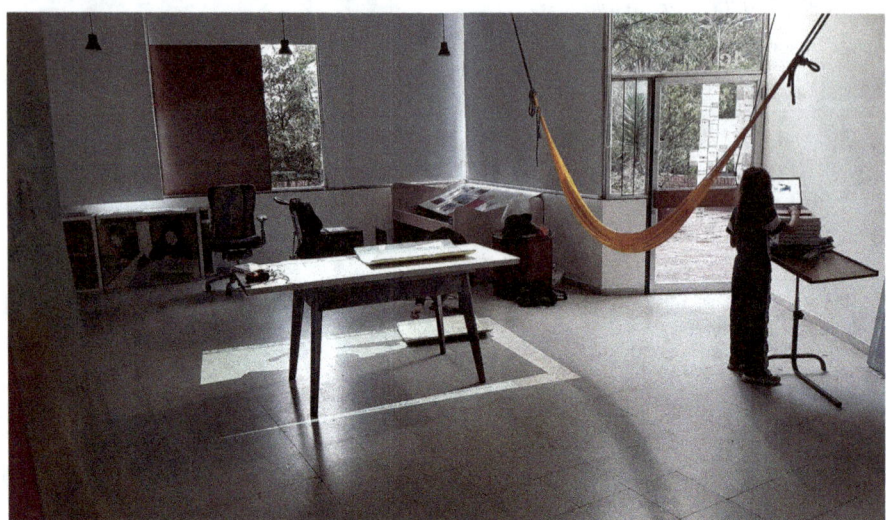

Figure 64: Studio view with Miltos Manetas' daughter Alpha.

Just 13% of the population in Colombia is Priv, Priv+, and Priv++, so even under the pandemic, we are having a great time. It may sound absurd, but the restrictions accompanying COVID-19 came as an opportunity for most of us. It enabled us to quit flying like mad all around the planet, and, even better, it stopped others from doing so over our heads, sitting inside the noisy metal containers we call airplanes. We could start enjoying family life. Our kids were free for a while from their usual school-sequestering, and the school itself became a videogame, a screen-addiction. I am leaving it to the kids to decide how far they want to go with 'school.' As an addict myself, I shouldn't be the one who makes the rules.

What about 'the rest'? I am hearing from the cleaning lady (domestic assistant/babysitter), that many members of her group, the 87% of the population, are suffering or even dying. But that's hardly news in this country and frankly, I don't even notice. Nobody pays particular attention. As for the Super Rich (Priv+++), they seem to be grabbing the opportunity to openly abuse the commonwealth. Again, that's quite normal here. (My friends tell me that in my native country of Greece, it is the same.)

Did more underprivileged (NoPrivils) people die? Are they getting into misery because of COVID-19? That we'll never know and, after all, it doesn't matter. It seems that our long-term project is to eliminate them all anyway. I say 'our' because I believe that by belonging to Priv+, one is consciously or unconsciously part of the Terminators Team: our mission is to support the Free Market at any cost, even by terminating the Earth's atmosphere and everything that lives above the surface.

But it will not be the end. We will continue 'our' human race into the 'Gaia' together with our robots and our AI until we are ready to start shooting our offspring out into the galaxies!

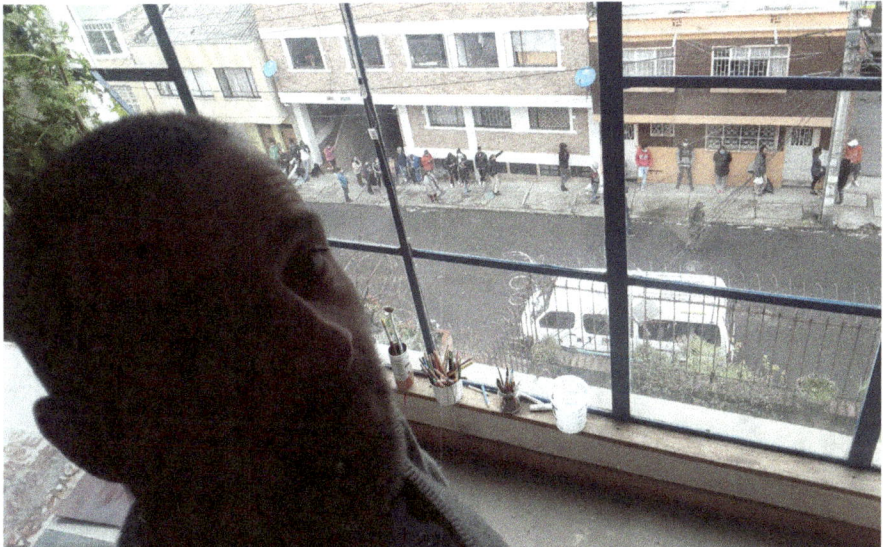

Figure 65: Self-portrait with less privileged.

When COVID-19 arrived, I was already thinking about such risks. Because my health is a bit weak, I spent a few days amusing myself with the eventuality of passing away. Realizing that I am ready to die anyway – I had a wonderful life already – I decided instead that for my life to feel optimal, I'd better be in the middle of it! Therefore, I decided to live another 56 years and reach 112 in 2076. Transferring myself to that age with my imagination, I felt the need to start writing an apocalypse story, hoping that if I put my fantasies on paper, or better, into posts as I am writing on social media, then they will never come true. It was certainly the case for John and his Apocalypse: it never happened! His Jesus never came back. The dead did not resurrect.

So, using John of the Apocalypse as my mentor, I start working on my own Revelation, placing myself in the same cave at Patmos where he wrote his delirium. I describe a post-climate catastrophe future when 70 million hyper-privileged suddenly retire into wonderful cities they had built under the surface, leaving all the rest to die after milking them without mercy over three decades of cruel technocracy. These super-wealthy people bring seven million scientists and a few thousand culture-parasites along, such as myself. Yet after having a great life with them, I decide to go and die on the surface. As I am awaiting my end, a very young girl, who knows nothing about History/God/Art or the internet, visits me. I spend four long days speaking to her about these phenomena, and about what happened during the last 56 years.

I am not in a hurry to finish it, this story, which constantly appears and disappears as texts, images, and animations on my Instagram account @manetasapocalypse, and as narration on Clubhouse.

It becomes a kind of Oracle for the rest of my life: I intend to keep writing it as I go on existing, looking at what happens in my life from the vanishing point of its perspective.

I had already been testing and experimenting with post-internet life, which the whole planet is now discovering, from 1998 onward. The sweet dystopia that I was professing from back then only became a reality for everyone now, and it feels... bitter-sweet, but still acceptable, sometimes exciting.

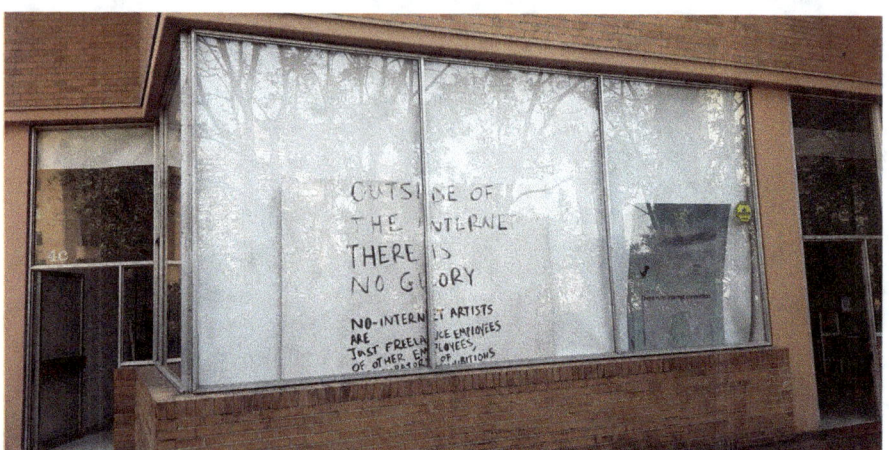

Figure 66: Street view of Miltos Manetas' studio in Bogota.

Lately, strange things started happening: a creation of mine, the idea of a Non-Fungible Token that had become an obsession for me in the days of NEEN, suddenly took over the planet and the economy with the booming of CryptoArt and NFT. The 1% seems busy redistributing its wealth between themselves while opening its gates and becoming a 1.5% or even a 2%. There's a river of Gold running on our computer screens now and, I suppose, we are all obliged to become multimillionaires, those of us who are specially-Privileged at least. One hundred fifty million multimillionaires should be enough to finance life-after-atmosphere, survival in luxury futuristic cities underground.

But these are all fantasies, of course. Reality is our Non-Fungible Token and for the moment, until Ethereum starts accumulating, I, like everyone else, need to survive. Initially, I took the opportunity presented by the collapse of 'our art market,' which is simply speculation over the up and downs of the euphoria of the Privileged+++, to 'hit rock bottom' and exploit the niche around it! In contemporary art, you are allowed to do anything except to sell for very little. I have been doing that with a specific body of works of mine. I am producing it for that exact purpose. I am calling it #manetas_artforsurvival. Until there's COVID-19, there's no blame and when that is over, the HyperPriviledged will be too euphoric to notice, anxious as they'll be to buy anything at the highest price possible to keep helping themselves feeling... inferior. And, as a result, they will keep on passionately destroying the atmosphere.

NANCY MAURO-FLUDE

The array of happenings and gatherings on platforms over the internet was astounding, although there are copious things to critique. On a positive note, with the expectation of overseas travel erased for most of the planet it was like after 20 years the greater arts public remembered the internet.

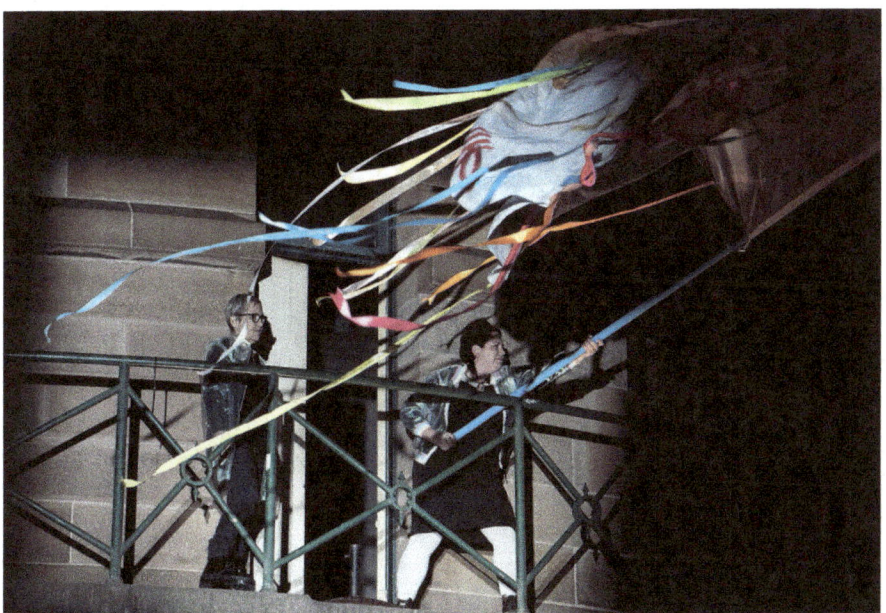

Figure 67: Performance still Nancy Mauro Flude (right) and Linda Dement, 'Cyberfeminist Bed Sheet Transfigured' (2020) in Tomorrow, Bett Gallery, Hobart Tasmania. Image courtesy of Jonathon Delacour.

I recall the advent of the emergence of the novel coronavirus 2019-nCoV distinctly.

Over the summer of 2019/20 when we witnessed our country, Australia, go up in flames, sprigs of hope began to sprout. Then the pandemic hit, in the wake of the fourth industrial automation and sixth species mass extinction.

In early February, I had a research meeting with colleagues at the University of Melbourne. This required me to take a one-hour plane flight from nipaluna/Hobart the South Island of lutruwita/Tasmania to Naarn/Melbourne, the capital city of Victoria.[1] It was a regular trip to the continent of Australia, or the mainland, as is common parlance with Tasmanian people.

---

1   The name of the country in which the city of Hobart sits is island 'lutruwita' Tasmania. In palawa kani 'nipaluna' is the language of Tasmanian Aborigines, the traditional owners, and custodians. 'Naarm' (or 'Narrm') is the Aboriginal place name for the area where the city of Melbourne is located on the traditional lands and of the Kulin nation.

Though there were murmurs about COVID-19 in the media, they focused on 'elsewhere.' As I was packing, something inside me clicked. Tacit advice from my body.

Listening to it, I took a facemask to wear on the flight and it felt totally unusual. I kept the facemask from when I spent some time in Singapore, where wearing them was common. Quite regularly, this island would be covered in a pungent thick smoke, the result of their neighbors in Indonesia burning rain forests for palm oil. I also decided to take three empty suitcases, with the resolve to carry things from my office on the mainland back in them eventually. I didn't really think about them until the last evening, the 7th of February. I had a kind of panic attack. I rang a friend and asked if she would be present while I packed up the debris and paraphernalia in my 'assigned workspace' — books/papers/tech equipment. I was completely unnerved and forgot about my commitment to give a remote keynote at the Inaugural Symposium of Spiritual Technologies within Creative Practices, Rosendal Theatre, Trondheim, Norway. Missing this wonderful occasion was incongruous, to say the least.

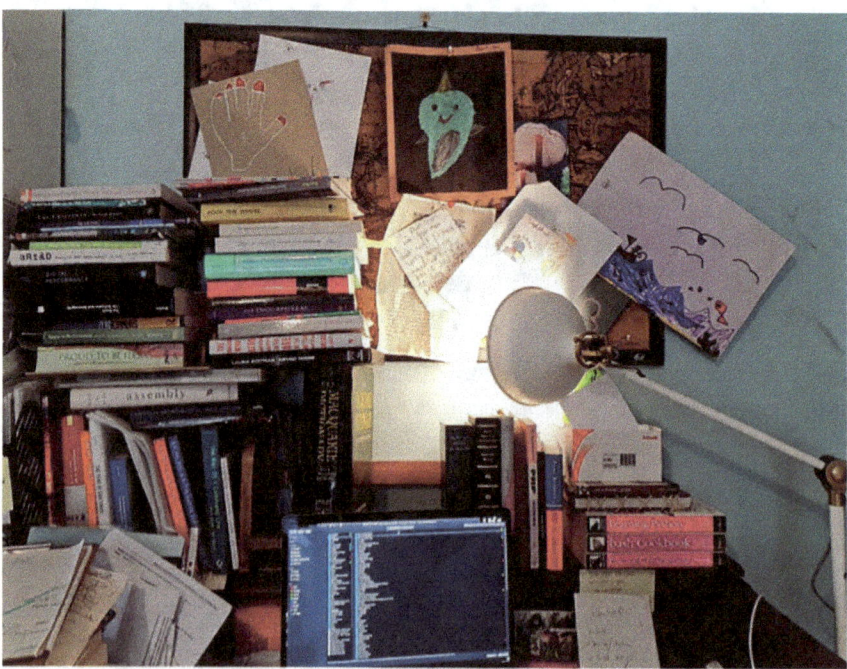

Figure 68: Workstation in bedroom. Image: Nancy Mauro-Flude.

Although Victoria Health Authorities confirmed the first case of COVID-19 on the 25th of January 2020, I was singular in the act of wearing a mask on my last trip home on the 5th of March. At the time, it felt like I was performing the virus in public. I discussed with work colleagues how a facemask probably wouldn't protect us from the virus while teaching in small classrooms with poor ventilation. One of them said they couldn't believe this virus outbreak was happening. I revealed how 'it comes as no surprise. I've been anticipating the collapse most of my life.'

In the last decade, I was experiencing a kind of rigidity on a cellular level. I associated this to the earthly substate and clocked it that something has 'to give' because consumption and production throughout our planetary archipelago are not to scale, distorted beyond belief.

Then came the slew of noncommittal emails from university leadership with carefully worded requests asking in hypotheticals: if I can rework the critical theory course, and coordinate for the semester to take place online. I confirmed I could, but said I need time to design it. Such appeals were met with no response. My concerns were met with a dismissive attitude. On the 10th of March, it was my 45th birthday. I snapped and threw the cutlery across the table to my partner, which was clearly out of order. My dreadful conduct decided for me that I would not leave the island again for quite a while at least.

Melbourne's Tullamarine Airport is the third most traveled passenger air route in the world, with direct flights to 33 domestic destinations in the Pacific, Europe, Asia, North America, and South America. To state the obvious; the virus hit central Melbourne hard.

The recommendations from the Health Authorities were initially received as hyperbole. In March 2020, the Australian Prime Minister was still dismissing the pandemic and joking in the press about how he'll certainly be going to the football on the weekend, despite the state and federal governments agreeing to cancel gatherings of more than 500 people across Australia. His attitude was in direct contradiction to many individual premiers of states and territories that were attempting to manage the country safely. At the same time, I watched as the doors of contagious families in Wuhan were welded, people left to perish on various news feeds. I read posts from Taiwanese friends who live in Australia and claimed that even as far back as November 2019 they knew of the virus, but their cries were silenced by Big Daddy China.

Friends began to text me apocalyptic prepping lists. Beyond the well-publicized non-perishable goods, Eucalyptus oil and gin were scarce resources. I went and bought a battery-powered analog radio. I had to work hard to convince the saleswoman that I didn't want the digital fandangles of the latest model. I was actually after a solar-powered radio, but that was another mission.

When our state premier Peter Gutwein declared a state of emergency and the 'toughest border restrictions in Australia,' the news spread over me like a welcome relief. This feeling continued when seeing the headline: 'We've got a moat, and we're not afraid to use it.' on the front page of Tasmania's The Mercury newspaper on Friday the 20th of March 2020. Among the many blessings of our island is our moat; these bodies of water are commonly known as the Bass Strait and the Tasman sea. I've always held tight that this island is the womb of the world. Compared to other parts of the world, our numbers are low, but in Victoria, COVID-19 cases are the highest to date; 20,483, compared with Tasmania's 234, as I write this in March 2021.

I'm going into detail here because I began to experience critical anxiety about leaving the island. I am the principal carer of my mother who has a pre-existing health condition. If I became a COVID-19 carrier, this would have serious consequences for her and other vulnerable people in my community.

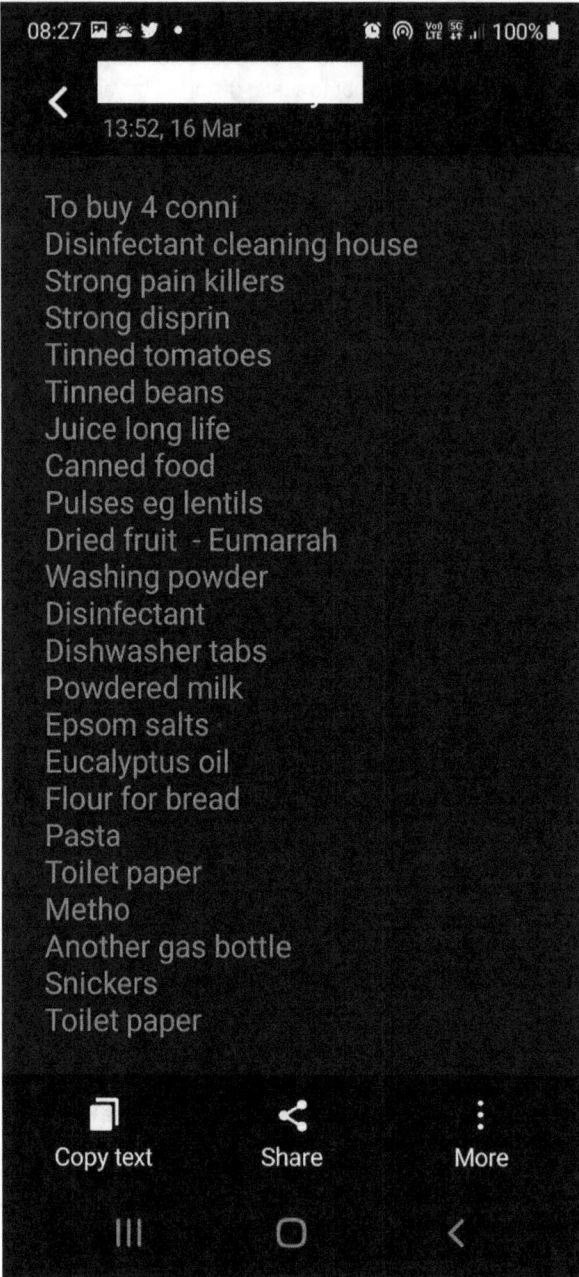

Figure 69: Prep list.

As I write, my mother started to leave her apartment a little more now. But for around eight months, my daughter and I would make contact with her with certain constraints; depending on where we had been and what the broader restrictions were for the island.

In some ways at the dawn of the pandemic, I considered myself totally agile to adapt and prepare for such a world schism, living in Tasmania and thus having a moat! Beyond getting a radio, I also put safeguards in place, acting swiftly in collaboration with my mother. We filled out forms granting me the legal status of her enduring guardian in case I would be forced to return to the mainland.

After the initial preparations, I became very annoyed with myself. It had always been my wish to be partially self-sufficient; I learned the principles of permaculture design and worked hard to have some land to grow produce, fruit, vegetables, and herbs. It is harvest time now which requires a substantial commitment to preparing the yield. I ordered a grain mill to grind flour and other similar contraptions. We don't have goats yet, but we do have two chickens!

I have gratitude for where I live, and thankful that I could continue to work. I am shocked at my lack of resilience during the lockdowns, but I don't mind being often close to home. For the most part, a feeling of dread was due to external forces that I allowed to leak into the atmosphere of my home, mainly due to communication from leadership in the university where I worked. I was left with the sole pastoral care of 180 first-year students. The overseas students, mostly from China, had attempted to enter Australia from other places in South East Asia and found themselves stranded in transit. Students residing locally lost their jobs. One female pupil finding herself at a loss for income was therefore invited to live at her boyfriend's house. His family, having never been to university, couldn't understand the culture of study, nor why she was devoting time to the university and not to the kitchen. Other students have never been on campus and could barely speak English. In one instance, I had to seek various avenues to find another student or staff member from Thailand because a newly arrived Thai student was struggling with the language. In my encounters with them, I sensed isolation and fragility when they asked me how long the lockdown may last.

When things start to crumble, survivalist strategies kick in. To my bitter disappointment, the labor of care staff did for students wasn't shared. My students revealed about four weeks into the lockdown that I was the only lecturer with whom they have weekly contact and who allocated time for them to ask questions. Apparently, in other courses, the materials were placed in a digital learning environment and students were simply told to access them. It was only on the 22nd of March 2020 that the university closed officially, commanding that all communications and teaching must take place online. It is still the case a year later – I write in semester 1 of 2021.

It is undoubtedly an extremely difficult time with an impact on many people's health. Halfway through the semester in lockdown, my child was at home from school and her father also worked from home, in close quarters. We all suffered under pressure. My 9-year-old daughter began experiencing mental health issues and migraines and was hospitalized on three occasions in 2020.

Before the COVID-19 pandemic, I would commute to work to be on campus during the semester, mainly via airplane. Recently, and quite out of the blue, I received an email from the head of the School of Design. They were afraid that travel restrictions might cause problems, making a false assertion that I need to reside in Victoria as a condition of my future employment in 2022 and claiming that it is the Commonwealth Government's doing. The claim is untrue. Section 92 of the Constitution of Australia claims 'trade, commerce, and intercourse among the States, whether by means of internal carriage or ocean navigation, shall be absolutely free.'

Not only do these wilful false untruths give rise to concerns over intimidation and harassment to staff. From these pronouncements, we may also intuit how so-called broadminded organizations of the university are adopting tactics of security, control, and command.

At the start of the pandemic, I co-devised a local transdisciplinary event 'The Thorny Question of Art and Economy: A Conversation Piece (2020),' a 'slithery philosophical filibuster' held throughout an evening at the advent of the emergence of COVID-19 at the Museum of New and Old Art (MONA) in lutruwita/Tasmania, in collaboration with other artists, art workers, nonhuman agents, and a wider public audience. The uncanny nature of radical administration applied in our small act included a swarm of supporting actors, intermediaries, and agencies that open onto other worlds, to offer a reverse-engineered glimpse of a counter-technology, counter-intelligence, and counter-inscription. A deliberate swerve away from the metrics of sector professionalism and glossaries of careers etc., all manipulated by a phalanx of economic rationalist tropes.

Another motivation to stage this event was a retort to how the 'arts' was removed from the title of the relevant Australian Federal government department in December 2019, when the Department of Communications and the Arts was replaced by the Department of Infrastructure, Transport, Regional Development, and Communications. The reasoning behind it was as follows: 'Having fewer departments will allow us to bust bureaucratic congestion, improve decision-making and ultimately deliver better services for the Australian people.'

The decision-making drama *The Thorny Question* (2020) was a durational performance in three acts. It took a swipe not only at the sovereignty of decision-making in emergent technologies but also at (arts) funding bodies. To make a case for an approach quite distinct from that increasingly and urgently voiced in the artistic field and the wider public realm. The stars of the show were *Ouijic Agents* (hi-vis pink robotic balls) whose acts of spectacularly biased-looking yet spookily unassailable performances of machinic decision-making, proved at least as inscrutable as it was transparent. Acts of adjudication were the filament woven at the center of this event. In Act III, the ticket-holding public was invited to each prepare a proposal for disposing of *their Collective Investment*, the money collected on the door within certain constraints. Propositions were offered around a circle, such as:

'I want to give money to my daughter's school library.'

'I'd build a sauna for artists.'

'I want to acknowledge the cleaners who will clean up after the event and give the money to them,' and so on.

PRESENTED BY: FERAL MBA, DESPOINAS MEDIA COVEN AND FAVOUR ECONOMY

SPONSORED BY MEANS OF THE KIND PROVISION OF SPACE BY 24 CARROT GARDENS

THE THORNY QUESTION OF ART AND ECONOMY
A slithery philosophical filibuster

20.02.2020
MONA Eros & Thanatos
Hobart TAS

Budget

Income

Advance ticket sales x $5.78	$282.96
Cash on the door tickets x $5	$ ./* **75**
Donations	$ ./*
Merch sales	$ ./*
* at time of going to print	

$ 370·00

Expenditure

Paypal @ 2.6% + A$0.30	$9.75 *
Stripe @ 1.75% + A$0.30	$11.73 *
Pretix @ 2.5%	$7.07 *
Contingency	$9.41
A3 gold print x25 (this budget)	$145.20
The Money	$245 * +
late minute advance sales + door ticket sales	$ ./*

Non Budget

Bonded, incommensurable, in kind, gifted, gleaned, granted, non-enumerated, non-remunerated, loaned, poached and post-transactional extra-budget value. Including & not limited to:

Melbourne-Hobart flights x2
Sydney-Hobart flights x2
Airport pickups x3, drop offs x3
Guest CBD lodgings secured through family connections and/or open market
    indeterminate forms of emotional labour
Guest lodgings: local (caravan, cleaning, preparations)
Feral business coaching session, Favour Economy coaching session
Coffee, wine, beer, ginger cordial
FoAM, Feral MBA, Despoinas Media Coven, Favour Economy networks emotional
    rescue | co-support
Pre-production, pre-event lunch items: gardened, home catered, store-bought
24 Carrot Gardens sponsor: Eros (& Thanatos) venue, MONA technicians, AV
    equipment, chairs
Additional equipment foraged
Organisers prepare pre-production, pre-event lunch, cutlery, plates, undertake
    post-production mop up
Photographer documents
Cultural expertise of artists, performers, technicians towards technical apparati,
    ouijic actants & other discourses
Miscellaneous organisers hours | home offices, refreshments and ./* emails
Feral MBA participants assist
Bottles of wine ./*
Childcare x3+strays
Mediating the lay of the land local vvild wisdom | lore of seas & country
Watching ethereum's wild money market moves triggers temporary
    disassociation from the idea that value = money
A4 printing courtesy of Moonah Arts Centre (MAC)
A4 paper courtesy of steal from work (elsewhere anywhere)
Autonomous webservers
Instagram, Google, Facebook and its administrators:
    Contemporary Art Tasmania (CAT), Regional Arts Australia,
    Women's Arts Register (WAR), National Association for the Visual Arts (NAVA),
    and other individuals
Resource Work Cooperative mailing list
Automaton ouijic agents retrieved from under the house
A3 budget layout (this poster) + ingenious ideas
Sick leave, Medicare, Family tax benefits
http://vvvvvvvvvv.net
http://fo.am
Etherpad developers and associated system admin friends
The atmosphere and the aether
Bacterial gut hub communities

THE THORNY QUESTION OF ART AND ECONOMY is a satellite event to the Feral MBA, an experimental curriculum in business for/with artists, in Hobart over February and March 2020.

Figure 70: 'The Budget' performed a supporting role, including the host of non-financial items that under-wrote the event, reconfiguring the zero-sum game of double-entry accounting, listing artists' cultural expertise, childcare, and planning meeting lunch items, and so on, regularly blanked by economists. Other notables are the asymmetrical lines of 'INCOME and NON BUDGET' rescued from its role as a background *inevitability, hidden in annual reports. 'The Budget' was installed at the event as a featured artwork and item of merchandise (on sale at the door for $10). Also, it draws attention to intermediary workings that are often mistaken for the slippery prospect of transparency. Detail from 'The Thorny Question of Art and Economy A Conversation Piece' (2020). Image courtesy of Nancy Mauro-Flude.*

When the circuit of proposals had run its course. The participating audience was faced by an outlandish supernatural collective of automated technologies, 13 Ouijic Agents. Their task: to single out a winning proposal, without fear or favor.

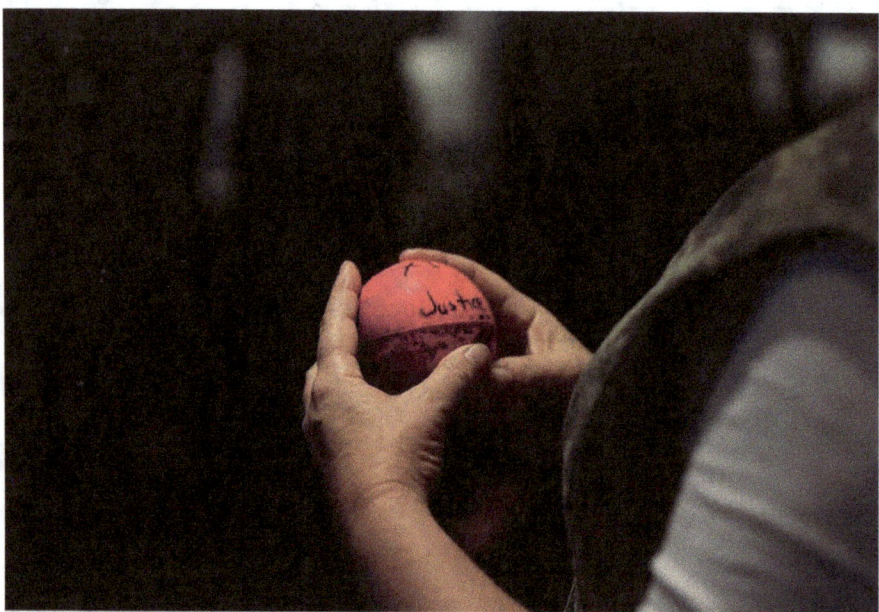

Figure 71: Ouijic Agent number 13 JUSTICE in the hands of 'The Chosen One.' Under the guise of Ouijic Agents, gifted from the Advanced Centre of Excellence for Automated Decision Making, these beguiling robotic mop automata balls, self-contained electrical devices, powered by servo motors that simultaneously rotated and pushed, found a murky way to furnish prominence with another peripheral kin. Image detail, 'The Thorny Question of Art and Economy A Conversation Piece' (2020). Image courtesy of Jesse Barclay.

Through wild acts of pathfinding, the event acted to encourage the audience to be aware and comprehend the slew intermediaries at play, at any given moment. In a bid to nurture an embodiment of a world that emerges from feeling, sensing, thinking, witnessing, and compassion, rather than a prescribed set of so-called common-sense agendas that are typically altruistic, selfless, or rationally self-interested.

In 2020, my work developed in tandem with the immobility and feelings of trepidation caused by the major planetary schism and rupture that is the pandemic. Throughout the year, artistic collaborations ranged from compulsions that emerged with no clear form insight, to convening a multi-site symposium, exhibitions of work, and presenting artist talks and remote performance lectures.

Despite or because of the plague, I permitted myself to follow through with ideas that typically often vanish as they move down my to-do list. I made a short sketch about timtumili minanya/ River Derwent – a deep body of water in the shipping port for the city where I live. For at least 40,000 years before colonization, it was a birthing suite for whales. I called a friend with a boat who was up for taking me out, inquired if two other people were willing to crew, and grabbed a digital video camera. The result was a short moving image entitled *Womb of the World*. It was selected for Tidal.2020 at Devonport Regional Gallery. To be shortlisted for this award exhibition artists must demonstrate a sustained association with the island.

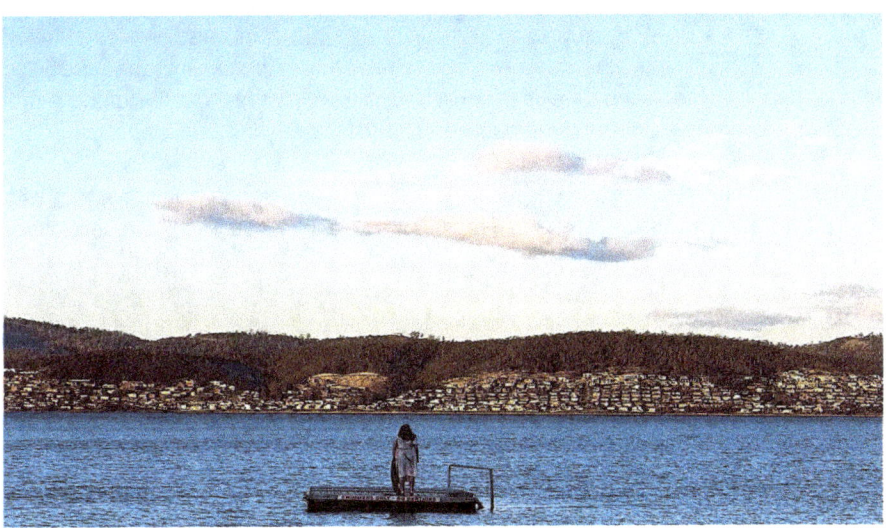

Figure 72: 'Womb of the World' (2020) recorded as internet scale one-channel video depicting a woman standing in the midst of elemental forces on a floating platform timtumili minanya/River Derwent. Image courtesy of Nancy Mauro-Flude.

The array of happenings and gatherings on platforms over the internet was astounding, although there are copious things to critique. On a positive note, with the expectation of overseas travel erased for most of the planet it was like after 20 years the greater arts public remembered the internet.

I installed a collaborative web-based text editor EtherPad on my webserver, also deployed as one of the intermediary actors in *The Thorny Event*. This open-source real-time environment enabled me to initiate three iterations of the online performance *Writing the Feminist Internet*. I invited contributors to rewrite and solicit principles and sentiments about computational culture and feminist waves. The event meant to generate awareness of how the principles and waves of feminisms are embodied, navigating over (and across) theoretical bearings, textually cutting up, reshuffling, and conjuring words in the browser space. We staged multiple voices using a different color for each participant. You could see habitual perceptions and thoughts unfold in real-time writing. Some people inhabited the charms of soothsayers, while others appeared as rowdy choir, clutching the roles of 'do-gooder' or devil's advocate. Manifestations would range from diligently responding to the commands by participants such as: 'What feminist wave is this?!' to crafting concrete poetry from texts and starting a whole new cadence and line of progression.

The textual movements in *Writing the Feminist Internet* gave rise to an array of techno-politics, swelling, and diffracting, speculative brainstorming about computation and feminism. Although a structure was provided for participants to improvise, it turned out that playfulness and openness are challenging to some people's expectations.

Like any technology, writing is a phenomenon obscured by the conventions of capital. The act of rewriting feminist mantras, provisionally dislodging received definitions, revealed the need for unwavering meaning and the overwhelming compulsion of people to want to be correct and dead-on target. These customs are often derived from imperialist agendas that demonstrate no patience for probing sentiments in a public arena and unfastening established assumptions.

Instead, participants were required to read and write tacitly in a transitory improvisation with others, to tune into the ephemeral experience. Thus, we dismantled fixed apprehensions to which many of us develop habitual behavior patterns.

Such alternate means of assembling knowledge bestowed by communing in a temporary place withdrew from the insistence on demarcations. Often deemed aberrant and unruly, these modes can open up entirely new sets of possibilities. They deliver us from restrictions brought about by reductionist systems that ignore the complexity of actants in human and non-human relationships that nest, recur, and repeat beyond the adoption of a solution.

I am in the middle of developing a feminist critical internet theory, a radical coming together of diverse viewpoints. Motivated from the bedlam of feminist internet groups, this infrastructure is best understood as a cauldron that holds inexplicable *asemic* brews. Asemic writing is often illegible. It has no fixed meaning. It is open-ended and vivid. Here, every actant arrives with their own medicine or flora to contribute. Collective terminal sharing and feminist server maintenance are forms of divination not unlike 'alectryomancy' in which an animal such as a bird, was placed inside a ring of letters scattered traditionally with corn, and from their indeterminate dance, fortunes were told from the letters near which it moved. Imparting omens for further deciphering.

It is early days, but I am working on a new body of work called *Glossalia* that was seeded by these collaborative performances. Tinkering into systems for other kinds of experience than one of control, for release or deliverance.

Another pressing issue that began bubbling up like an active volcano is the desire to navigate my way out of the maze and thicket of institutional tangles I've tied myself up in. I want to recover sovereignty over how and when I conduct and trade in various exchanges with other living beings.

When ruminating about the freedom to choose our own deliverance and dependencies, I am reminded of the artist Mez Breeze (inventor of the hybrid language mezangelle), who favors synthetic communication with her artistic community. She doesn't gather in 'meat space' but communicates over networks. This topic came to light when we were speaking about seed swapping through the postal network.

A move towards more independence was the multi-site event MoneyLab#X Economythologies (#MLX) in November 2020, which Denise Thwaites and I co-curated. Several universities, galleries, and arts organizations participated. It was presented as part of the international *MoneyLab* series that brings together scholars, activists, artists, geeks, and journalists to explore alternative economies and systems of financialization. #MLX was the first of these events ever to be shown in the Southern Hemisphere. It focused on the iridescence of money – its symbols, systems, artifacts, and technologies – as it gives rise to worlds in transition. We curated a program of talks, performances, and artworks that considered specifically how the blockchain's uprooting of legacy, economic systems, and narratives creates nascent ways to imagine how to value, design, and organize our creative and cultural practices. We did this by investigating how the concept of a transaction (what it means to engage in the relations of commerce) can be revisioned within the context of critical thinking and making.

Our transdisciplinary research agenda on alternative economies stretches across our planetary archipelago. With an emphasis on sharing research and art voices from the South East Asia-Pacific-Oceanic region, we represented research and art from these realms to collectively imagine new ways of reconfiguring money. At the advent of the current roaring 20s hype of crypto art, this is now a topical subject with the public interest.

In a time of eco-crises, techno-utopias, disaster capitalism, and necropolitics, many of us are compelled to examine the narratives, systems, economies, and limitations that have driven us towards catastrophe. I've engaged a trans-local community bound by peer-to-peer (p2p) gifting. A 'Sacred Economics' practice that operates on trust and commitment among and between the members. Communications occur through signal – a messaging application. After the initial financial investment, called a 'sacred yes,' the experience is akin to an expanded workshop based on offerings from the group, called a loom, that may be shared in the form of written material, music/song, short videos, voice notes, images. The requirement is to offer our presence, our intention, our embodiment on a collective basis. We take cues from the elements fire, air, earth, and water, and act accordingly in sharing our findings. I have confidence in intermediaries that I am traveling with and the daily bricolage of cosmographic lilts.

There's a lot of different forces at play right now for me which requires a humble amount of holistic boxing with some dark elements. Over the past year, I have been asking what different ways of life could be possible. And if they were here all along, then how can we reignite them?

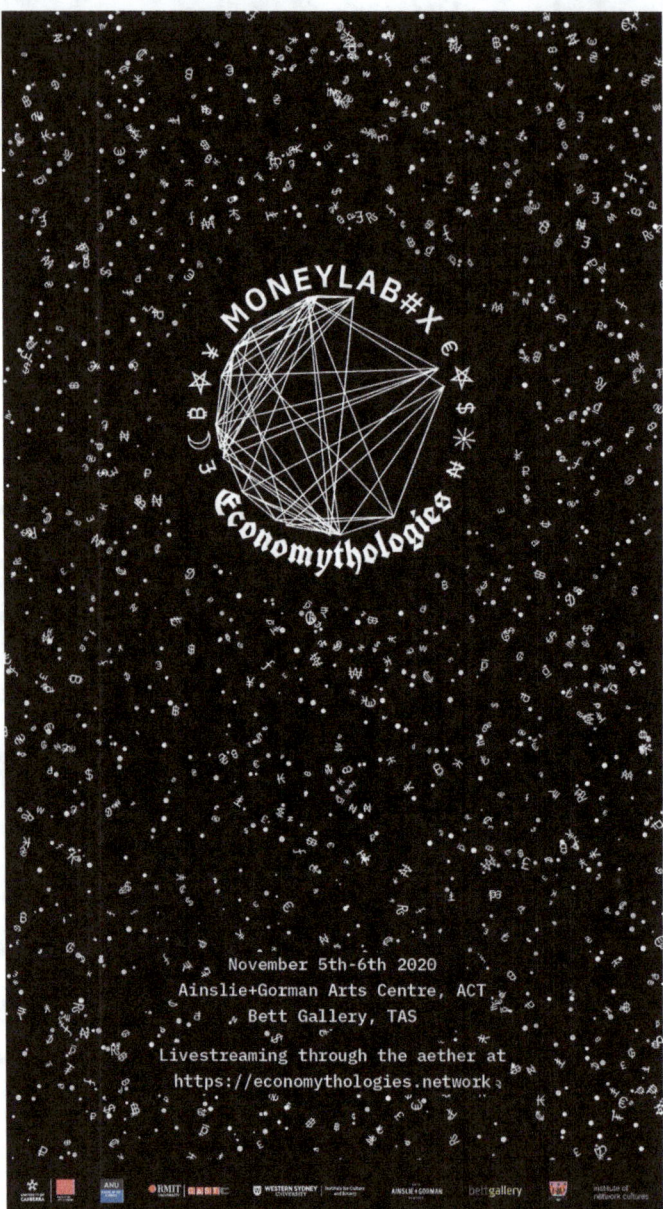

Figure 73: One of the media collaterals for Economythologies #MLX a techno-pagan-mystic visual system the stars + currency symbols + technological networks = economythologies.network. Shaee Illyas, a trans- disciplinary designer, made a script to generate different variations of this mage for different collaterals, such as invitations, reports, backdrops, presentations, social media, website etc. Each iteration is different. Image: Shaee Illyas.

My conclusion was that I could simplify and have three purposes in life:

1) To be stretch more, become more self-sufficient, and scale consumption.

2) To share and leave evocative contributions with and for others.

3) To nurture and appreciate more fully how I am surrounded by people who are capable of unconditional (asynchronous) love.

If I can live like this with others, then nothing else should matter.

Easier said than done. I am reminded of our inertia and the visceral dance that initiates from our cells. To perceive veracity and experience moments tacitly with ease is a process of embodiment. Being a process, not doing a process. Out of it emerges feeling, sensing, and action. The source of this sentient process is love.

LYNN HERSHMAN LEESON

Most of my shows were canceled or delayed. There were exhibitions in Amsterdam, in London, and in Germany, all canceled.

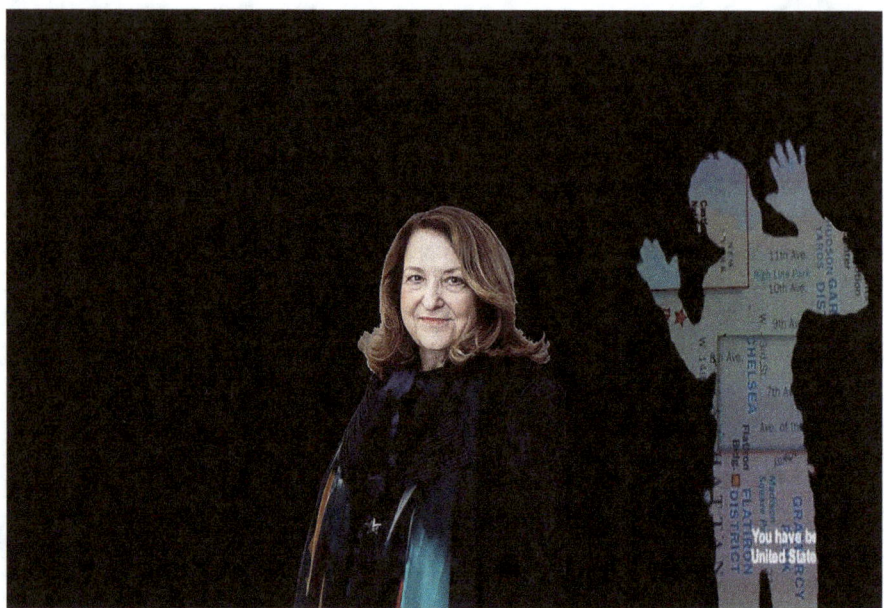

Figure 74: Lynn Hershman in front of 'Shadow Stalker' at the opening of Uncanny Valley at the de Young Museum, San Francisco, 2020.

In the beginning, I did a lot. I finished about six sculptures that had been sitting on shelves for decades, did about sixty new drawings and a short videotape about 'how to be a good ancestor,' designed and made a tarot deck, did an entire 185-page book on the floating museum (which I did in the 70s, but which had never been documented), wrote from scratch 225 pages in two drafts of a memoir, and, last but not least, I worked with another writer to make a script for a feature film we want to do next year.

Then it hit. One leg became swollen, I had a 103°F temperature (38°C), no one would call me back because it was not COVID-19. It turned into a severe blood infection that required hospitalization and about three months to heal. It could have been much worse, and I am grateful, but I am spending my energy getting my strength back. I am doing exercises and walking when I can. It was not caused by the pandemic. Nobody knows what caused it, but it happened in the middle of it.

I am struggling to get back to work, but lost energy and concentration do not come back overnight. I am putting myself on a schedule of recovery, slowly and safely with the help of my doctors.

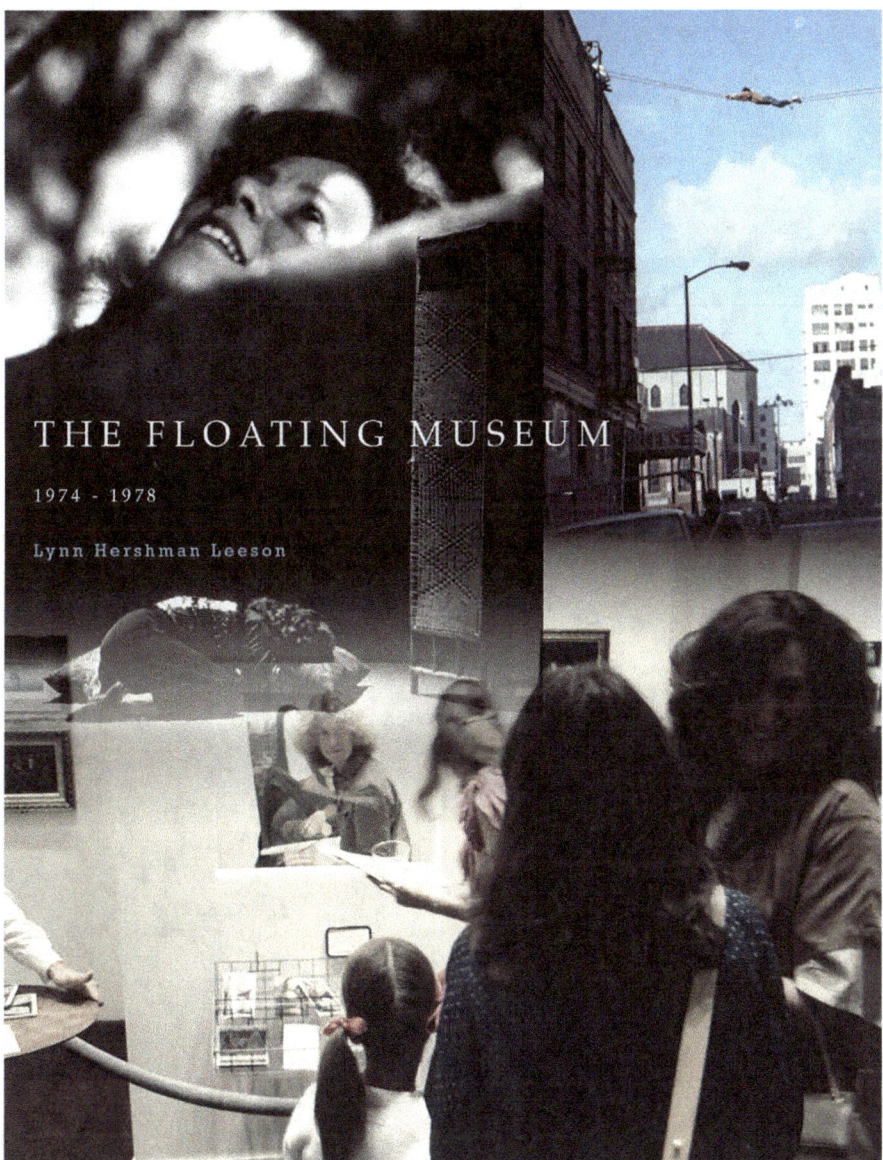

Figure 75: Cover of the book for 'The Floating Museum.'

Most of my shows were canceled or delayed. There were exhibitions in Amsterdam, in London, and in Germany, all canceled. I have a show in Rozenstraat, Amsterdam, end of February. The exhibition at the New York-based New Museum is now scheduled for July 2021. It will be on one floor, and information is on the New Museum website.

San Francisco was the first to close, and it is still shut. Museums are closed, which I find particularly difficult. I am now reading, listening to podcasts, researching, and watching lots of films.

Now people are getting vaccinated in San Francisco, and I have already received part one. I am thinking more about priorities and what really matters, caring for others, and being gentle to oneself and the environment.

Cooking every day.

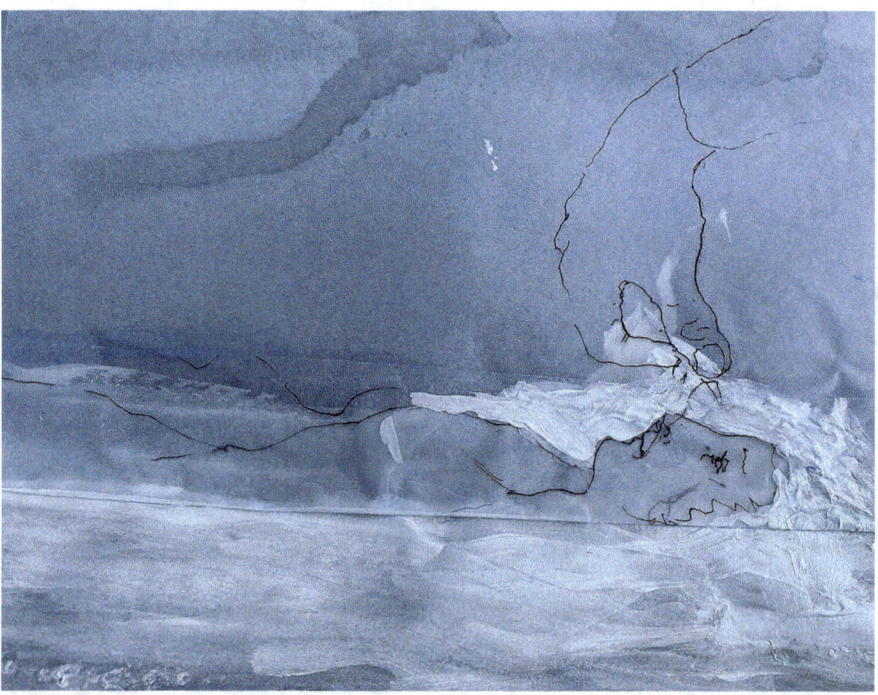

Figure 76: Drawing before I got my COVID-19 shot, ink, watercolor on paper, 8 x 10", 2021.

ADHAM HAFEZ

Performers are trained to listen to their bodies, to every little note and change. Extreme measures such as lockdowns may be harder on our bodies than perhaps on those that are not trained to be body-focused and body-centric.

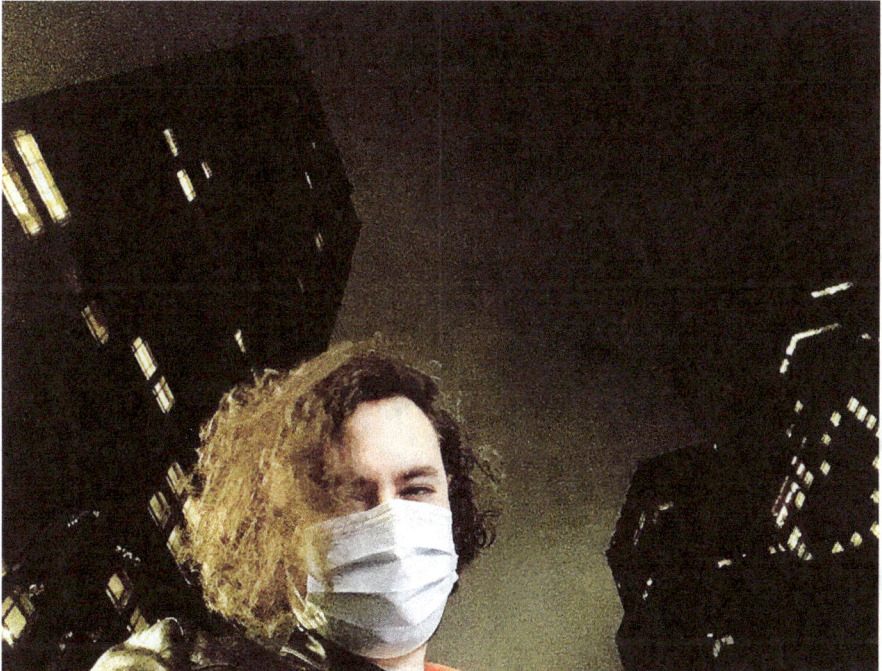

Figure 77: Adham Hafez, selfie with mask.

In New York City, the authorities took some time to acknowledge the situation, the pandemic. But I also feel that people took some time as well. Not everyone had the same response. My relation to the pandemic has changed a lot over months, throughout this last year. But I remember when it first started, and I could not get basic supplies for weeks and eventually months. You would not find bread, and when you did there was no toilet paper, and when you did there would not enough eggs, etc. It was like living through war, which I have witnessed. And living through revolutions, which I have witnessed too. It reminded me of when we were in lockdown on Tahrir Square, without the internet, or phone lines, and then the electricity and water intermittently went off as well.

This feeling of being nothing but your very own physical being and your survival skills, facing either absolute dictatorship or absolute governance havoc. Since then, a lot has happened in New York. People tried to adapt, to adapt to the long lines in front of the supermarkets that continue today. To adapt to closed theatres and create work online or on the street. And to adapt to the fact that this will be our future for a while. We won't wake up and suddenly it's all over. So many actors in this equation also have interests in prolonging this situation. Disaster capitalism rules again. The disaster is actually very lucrative to certain business sectors.

I am very disappointed at how artistic work has been treated during the pandemic, especially here in the United States. We are barely surviving. If it were not for organizations creating small resources, or for foundations redistributing funds, artists would not have survived at all. It is still extremely difficult to imagine how the future will look, and how to stand on our feet again.

La Mama Theatre in New York was one of the first that started helping artists during the lockdown. Not only helping, but even commissioning new work, and reflecting on the conditions of being in a lockdown; what it means to theatre and performance, and what it could teach us about the world and how it is changing. They embraced and welcomed experiments, the way they embraced and welcomed mistakes. Mia Yoo, the artistic director of the theatre, when I spoke with her about the first commission they gave me, already in April 2020, shared my fears about not knowing how to suddenly shift my work from live performance to live digital TV broadcast. She said that this is part of the learning process and that this is part of the experience. That we need to take these risks, and we take them together, otherwise we are not equipped for this new world.

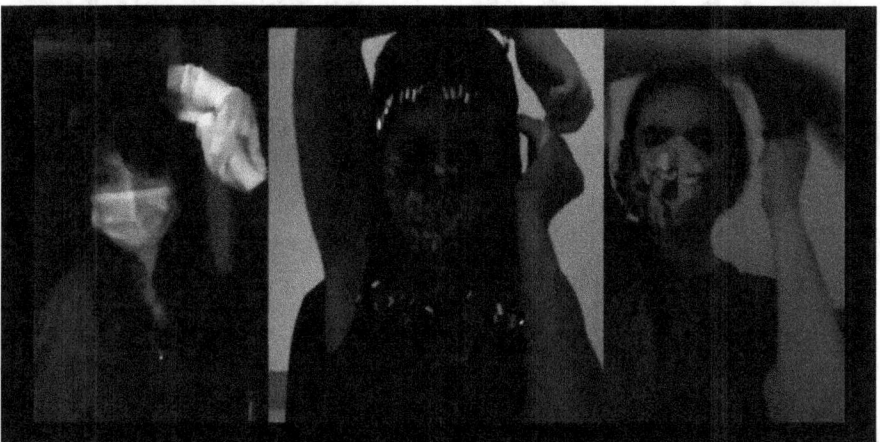

Figure 78: Scene from the KitKat Club by HaRaKa Platform, December 2020.

My life has been shaped by difficult mobility. I was born in the Arab African nation, Egypt. I was born in a Muslim majority country. To be a citizen of Egypt and to wish to travel with my work, to tour with my company, to go to attend a residency or an educational program has always been near impossible. Let alone to go on a vacation with my family, for instance. We don't even dare to dream such dreams. There is no postcolonial, there is the colonial, and the neocolonial. Since the onset of the pandemic, traveling has become an absolute impossibility for people like me. I am writing you this from New York. I was supposed to be in Belgium two months ago already for my residency at Kunsthal Gent, but the Belgian embassy has repeatedly refused to assist me to secure a visa. The rules are never clear, a lot changes quickly, and it is always a financial risk, which makes it a very unwelcoming experience. Perhaps this is what Europe is sending as a message: Arabs, Africans, and Muslims are not welcome.

Meanwhile, I am trying to learn how to adapt my work to this new world. It is not the first time. In 2016, I curated a festival in New York where the Syrian choreographer Noura Murad couldn't come and changed her work to a performance sent as instructions by email, performed by New York dancers to a live Skype call with Noura in Damascus. In 2012, in Cairo, our international festival 'TransDance' that I used to curate with my platform HaRaKa, could not bring Rima Najdi, so we reinvented her performance as a radio piece transmitted to the audience, where the audience became the performers of the work. Rima Najdi is a Lebanese performance artist. And while traveling between Egypt and Lebanon has always favored the Lebanese coming to Egypt at a much easier pace and process than the other way round, the year when we did our festival in 2012, there were political tensions between the countries, and they suspended issuing visas for the Lebanese to come to Egypt. The same happened with Tunisian artists. It was during the tumultuous year of the shift from the revolutionary wave, to the state of exception, to the military interim rule, to the rule of the Muslim brotherhood, and just this long series of very quick and radical political changes that kept happening, and essentially continuing at a much slower pace now since 2011.

We constantly adapt. When you are from a place like Egypt, you have no choice but to adapt, because the conditions have always been extremely difficult. Conditions that are not endemic, but are also supported and sustained by the world's order as it is today. The difficulty for an Arab artist to get a visa to travel to Europe, and the lack of Arab artistic work in contemporary art academies in Europe today are problems within the same ecosystem of othering, alienating, dehumanizing, and colonizing.

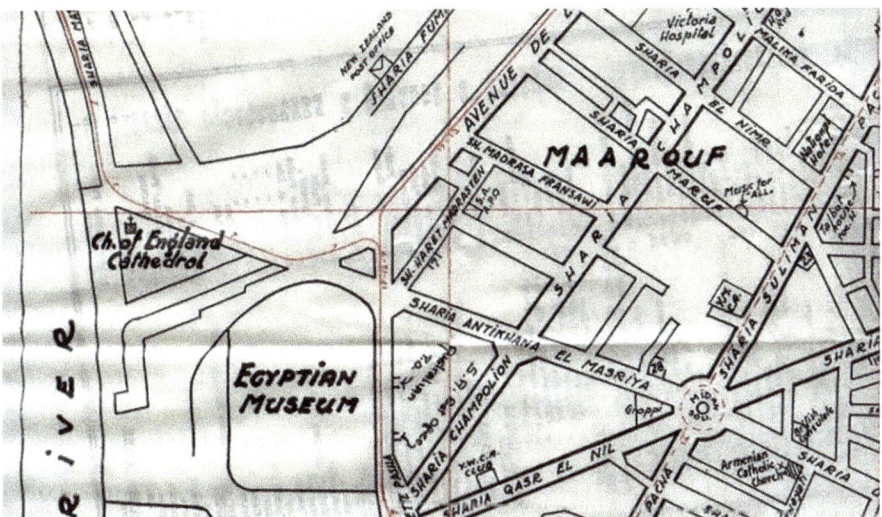

Figure 79: Archival map of downtown Cairo, Egypt. Presentation by Adam Kucharski.

In 2019, we created a project called *In 50 Years or So* that looked at the Suez Canal both from the perspective of the Anthropocene and positioned it within a capitalist colonial world order. We would have never thought we would see the Suez Canal blockage in March 2021, with the Evergreen massive container ship stuck there, and impacting the flow of global capitalism. Moments like this make us realize that the deep thinking and multiple platforms research that we engage within at HaRaKa Platform allows us to envision and propose futurist narratives that quickly transform into unfolding realities. With this in mind, the minute the pandemic hit, we got together: the core group is Lamia Gouda, Mona Gamil, Adam Kucharski and me. We decided that our upcoming project, which is a cabaret on the history of cabarets, is to shift immediately to an online process. We had no qualm, and we did not think this will be a short wave of nuisance, then life goes back to normal. Perhaps again because living in Egypt makes you create a plan B, and D, and Z! So, we rehearsed online, invested in taking workshops on digital theatre and live broadcast tools, and sent our technical director Mido Sadek to a digital theatre workshop online, to equip ourselves instantly for this new reality.

The project that was born looks at an ironic moment in history. 'Cairo KitKat Club' focuses on the 1920s and 1930s history of cabaret. The KitKat Club was a nightclub in Cairo by the Nile, in an area that is generally now called KitKat, after the name of the club. The KitKat Club was closed in the second half of the 20th century and demolished. Nothing remains of the club beyond its stories, tales from the neighborhood, and very few photographs and film clips. We wanted to show how public conviviality and entertainment intertwined with world wars, racist attacks, economic meltdowns, and a global pandemic! It became this poetic process of exploring what had happened a hundred years ago and looking at today's world. Looking at how back in the day, cabarets and underground theatres were the first to go. They were the spaces that got attacked, othered, vilified and pushed to extinction. How similar that moment was to ours today. In western cities, theatres, clubs, cabarets were closed temporarily during the Spanish Flu. In the West, they were ostracized and seen as spaces of radical politics and radical behavior, be it sexual or other. In Egypt in the 1920s and 1930s, cabarets were not vilified. Here, the rise of cabaret was part of the rise of a new wave of urban and political change. A new heart of the city (what we now call Downtown Cairo) became the political, financial, and cultural center not only of Cairo but also of many other cities in the region. People were flocking to these cabarets. Stars like Josephine Baker, or Cecile B. DeMille. Funnily enough, in Egypt during this pandemic now, theatres are already open and working fully, same with music venues and museums. There was only a very short-lived closure, unlike ongoing extreme measures in Western cities. We are yet to understand what these differences are about, and how this story will continue to unfold.

The performance we created was a mix of pre-recorded material we filmed in Cairo, Berlin, Riyadh, and New York, and a live performance on Zoom, that took place in a launch we did in partnership with La Mama Theatre in New York City, and a large installation we exhibited at the Goethe Institute in New York City. The pandemic enabled us to experiment with ways of togetherness across borders, time zones and infection rates. And yet, it was not the topic of conversation, as much as it was the material condition that allowed or challenged the work we were creating.

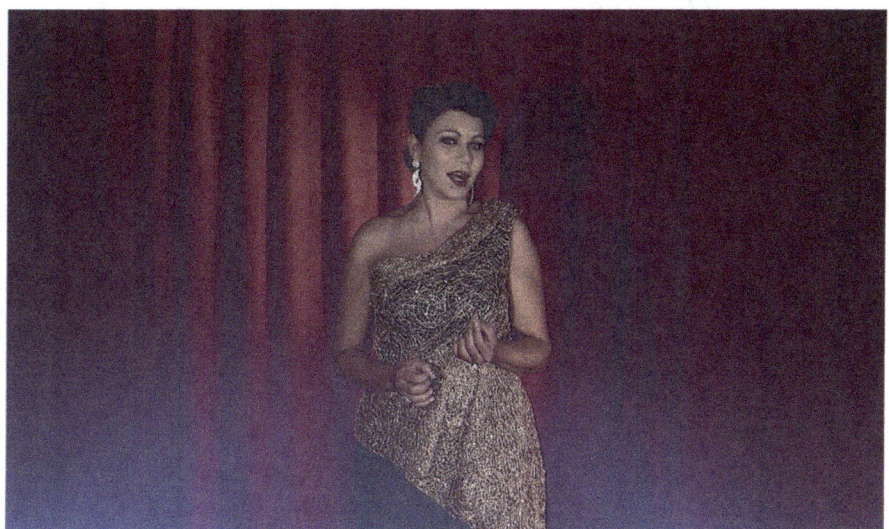

Figure 80: Scene from the KitKat Club, with Lamia Gouda performing Asmahan, December 2020.

For myself and for many other performing artists with whom I have been in dialogue, we felt the impact of the lockdown on our bodies and our health. Dancers, singers, actors, and performers in my friend circle have been discussing many physical complaints and mysterious ailments. Are these the signs of our times, ongoing complications of a previous infection, or is it part of a deconditioning that we are experiencing because of the lockdown? Performers are trained to listen to their bodies, to every little note and change. Extreme measures such as lockdowns may be harder on our bodies than perhaps on those that are not trained to be body-focused and body-centric. For many of us, we are thinking of ways of supporting people to heal. Lamia Gouda, the core researcher at HaRaKa Platform, set up a company designing masks to help people stay healthy without feeling and looking grim. Fadi Khoury, the Iraqi choreographer based in New York, has been offering dance workshops to nurses, as part of a project called 'Heal the Healers.' Cindy Sibilsky, writer, performer, and producer in New York, has been supporting budding performance initiatives by writing and documenting their struggle with the lockdown and with finding ways to support radical socially distant performance work.

I have been doing a lot of work to help people find ways to be articulate about their bodies and their ailments, through an upcoming project called *SICK* that hopes to empower people with ways to understand and address the institution of medicine. And I believe that all these attempts are ways for us to understand how to heal ourselves, or at least how to live in the present moment while figuring new ways of support, new alliances, and finding a new meaning to our work in the shadow of the global crisis.

ANNIE ABRAHAMS

I miss contact with colleagues, I miss visits to museums and theaters, I miss intensive work periods, I miss hanging out together and chatting, I miss the unexpected.

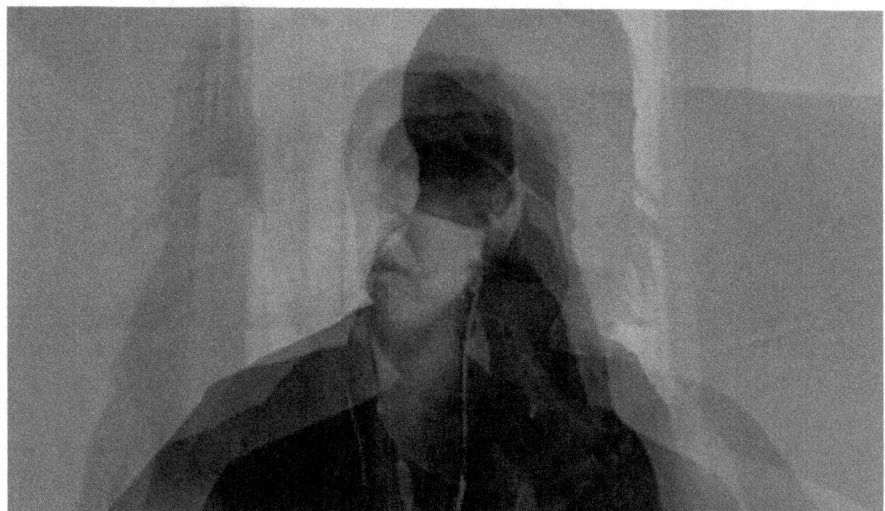

Figure 81: Superposition of images of the performance of 'Breathing' by Utterings.

France, where I live, has a fairly strict corona policy, and given my vulnerability (a piece of my lungs was removed 5 years ago), I like and appreciate that. I am just afraid of the virus and take extreme care. In the past year, I have seen maybe ten people in 'real life' besides my husband. I am very much looking forward to a vaccination, which unfortunately is too long in coming.

It is not easy to write something about a situation when you are still in the middle of it. Analyzing is not easy. When I try, I immediately feel more fragile. Thinking about it makes me feel more vulnerable. I don't want to be preoccupied with what might have been, with what I miss... I have to push myself every day to do something, to make something, to stand still is dangerous. It wasn't like that at the beginning when there still seemed to be perspective. I miss contact with colleagues, I miss visits to museums and theaters, I miss intensive work periods, I miss hanging out together and chatting, I miss the unexpected.

Because my work before the pandemic was already focused on communication, collaboration, and behavior via teleconferencing applications, there were not that many changes in how I create it. Some exhibitions were canceled, but others took their place. I was asked to do a workshop or give a talk more often, but that didn't lead to new production opportunities. Colleagues thought that with my years of experience I would be very busy. That was/is not the case. My work is and remains investigative and is not product-oriented, which remains problematic for the art world. So now I have more time to engage in poetry and language, and to scan old negatives. Writing poems helps to channel my anger (and fear).

My work has always been context-bound, embedded in the environment, and inspired by personal questions. So yes, the pandemic has also influenced me.

Right at the beginning, Daniel Pinheiro and I decided to hurry up with a video essay we had been working on for a while. We both have a lot of experience with webcam performance and have been researching what is so specific about it for years. In the video essay published in October 2020 in the Journal of Embodied Research, we show the physical and material conditions that influence interactions in contacts via webcams.

Another project entitled *BEFORE THE FIRST*, made with Helen Varley Jamieson and Suzon Fuks, started as a reaction to the fact that many artists had to work online for the first time and presented it as extremely innovative. We wanted to show that online performance was not 'new' and already had a history going way back. To make the video, we contacted artists and colleagues of different generations and disciplines who we knew had used the internet in their performance practice much earlier. We asked them about their first online performance experience. This was not about showing a complete overview (there is much, much more), but more about reminding people that online performance has an ancient and rich history.

There were also special pandemic initiatives. For example, I participated in *Pandemic Encounters*, an online performance installation organized by Paul Sermon and Randall Packer. For this performance, I made a soundtrack *Pandemic Encounter*, in which I mix the sound of my breathing with my computer distorted heartbeat and *Silences*, a sound work by Frans van Lent. Afterward, I was able to present this sound file as an independent artwork in two exhibitions: *LOCKDOWN* at Atelier Melusine, La Trimouille, and *Temps Suspendu* at Palteforme, Paris.

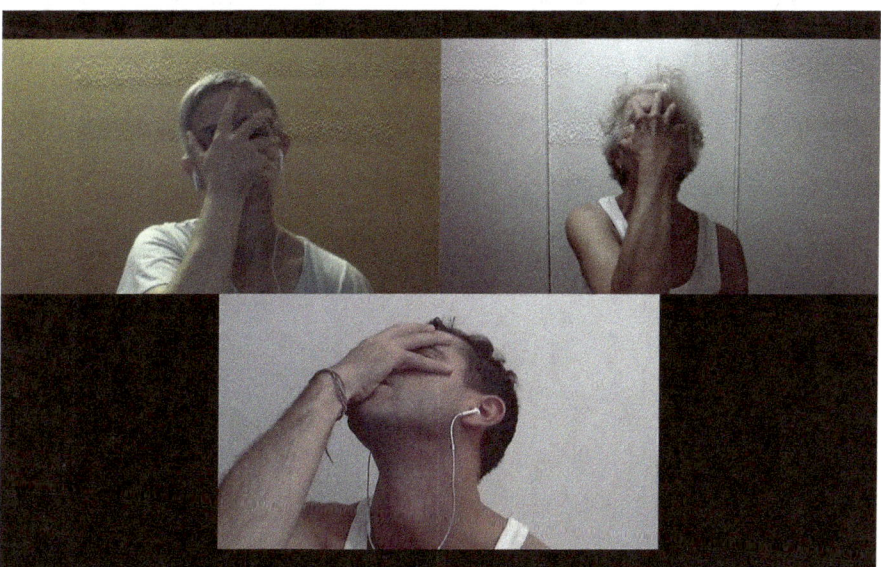

Figure 82: Screenshot 'Distant Movements #6,' with clockwise Muriel Piqué, Annie Abrahams, and Daniel Pinhiero.

Other online performance projects that had been running for some time such as *Distant Feelings* (2015-ongoing) with Daniel Pinheiro and *Distant Movements* (2018-ongoing) with Daniel Pinheiro and Muriel Piqué continued as usual but gained an extra dimension during the pandemic as we also opened the sessions to other interested parties. In *Distant Feelings*, we wonder if and how energy circulates between bodies in an online performance where physical contact is absent. With eyes closed and without talking, we 'feel' the others. In *Distant Movements*, we are similarly concerned with whether and how to experience dancing with others when sitting alone in front of a computer screen. Eventually, with great success, we organized seven additional weekly open sessions for both projects.

Just before the pandemic, in November 2019, Utterings, an internet performance and research group around language and voice, was founded. With Constança Carvalho Homem, Curt Cloninger, Nerina Cocchi, Daniel Pinheiro, and Derek Piotr, we formed an online band that focuses, blindfolded, on creating a 'new' language 'on the fly' that puts attention, trust, and feeling above rationality. After our first performance during Audioblast #8 for APO-33 in Nantes and another during the Network Music Festival, we did a special performance called *Breathing* for STWST 48x6 in Linz, Austria. During this performance, we communicated for thirty minutes using only breath sounds. After this, we had another series of three performances called *New Language*, *Above Rationality*, and *Transmissions* on the Listening Arts Channel of 'We're All Bats.'

Meanwhile, I'm looking forward to the three workshops and performances we'll be doing with Utterings in April 2021 also for 'We're All Bats.' Hopefully, this summer the residency with 3G(enerations) – Constellations planned at Espace Gantner in Bourogne, France, can also go ahead. It would be nice to finally work there with Pascale Barret, Alix Desaubliaux, and Alice Lenay on a publication about *Constellations*, our non-binary laboratory of collaborative and performative explorations in the realm of contemporary net art. I am sure I can still discover interesting new aspects of it.

It sounds strange maybe, but sometimes I am afraid that soon I won't know how to deal with 'real' people – bodies – anymore.

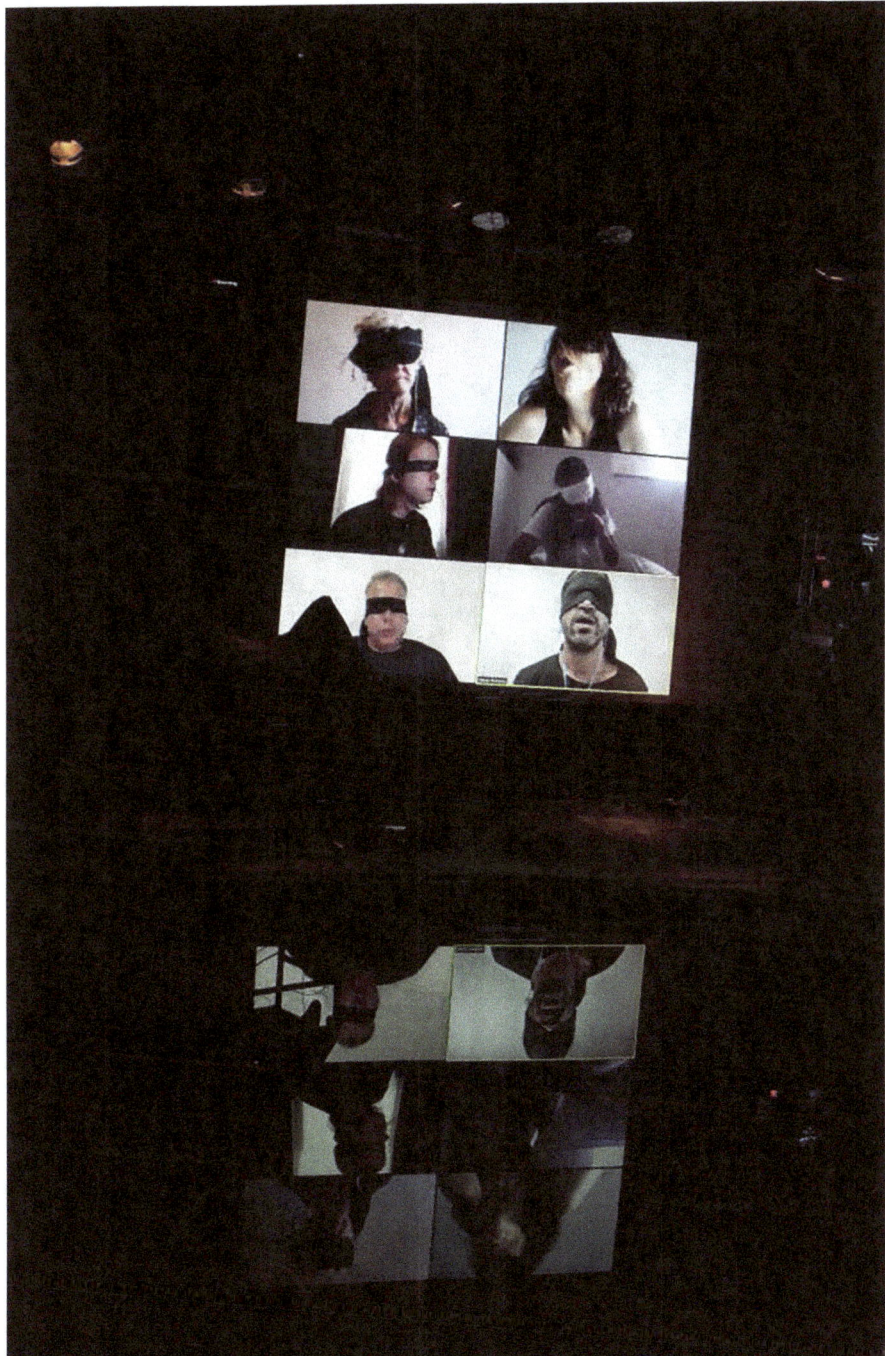

Figure 83: Projection of 'Breathing' by Utterings live performance at STWST48x6 MORE LESS in Linz, September 2020, photo by Sandra Brandmayr.

TINA LA PORTA

COVID-19 really threw me off my game. My work was way off schedule and I was still struggling with my mental health.

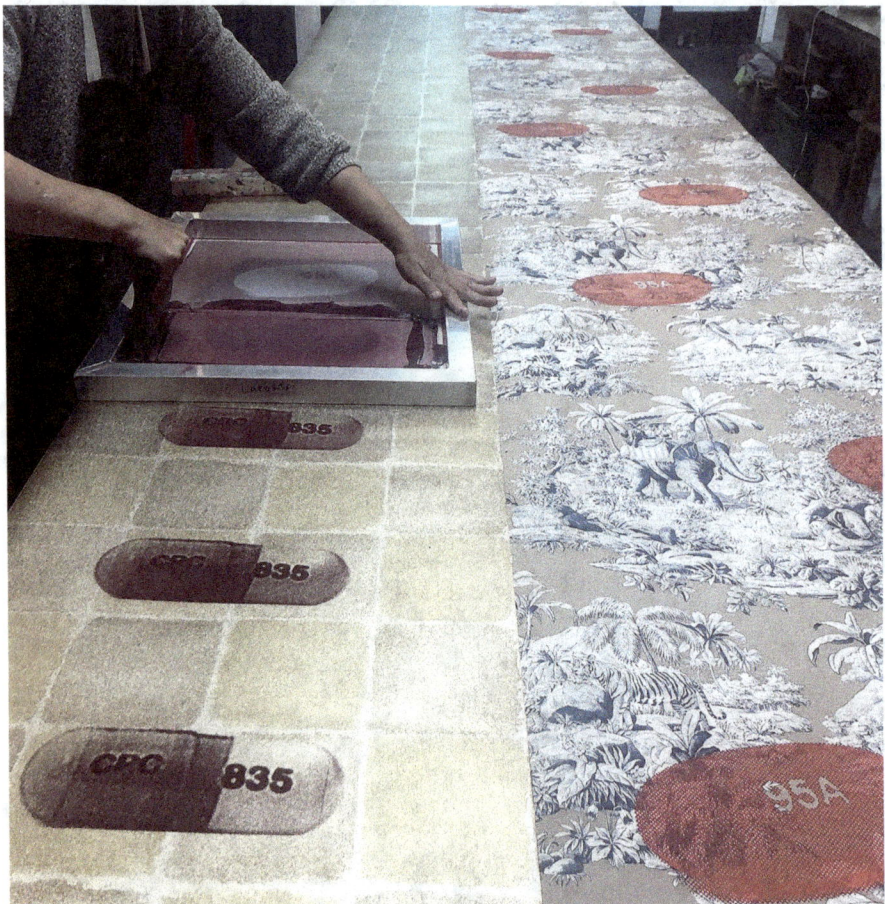

Figure 84: Screen printing on wallpaper at Oolite Printshop, Miami; 2021.

The situation here in the U.S. was total chaos and confusion. I remember watching the news and it seemed like everything was happening in Italy. Then I started to get bombarded with COVID-19 closure emails from arts organizations. I was trying to process it all while I deleted events from my calendar and still did not get much information on how bad it really was in the U.S. Then, we were in lockdown and people were panic buying at grocery stores as if a hurricane was on its way to South Florida.

All of a sudden everything turned to Zoom, Facebook, and Instagram Live. After a while, I experienced Zoom fatigue and fell into a Major Depressive Episode.

I did have a major project in the works that had to be canceled and another that was still in its planning stages. But because I relapsed into a severe state of depression, it got to the point where I couldn't even get out of my chair because I was completely exhausted and in severe physical pain. I was unable to work. I started a new treatment for depression, TMS (Transcranial Magnetic Stimulation). It's new here in the U.S. but it has been available to people struggling with their mental health in Europe and the UK for a while now. After my first round of TMS, I relapsed again and I am now on my third round of treatment.

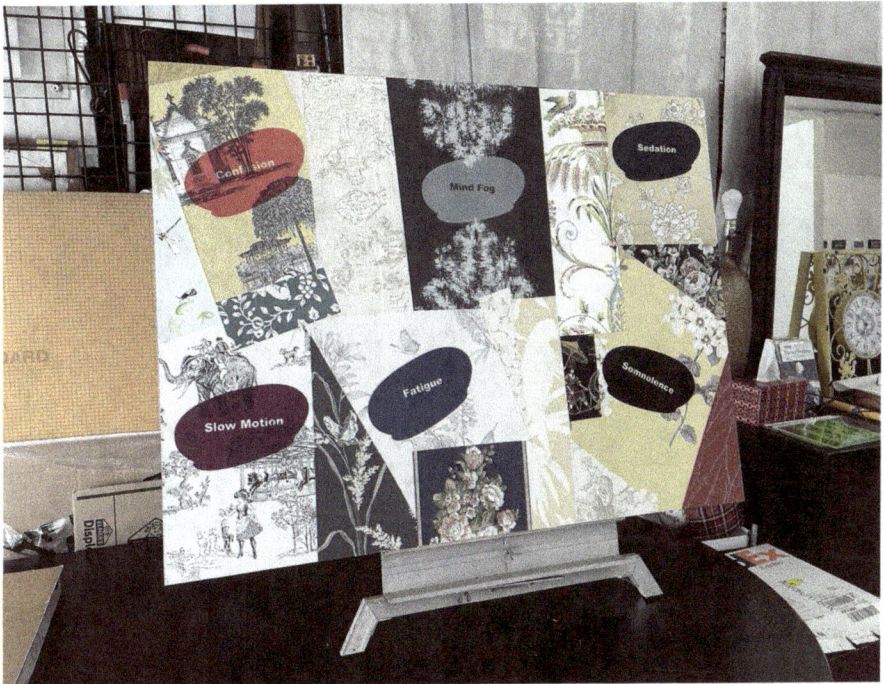

Figure 85: Collage of screen prints on wallpaper, 2021.

The arts organization that I had a commitment with for January 2021 wasn't very empathetic to what I was going through. I was able to turn my three-month solo show into one month to buy myself more time, but I really wanted to re-schedule completely. That wasn't an option, and I had to scale down my exhibition plans. I am showing a single-channel video projection.

COVID-19 really threw me off my game. My work was way off schedule and I was still struggling with my mental health. Ironically enough, the work I am doing right now has to do with mental health. So, I am suffering from a Major Depressive Episode and at the same time making work that mirrors my personal experience. In some ways, COVID-19 has made my work appear to be more relevant, and because of media coverage, the issues surrounding mental health have become more mainstream.

DENNIS DE BEL

*I've decided not to teach anymore for a while, at least not until I can physically do it
again.*

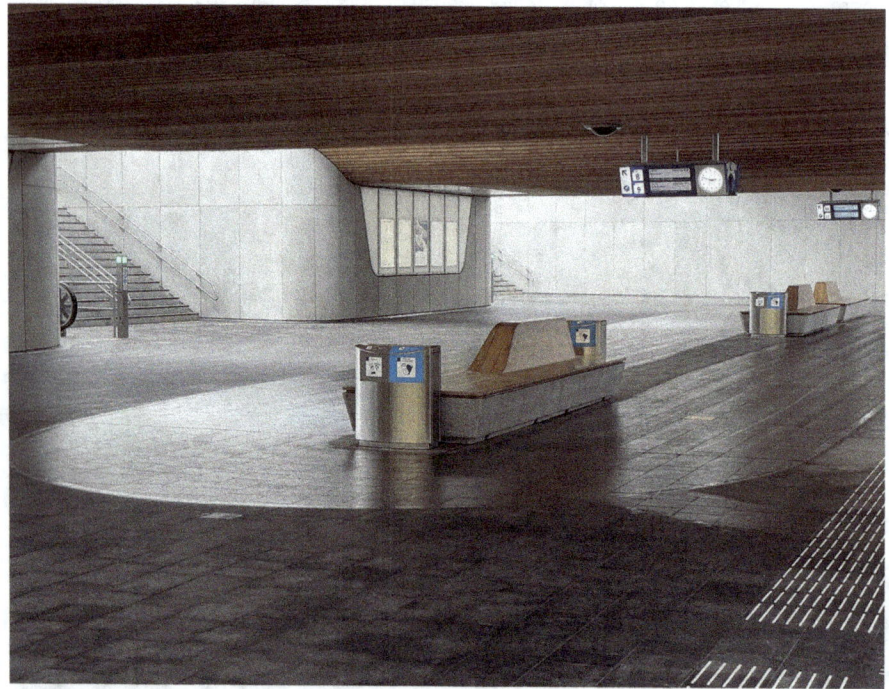

Figure 86: Untitled.

I had just returned from China, early February 2020, when news of the virus reached the
world. I never expected that, the arrogant westerner that I am, it would come even closer, to
the Netherlands. It soon became clear that the Dutch government didn't see that happening
either, and, after the first dozen or hundred cases were known, I was still teaching at the
design academy in Eindhoven as if nothing had happened. That was nice, physically teaching
hands-on stuff, but also super scary and unbelievable. How could everything just continue
while scary pictures of literal life or death situations in China and Italy were circulating?

Meanwhile, I was already wearing facemasks everywhere (my girlfriend is Chinese and has
experience with pandemics...). We were scolded, coughed at, and mocked everywhere. At
some point, the school finally closed ('The train is the safest place' were the last words my
coordinator said to me) and I haven't been outside much since.

A sort of peace and calm descended on me. Finally, there was a good excuse not to race from
one place to another and just stay at home. This also had the advantage of less travel time
and this benefited overdue projects I had. In other words, there was only more work to do.

Before school closed, some exchange students had already fled the Netherlands (Korean and Chinese students) for fear of the incompetence inherent to a 'democratic' handling of the pandemic. This translated into 'hybrid' or 'blended' learning, which sounds super nice and new, but means that, in my case, you have to have a Microsoft Teams session open to serve and 'engage' both online and 'offline' students. I really couldn't and didn't want to. Not in the least because my old laptop was no longer supported by Microsoft Teams and thus I had to bring two laptops etcetera, etcetera. Counterproductive. How did Microsoft get ALL Dutch academies to do this? I often wonder how Microsoft managed to get a foot in the door of education.

Until I graduated, everything seemed to be done in-house, you could just get some webspace from the ICT person for a particular project, for example. Then, all of a sudden, everything became MS Office 360. Then when I got emails from students, the kind of mail with the message that someone sent you an email, I had to make an MS account to read the attachments (stored in MS Cloud). Of course, that didn't work because your account had to be linked to the institute. As a freelancer, it was impossible to get such an account. And because everything was linked to accounts, you often couldn't use the beamer because it was connected to a PC in the room... for which you needed an account to log in. Students were nice enough to log in for you though... every 10 minutes, haha! Long story short, how come ALL academics went into business with MS? I suspect something with Data Retention laws or GDPR and that only MS had that in order or hugely good lobbying practices, probably it's something much simpler and I don't see the most obvious explanation. It became clear how, next to the academies, the infrastructure also becomes more corporate and inhuman.

Because I have no contract and teach freelance on an invoice basis, and was 'out' for about six months, I was losing income. I applied for a TOZO, a Dutch government COVID-19 business support program, but because I got a few website jobs again (corona pocket money?) I had to give the money back. With TOZO support, you are not allowed to earn anything extra, and yes, you can spend everything you earn and report it, but that didn't feel right, and it is also too much administration.

I did some more teaching through Teams. I am completely done with it. I'm also behind a screen a lot in my free time (read: working on my projects), physically that's really becoming too much now. I've also seriously seen ZERO online events, openings, talks, or streams, except for rc3, the German CCC hacker conference, but I would have watched that anyway. I also gave a talk there. Maybe that's a good comparison: these CCC conferences always happen in the 'void' between Christmas and New Year. This whole pandemic lockdown thing feels like that void, but this time it is a void lasting 12 months.

At the beginning of the crisis, I had a sort of hope that a lot of change would come now, for the benefit of humanity. It became clear how fragile EVERYTHING is. One year onwards, precarity rules, definitely also in government ICT. There is support here and there, but at what cost? All running plans seem to be on the back burner. I am looking forward to going to China again and just feeling free, feeling that everything is under control.

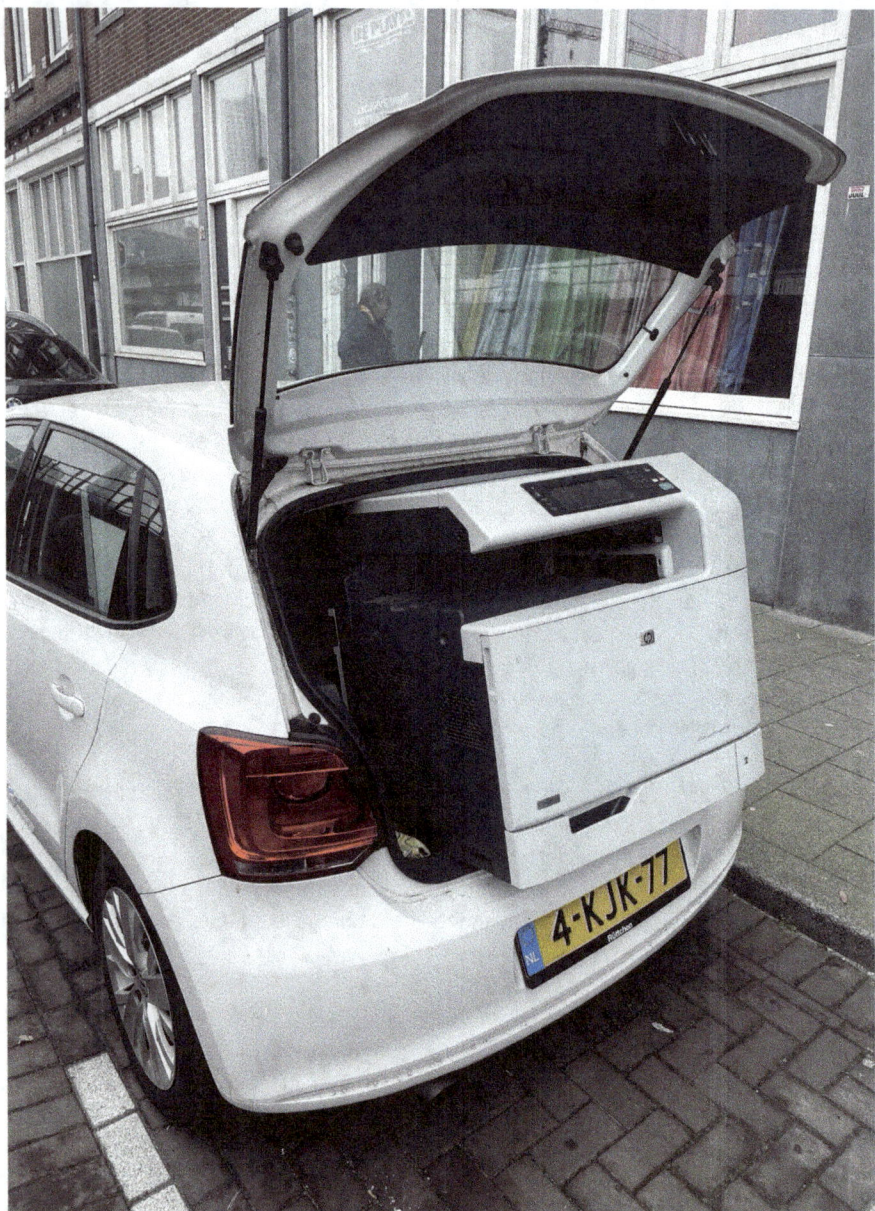

Figure 87: Untitled.

In the meantime, I've decided not to teach anymore for a while, at least not until I can physically do it again. I want to focus on one small project of my own for this year and wrap up
current projects. That's enough. Meanwhile, hope has given way to fear of what this crisis
will bring. In terms of work, I would love to collaborate and seek help from and with all sorts
of people, but because of this half-baked insecure home isolation shit and curfew, I'm only

thinking about myself. It's going to be a big ego trip 'save myself and escape from this hell' kind of story, but how, where to go? In that respect, it seems to be getting harder and harder to escape the grip of neoliberalism. 'Together against corona... a better environment starts with yourself?' That is also absolutely the opposite of what we need to overcome this crisis. The international collaboration to suppress this virus seems more like fertile ground for tensions... well-founded as well as unfounded.... and bird flu is already on the horizon, atchoo! Exciting times, something is finally happening, one might say, but I don't see much happening that offers any prospects. My head is full of nothing and everything at once.

LUCAS BAMBOZZI

Dealing with the cultural context in a profound and responsible way has become urgent.

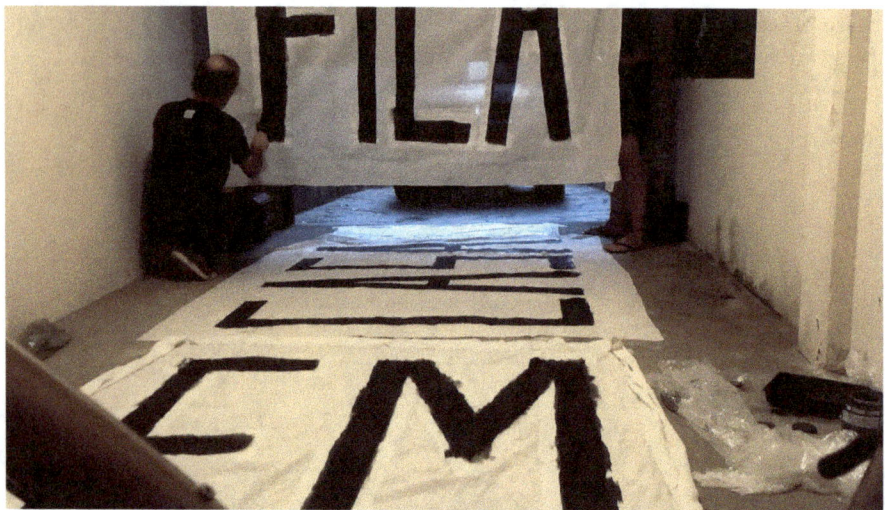

Figure 88: Providing domestic support to some needs. A flag encouraging people to stay home, produced in my garage.

Back in April 2020, when the COVID-19 crisis rose bigger concerns around the world, I took part in an online event conducted by the Technopolitics group from Vienna (Felix Stalder, Ina Zwerger, Axel Stockburger, and other great artists and researchers). The idea was to draw a local context in a discussion with Brian Holmes (U.S.), David Sperling (UK), Udi Edelman, and Tsilla Hassine (IL). I was then asked more or less the same questions Josephine asks for this publication, which spins a sort of retrospective in my mind.

By that occasion, exactly a year ago, I said that I felt we would soon experience a total mess in Brazil. Financially I would possibly get into trouble since most commissioned projects and invitations would stop during the pandemic season and I would rely mostly on teaching activities, which is commonly not enough to make a living in São Paulo. I was conscious about this; I had some reserved funds, so I was just postponing the possible symptoms of running out of income. Still, I was fortunate enough to live in a nice flat, in a pleasant environment, together with my daughter. What I really feared was what was about to come for the less privileged ones. And it all started to happen. Yes, it happened indeed. And it got worse than we could all imagine.

A brief retrospect. The discussion triggered by the Techonopolitics group brought back some blurred memories. Long ago, by the beginning of the 2000s, in his visits to Brazil, theorist and critic Brian Holmes was then pointing out the importance of a (re)connecting with public life, to meet the pulsating life 'out there,' the tougher realities on the streets.

He was emphasizing the need to avoid falling into emerging forms of alienation through increasing corporate mediation. As the 2000s were approaching that would lead to no legitimate re-enactment with anything other than fabricated realities, driven by the spread of screens and gadgets mediating our lives.

Cut. Here I am now, stuck in front of many screens (tinier ones, compared to those from the late 90s), surrounded by different kinds of fabricated realities. Science, medicine, human rights, regimes, and ideologies are questioned by negationism and substituted by global fantasies channeled via social networks. It is difficult to have the strength, to be always on, to feel the burden to check the truth among so many lies. Down here in Brazil we have a president elected by lies, supported by the fake news industry – mainly spread through apps like WhatsApp in our case.

In addition to fighting COVID-19, we have been fighting the President of the Republic, Jair Bolsonaro. Since the early days of the pandemic, he has been not only minimizing the risks of the virus but also systematically disseminating disinformation.

Recent research (March 2020) shows that for 44% of the Brazilian population believe the president was primarily responsible for the current direness of the coronavirus crisis in Brazil. For the sake of keeping the economy functioning for some sectors, using vague neoliberal precepts such as 'freedom' (misemployed here as the choice to wear or not wear protective masks), he never presented any plan to face the pandemic. For the Brazilian neoliberals, adorers of Bolsonaro, the virus is a fabrication. A massive number of poor, religious people still rely on his first statements, believing that the virus is a Chinese (i.e., communist) invention to debilitate the economy and attack capitalism. For the masses behind contemporary evangelical money-making churches, the cure is still just Jesus. Behind the curtains, its rich priests pay for their vaccines while refusing to support basic sanitary measures for the rest.

It is difficult to survive with so many lies shaping reality in such a massive way. From the beginning, his lying kept fueling our anger. We believed that we could defeat Bolsonaro while dealing with the virus. But today, the truth is that the virus acquired such vast proportions, exactly because we still have Bolsonaro. All this leads to the whole country having little empathy with the dead, no solidarity with the poor, so many blatant egocentric interests driven by the super-rich, so many intrusive bits of ideological speech shaping the minds of millions, so many bots on Twitter diverting the truth, so many bad words in the name of gods appealing just for money.

My writing here is therefore affected by a thread that is seen and perceived through the media, but which also directly affects our minds and bodies on a daily basis.

In discussions comparing Brazil to Asian countries for example, in the first months of 2020, there were many clues that the battle here would be really tragic and irresponsible. The virus was never treated here as a war to be fought by the masses – as it seems to be for the rest of the world, including the U.S., recently, after Trump left.

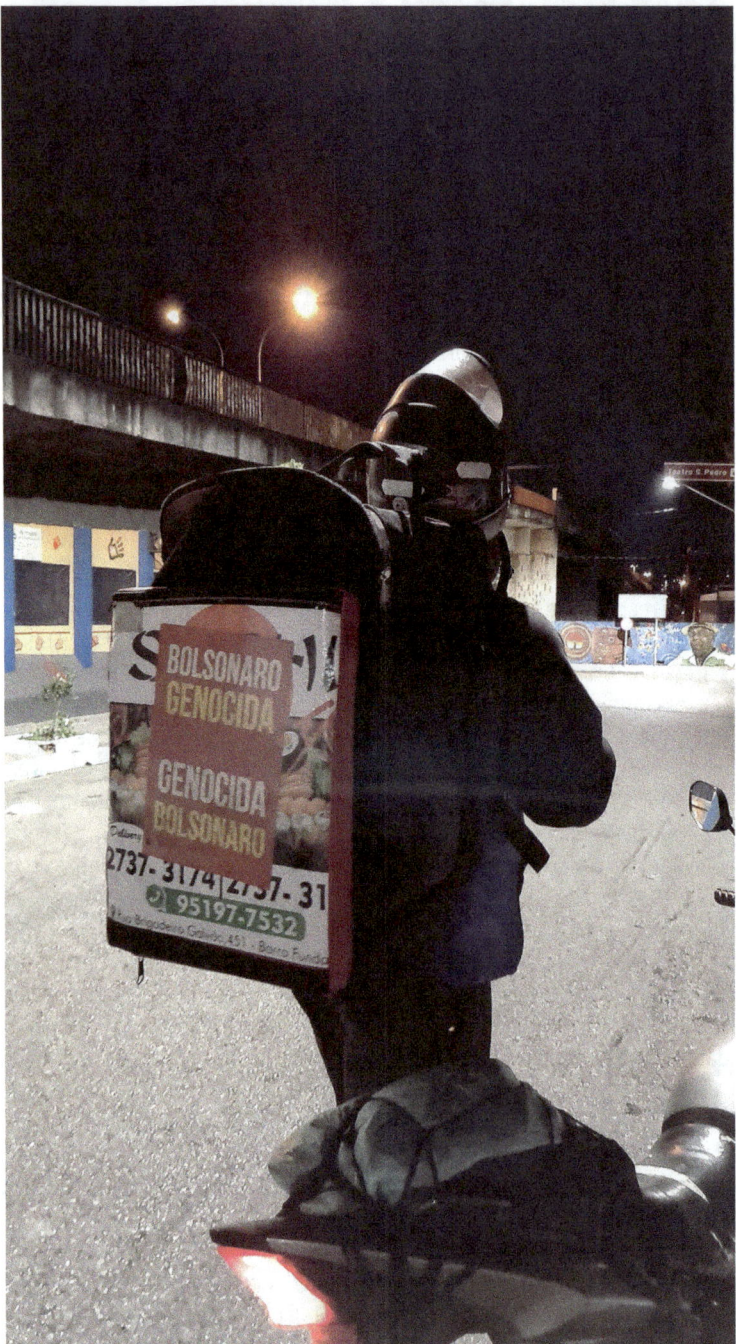

Figure 89: Delivery. Delivery motorbikers have been joining a silent protest against the death of more than 400,000 people due to the lack of any public health plan.

It became a real genocide. The chaos is profound because it is difficult for the whole population to decide what to follow: warnings from medical institutions or the economic rules of the Ministry of Economy, or the euphoria of the president, stuck in an endless pose of a candidate-in-campaign, following Chicago school rules on the economy and foreseeing his possibility to stay power after the next election in 2022.

Then there are speculations about the specific situation in Brazil. Everything that would supposedly help us (the summer, higher temperatures) did not reduce contaminations. Determinisms, such as the Confucianism obedience, described by Byung Chul Han as a key quality in Asia, which may have helped long-term disciplined societies to defeat the virus in some way, would not work here, in an undisciplined, turbulent culture.

Japan, Korea, China, Hong Kong, Taiwan, or Singapore have an authoritarian mentality, which comes from their cultural tradition (Confucianism). People are less resistant and more obedient than in Europe. They also trust the State.[1]

Therefore, next to the virus we have an aggravating issue, an extra enemy, which is the president (as well as his sons, who work as a crew) inoculating a kind of poison in the online social environment. His government is mostly maintained by his online supporters, who think we are also subjected to other kinds of viruses in our daily life. They are doing what they promised to do: to extinguish social programs, social movements, public institutions, the arts, ancestral knowledge, indigenous people, scientific knowledge, public health. Because they found 'communism' behind every social program, behind any thought greeting the commons. For more than 14 years (since 2002, the first election of Lula), mainstream media has shaped the idea that 'communism is behind the door.' They say that popular social programs hide a communist agenda. In churches all around the country, evil is associated with all the red flags found in the frontline of most social movements. All the acts of this government carry this as a strategy. It leads to the implementation of an exception state, which operates through concomitant diverting signs, contradictory modulations.

Entire companies are not following proper market policies. Institutions, stores, and services are dropping their obligations to their public, to their consumers. And the public system is weaker than ever since it is the target of the current constituted power.

There is no fun in such an ungoverned society. Obscurity has come to the tropics.

So, since early 2020, many of us understood that apart from living, making money, and keeping our mental health, we need to also face Bolsonaro. How? First, by spending time on social care: supporting homeless people, squats, housing occupations, by doing simple things such as raising awareness about necessary measures. For example, we knew from the first days of the pandemic back in March-April 2020 that it was urgent to stay at home. We needed to

---

1   Byung Chul Han, *The viral emergenc(e/y) and the world of tomorrow,* https://elpais.com/ideas/2020-03-21/la-emergencia-viral-y-el-mundo-de-manana-byung-chul-han-el-filosofo-surcoreano-que-piensa-desde-berlin.html, [transl. from Spanish], Accessed March 2020

help people to stay home. We needed to emphasize this since the official instructions were quite contradictory.

This is also manifested in my work. When the reclusion started, I was involved in several projects. They developed in different ways from the beginning of the pandemic to the present.

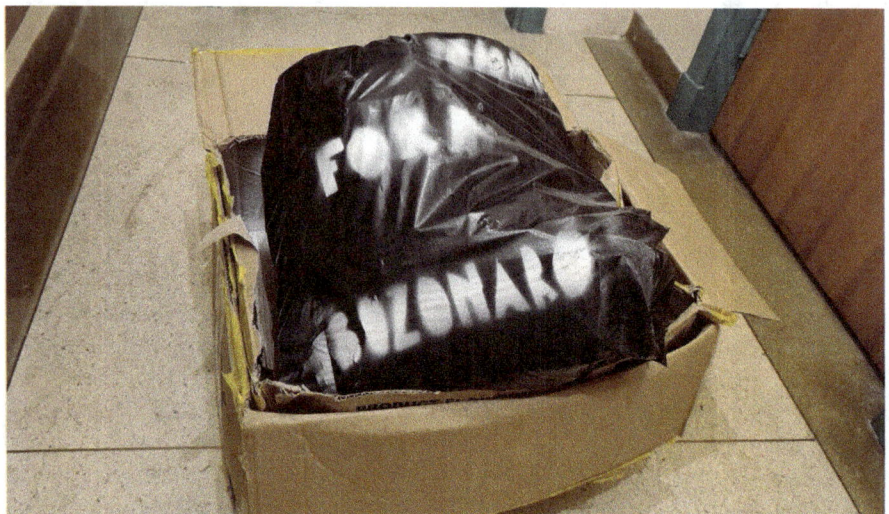

Figure 90: Garbage. All kinds of actions are valid to raise further consciousness about the madness in the government.

Since 2017, I have been part of a group of artists developing collaborative practices at the Ocupação 9 de Julho, a social occupation of a building in downtown São Paulo, conduct- ed by MSTC, Movimento Sem Teto do Centro (a collective housing movement). The initiative developed a series of activities that were crucial for establishing a cultural and artistic scene, which was in turn very important to sustain the housing movement.

There is the Occupation's kitchen. There are no public activities conducted by the kitchen at the moment, but the facilitators are providing food for other initiatives and peripheral groups in need of help in different parts of the city.

We run an art gallery at the Occupation. I am one of the coordinators of the space, and we all took part in the last exhibition *O Que Não é Floresta é Prisão Política* (roughly translated as 'What is not a Forest is a Political Prison'). Though the exhibition had to be closed, we kept working on an auction to raise money for the local community and activist movements to survive these hard times.

Then there was the Occupation's Cinema club. Before the reclusion days, we were deeply involved in offering free screenings of films followed by discussions with filmmakers and activists.

Some of these previously in-loco, physical activities were developed into online substitutions, and some had to just be suspended. I am still engaged with the group and all the activities, and we are still finding ways to keep it valuable for the community.

Next to this, I have been getting more involved with large-scale projections in public space around the city in recent years. Sometimes these projections are linked to an art project and the result of a kind of commissioned video piece. But especially during the pandemic, these projections have become a kind of intervention, as in a video-guerilla format, with any available resources, as an immediate response to Brazilian politics.

So, throughout 2020 I worked with a network of activists called *Projetemos*, involving more than 180 people from different cities. Since the beginning of the reclusion, the group started to do projections on urban facades, each member in their own neighborhood, daily. Most of the content was a part of direct actions against the government and the stupidity of the current president. I joined the group's actions as much as I could.

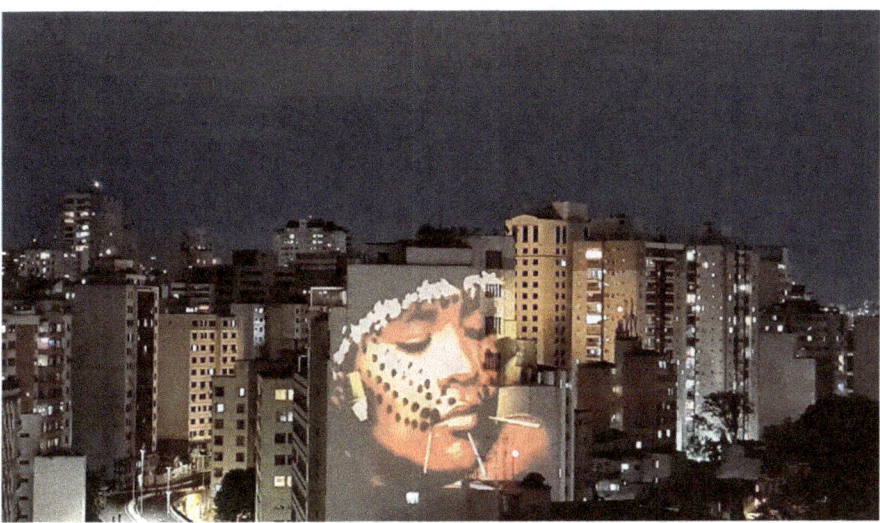

Figure 91: Large-scale projections I did in support of the Yanomamis, with photos provided by artist Claudia Andujar. There are already 25,000 gold prospectors in Yanomami lands, taking all kinds of plague (including corona virus) to their lives.

I have also worked on the projections of a series of videos to support the Yanomami ancient tribes in the north of Brazil. Illegal miners in the region, who are also bringing COVID-19 to the tribes, have assaulted them. It is known that the indigenous people in Brazil are not immune to many viral diseases; they historically don't take vaccines, so they are really at risk. The projections are done in support of an NGO called ISA, with images offered by Claudia Andujar, a famous photographer who has lived for many years with the Yanomami.

Next to this, I finished the editing of Lavra: a feature film about broken dams of open-pit mining (iron ore) in Minas Gerais, the Brazilian state most historically impacted by colonialist exploitation practices since the diamond and gold ages. It is still one of the largest exporters of iron ore in the world. The project became a hybrid documentary, made possible through a series of journeys around regions impacted by the iron ore tailings in the state, drifting through themes such as topophilia and solastalgia. The harm is everywhere; the damage has deeply impacted many communities and their livelihoods, reflecting the ongoing war between capitalism and nature. The reclusion period was a good time to immerse myself in editing the film. It is now in its last stages, approaching the sound and visual corrections for an upcoming submission to film festivals around the world.

The film appears in different formats: next to a feature-length documentary, I am working on a shorter experimental film and preparing an installation version.

And then, by the end of August, after months of social isolation, we could go out into the streets again. We did smoke bomb protests, to bring attention to how some institutions are hurt by the current neoliberal politics. The closing of Brazilian Cinemateca in São Paulo for example poses a danger to its amazing archive and the preservation of Brazilian culture.

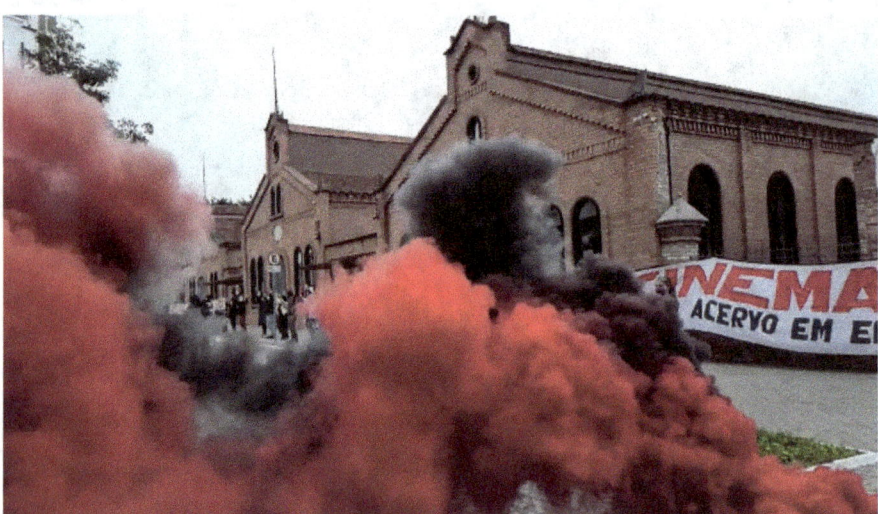

Figure 92: Protest against closing of Brazilian Cinemateca, in São Paulo, a major institution devoted to the cinema archives.

Some funds for supporting disrupted initiatives eventually came out via a few open calls. More recently, I managed to find resources to start a new edition of the AVXLab Festival, focusing on initiatives dealing with live AV transmissions, online performances, video art, net art, and other related media art. It will include a symposium and a series of online presentations. We want to bring together many artists dealing with the pandemic through different approaches, showing how people face the effects of COVID-19.

Dealing with the cultural context in a profound and responsible way has become urgent. Alienation is a big problem now and discussing it in depth is our responsibility, since most government actions were not responsible enough.

In March-April 2020, there were several publications about the pandemic that grabbed our attention. There was *Wuhan Soup*, with brilliant articles by Paul Preciado, Franco Berardi aka Bifo, Jean Luc Nancy, and Judith Butler. We thought we would learn how to become better people. David Harvey said that forty years of neoliberalism has left the public totally exposed and ill-prepared to face a public health crisis on the scale of COVID-19. We have to learn something from this tragedy. I am very inspired by Bruno Latour, who invites the reader to reflect on the following questions:

What are some suspended activities that you would like to see not coming back? What are the activities, now suspended, that you hope might develop/begin again, or even be created from scratch?[2]

Unfortunately, I don't see many people around reflecting on any of these 'constructive' questions anymore, at least not in Brazil. It does not make Brazil a better society, quite the opposite. Sure, I hope we learned to respect the public health system, which has been saving lives. But there is a profound social inequity everywhere, right there just outside the door. It is unfair. The slums on the peripheries have suffered the most. The sanitary conditions of most of the country are unbearable. And there is starvation, unemployment, cruelty. And there is little empathy from the rich, from the elite running this country since the colonial ages.

Some final words. At the beginning of the pandemic era, like many people, we wanted to learn how to decelerate, to slow down, to better know how to keep peace of mind, and how to cope with capitalism advancing our sleep time, as we were pushed into a constant state of home office activity. We now live inside our offices; we had to make ourselves available in a 24/7 mode, in a restless fashion. And we suffer its consequences daily. Jonathan Crary states that sleep is a standing affront to this state of capitalism.[3] In the restless productive society, one is primarily at war with oneself. We had to jump from theory to the real thing to learn about this. What is reflected in the financial market panic is not so much fear of the virus as fear of the self.

In the beginning, we were dealing with the symbolic side of reclusion. We used metaphors; we tried seeing the many sides of it. The invisible aspect of the virus raised different concerns about how to fear it. 'What is more harmful: what are you most afraid of, the visible or the invisible?' Today, the visible aspect of the virus found its way to all of us. It is getting closer and closer. It's out there, and it is standing at our doorsteps, literally. Where to run? Where to stay? We had to move our political fight once again to the web. A government such as that of Bolsonaro is damaging the fabric of everyday life. We must also fight to keep our joy.

---

2   Bruno Latour, What protective measures can you think of so we don't go back to the pre-crisis production model?, 2020, https://www.versopolis.com/times/opinion/846/what-protective-measures-can-you-think-of-so-we-don-t-go-back-to-the-pre-crisis-production-model
3   Jonathan Crary, *24/7: Late Capitalism and the Ends of Sleep*, London: Verso Books, 2013

Knowing there weren't many possibilities for actions in the streets, alongside the communities I work with, I allowed myself some time for more personal works, bringing back experimental videos I did in the past, the kind of pieces I used to do at home. It brought some genuine relief. Sometimes awareness of (micro)politics can be reached in a subtle way, just by staying at home and wondering about the storm out there, coming through the windows.

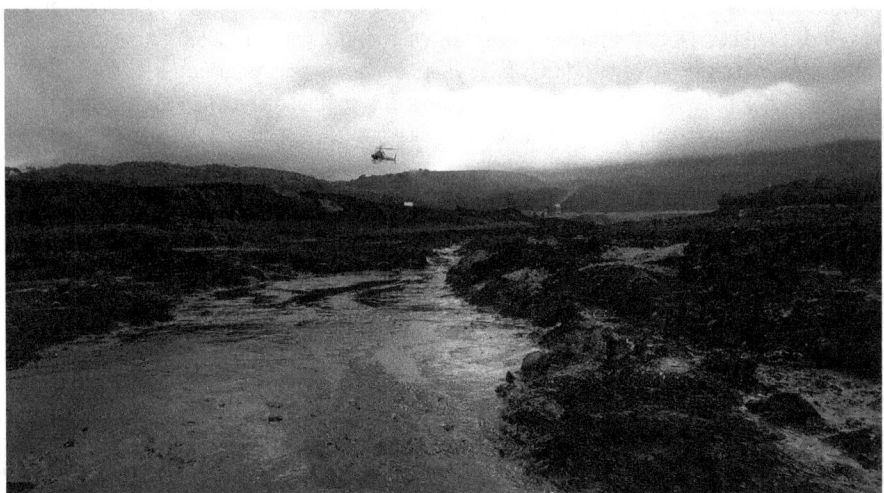

Figure 93: Still frame of the feature film 'Lavra,' mostly edited during the pandemic, to be released in 2021.

And there was all the rest: teaching, reading, planning a postdoc, applying for funds, deep breathing, doubting the future, taking care of my daughter, getting some sun. I am shouting out loud from my window against this corrupted, stupid, fascist government (sometimes literally shouting, sometimes through video projections, sometimes through leafleting actions on the streets). It may not be much, but it is something to do for now.

What is possible to synthesize from these micro and macro-rugged paths is that this writing cannot separate the different points of view to which we are subjected. We are affected by everything happening around us, simply by observing it. The observer alters the result. We are altered.

Just now, when writing these lines, we are entering a weekend that promises to be one of the saddest ones, this year, thus far. About 4,000 people are dying in a single day. Of this terrible figure, almost half happens in São Paulo state. And it is escalating daily. Again, and again.

BIOGRAPHIES

Annie Abrahams, based in Montpellier, France, has a primarily online art practice that meanders between research and performance. In her carefully scripted art, she reveals ordinary human behavior and develops what she calls an 'aesthetics of trust and attention.' She is interested in language politics and sees her often collaborative practices as a learning place for 'being with.'

Lucas Bambozzi is an artist and new media researcher producing installations, single channel videos, and interactive projects. His works have been shown in solo and collective shows in more than 40 countries, held by organizations such as MoMA in the U.S., ZKM, Frankfurter Kunstverein, and ISEA-Ruhr in Germany, Laboral and Arco's Expanded Box in Spain, HTTP Gallery in London, Havana Biennale in Cuba, ŠKUC gallery in Slovenia, Share Festival in Italy, WRO Media Art Biennale in Poland, Centre Georges Pompidou in France, ZERO1 Biennial in the USA, Bienal de Artes Mediales in Chile and many others in Brazil, including the São Paulo Biennale, Videobrasil, It's All True Festival, On-Off Live Images and FILE. He is one of the initiators of the arte.mov Festival (2006-2012), the exhibition 'Multitude' (2014), the Labmovel project (2012-2016) and the AVXLab Festival (2018-2021). He holds an MPhil in Philosophy of Computing from University of Plymouth, and a Ph.D. in Science from FAU USP.

Dennis de Bel is an artistic researcher, educator, and radio amateur. His practice oscillates between various configurations of collaborations focusing on collectively exploring hardware, software, and various forms of waves. He actualizes this through a broad spectrum of talks, devices, DJ sets, workshops, and exchanges like ISEA, Transmediale, Radical Networks and Relearn, including various educational institutions such as Design Academy Eindhoven and the Piet Zwart Institute Rotterdam. In 2017 he co-founded Varia, a physical space to actively develop collective approaches towards everyday technology informed by experiments with building physical, digital, and social infrastructures of affinity. De Bel holds a MA from the Piet Zwart Institute (NL) and most recently participated in the artist in residency program of the Institute for Provocation in Beijing (2018).

!Mediengruppe Bitnik are contemporary artists working on, and with, the internet. Their practice expands from the digital to physical spaces, often intentionally applying loss of control to challenge established structures and mechanisms. In the past they have been known to subvert surveillance cameras, bug an opera house to broadcast its performances outside, send a parcel containing a camera to Julian Assange at the Ecuadorian embassy in London, and physically glitch a building. In 2014, they sent a bot called 'Random Darknet Shopper' on a three-month shopping spree in the Darknets where it randomly bought items like keys, cigarettes, trainers, and ecstasy, and had them sent directly to the gallery space.

S()fia Braga is an Italian transdisciplinary artist based in Linz (AT). She develops her artistic research between digital, post-digital practices and cyberstalking, focusing especially on the social impact of web interfaces and the subversion of centralized social media platforms. She graduated in Visual Arts (BA, MA) at the Academy of Fine Arts of Bologna and in Interface

Cultures (MA) at the University of Art and Design of Linz. In 2019, she was artist in residence at IAMAS, the Institute of Advanced Media Arts and Sciences in Ōgaki, Japan, and curated the Internet Yami-Ichi at Ars Electronica Festival as well as its first Italian edition in Bologna at DAS, Dispositivo Arti Sperimentali. She was a finalist for the Share Prize 2020 in Turin, Italy. In 2021, she co-founded and co-curated the Next Cloud Residency hosted by the net culture initiative *servus.at*. Her works have been exhibited at Ars Electronica Festival (AT), Deutsche Bank (IT), Share Festival (IT), Xie Zilong Photography Museum (CN), Pinacoteca Albertina di Torino (IT), XII Video Vortex Conference (MT), WRO Media Art Biennale (PL), The Wrong - New Digital Art Biennale, Schlossmuseum Linz (AT), Link Cabinet (IT) and more.

Arcángelo Constantini is an artistic inventor and technological hacker. His production is based on speculative realism under different transdisciplinary and multifaceted discursive lines. To develop his processes and experimental hypotheses, he uses a variety of technological means or poetic discourses. He was Curator of Art and Media at the Museo Tamayo Arte Contemporáneo, Director of the project ¼ , Director of FACTO, curator of the inaugural event of the Fonoteca Nacional and the Universidad Centro, and currently organizes with Marcela Armas the sound art cycle *Meditatio Sonus.*

Tiny Domingos is a Berlin-based artist and researcher. His artistic practice combines space-related work and geophysical, economic, and biological flows. He is currently working on an eco-fiction project in a perspective of reconnection with the living and the mineral. He is the founder and director of a Berlin-based art space *ROSALUX*, and a member of the Intelligence Debiased Research Group, London. His work has been featured, among others, at the Bozar Center for Fine Arts (Brussels), KW Institute of contemporary art (Berlin), Calouste Gulbenkian arts center (Rio de Janeiro) and the Rijksmuseum Amsterdam.

John Duncan is known for his extensive body of work in performance, video, installations, and experimental music. He is a member of LAFMS (the Los Angeles Free Music Society). In Tokyo, he pioneered work with key Japanese noise musicians, directed an adult video series produced by Kuki and operated his own pirate FM radio and television broadcasts, most recently performing with Ishibashi Eiko, Jim O'Rourke, and Joe Talia on the *Red Sky* concert tour throughout Japan. *A Shaman at the Edge of Town*, a fictional account of Duncan's artistic career by Yelena De Luca Mitrjushkina, will be published by iDEAL in late 2021.

Ben Grosser creates interactive experiences, machines, and systems that examine the cultural, social, and political effects of software. Recent exhibition venues include the Barbican Centre in London, Museum Kesselhaus in Berlin, Museu das Comunicações in Lisbon, and Galerie Charlot in Paris. His works have been featured in The New Yorker, Wired, The Atlantic, The Guardian, The Washington Post, El País, Libération, Süddeutsche Zeitung, and Der Spiegel. Grosser's artworks are regularly cited in books investigating the cultural effects of technology, including *The Age of Surveillance Capitalism*, *The Metainterface*, *Critical Code Studies*, and *Technologies of Vision*, as well as volumes centered on computational art practices such as 'Electronic Literature,' 'The New Aesthetic and Art,' and 'Digital Art.'

Grosser is an associate professor in the School of Art and Design, and co-founder of the Critical Technology Studies Lab at the National Center for Supercomputing Applications, both at the University of Illinois at Urbana-Champaign, U.S.

Adham Hafez is a curator, theorist, historian, and artist working with choreography, installation, sound, and text. His work encompasses postcolonial studies, the Anthropocene and performance, politics of choreography, Middle East, and Arab art history, alternative modernities, and climate change. His work has been presented internationally at world renowned venues including Hebbel Am Ufer, Cairo Opera House, MoMA PS1, Sharjah Architecture Triennial, Damascus Opera House, La Mama Theatre, among others. He publishes essays and texts in Arabic, English, and French, and he is the founder of HaRaKa Platform, Egypt's first platform dedicated to performance studies and choreography established 15 years ago, as well as Cairography Publication that he co-founded with Egyptian writer and critic Ismail Fayed.

Sachiko Hayashi pursues art practice at the intersection of New Media and Contemporary Visual Art after having obtained a MA in Digital Media (UK) and additional two-year postgraduate studies in Computer Arts at the Royal Institute of Art in Stockholm. Seeing art as crystallization of perspectives and communication thereof, her work is born out of her experience as 'Other' (gender, racial, ethnic, and aesthetic) and often deals with how to resolve issues surrounding identity within a highly developed technological, scientific, and/or media society. In recent years, her focus has been gesture-controlled interactivity for instant moving-image making (often called 'live cinema'), exploring temporal compositions in subjective imagery. Since 2013, she has also served as the editor of *hz-journal.org*.

Lynn Hershman Leeson is an artist and film maker. She lives in New York and San Francisco. Her current exhibition, 'Twisted,' will be at The New Museum, New York, 30 June – 4 October 2021. Hershman Leeson has received numerous prizes and awards and is Professor Emeritus at The University of California, Davis.

Garnet Hertz is Canada Research Chair in Design and Media Arts and Associate Professor of Design at Emily Carr University. His art and research investigate DIY culture, electronic art, and critical design practices. He has exhibited in eighteen countries including SIGGRAPH, Ars Electronica, and DEAF and was the recipient of the Oscar Signorini Award in robotic art and a Fulbright award. He has worked at Art Center College of Design and University of California Irvine. His research is widely cited in academic publications, and popular press on his work has disseminated through 25 countries including The New York Times, Wired, The Washington Post, NPR, USA Today, NBC, CBS, TV Tokyo, and CNN Headline News.

Dr. Jennifer Kanary is the founder of Roomforthoughts (1998), an artistic research practice dedicated to understanding the physics of thought and how the brain constructs realities. Jennifer has an interest in understanding how art is a form of knowledge production, particularly in a scientific context in relation to the mind and how it works. She was an artistic research-er-in-residence at the National Psychiatry Museum in Haarlem and Waag Society Institute for Art, Science and Technology, Amsterdam. She was a tutor of the Honours Programme ART and RESEARCH at the University of Amsterdam and the Gerrit Rietveld Academie from

2008-2011. She is best known for the project *Labyrinth Psychotica*. As part of her practice, Jennifer coaches students and professionals in creative mind-journeys to help develop vision, leadership, and entrepreneurship for social change through an empathic subjective lens.

Brian Mackern is a New Media artist, composer, a/v performer and developer of self-generating structures and sound-visual reactive environments. His work is focused mainly on processes, structures, and found footage. He explores interface design, alternative browsing, the creation of sound toys, video-data animations in real time, netart, and sound art. He has presented his work and given workshops and lectures on numerous tours in Argentina, Chile, Mexico, Spain, France, Portugal, Italy, Poland, Slovenia, Germany, Belgium, Korea. His work has been exhibited at major international art festivals, having received recognition from numerous institutions.

Milton Manetas is a Greek artist living and working in London and New York. In 2000, he conceptualized the art movement *Neen*, which brings together visual artists but also software engineers, web designers, game animators, and other professionals in the technology sector. Manetas analyzes the relationship between computers, video games, and humans, often portraying subjects deeply engaged in activities that consumer electronic tools have made possible. His work proceeds in two directions: the pure matter of his more 'classic' works is realized through oil painting, and engagements with *Neen* exist on the web and in the virtual universe.

Nancy Mauro-Flude is a performance artist represented by Bett Gallery, Tasmania. She currently lectures in critical theory and twenty-first century mediums and leads the 'Engineering Flora Fiction and Data Fauna' studio at the College of Design and Social Context, RMIT University. Founder of the Holistic Computing Network, Nancy is writing about chthonic feminist internet cultures and the provenance of radio stars.

Lorna Mills is a Canadian artist who has actively exhibited her work in both solo and group exhibitions since the early 90s. Her practice includes obsessive Ilfochrome printing, obsessive painting, obsessive super 8 film & video, and obsessive on-line animated GIFs incorporated into restrained off-line installation work. Recent exhibitions include 'At Play in the Fields of the Lord' at Transfer Gallery, Brooklyn NY, 'Dreamlands' at the Whitney Museum, NY, 'Yellowwhirlaway' at the Museum of the Moving Image, NY and 'The Great Code' at Transfer Gallery, NY. For the month of March 2016, her work *Mountain Time/Light* was displayed on 45 Jumbo monitors in Times Square, NYC, every night as part of the 'Midnight Moment' program curated by Times Square Arts. She has also curated 'Ways of Something,' a collaborative remake of the 1972 John Berger documentary 'Ways of Seeing' episodes one through four, featuring over 115 networked artists and most recently WELLNOW.WTF, a sprawling netart project co-curated with Faith Holland and Wade Wallerstien.

Daniela de Paulis is a former contemporary dancer, a media artist, a licensed radio operator, and a radio telescope operator. From 2009 to 2019, she has been artist in residence at the Dwingeloo radio telescope, where she developed the Visual Moonbounce technology, the live performance OPTICKS, and a series of innovative projects combining radio technologies with live performance art and neuroscience. She is a member of the IAA SETI (Search for Extraterrestrial Intelligence) Permanent Committee. She is the recipient of the Baruch Bloomberg Fellowship in Astrobiology at the Green Bank Observatory where she will develop a new art-science project in 2022. She has published her work with the Leonardo MIT Journal, Inderscience, Springer, Cambridge University Press and RIXC among others.

Tina La Porta is an artist immersed in the global internet art movement. Her current work explores symptoms of mental illness, side effects of prescription medications, and the therapeutic qualities of the artistic process. She has exhibited in numerous solo and group exhibitions in the U.S. and abroad, including The New Museum, NY; The NSU Art Museum, Fort Lauderdale, FL; Museo Nacional Centro de Art Reina Sofia, Madrid, Spain; Museu do Essencial e do Alem Disso, Rio de Janeiro, Brazil; Institute of Contemporary Arts, London, England; San Francisco Art Institute, San Francisco, CA; Centre Cultural de la Fundació 'la Caixa,' Barcelona, Spain; The Kitchen, New York, NY. She also taught at the Graduate and Undergraduate levels in Fine Art at Cooper Union, New York University, The New School, Rutgers University, Pratt Institute, Parsons School of Design, New Jersey Institute of Technology, New York Institute of Technology, Fordham University, St. John's University and Fairfield University.

Archana Prasad is an artist and activist whose work is in a conjunction of visual art, technology, and urban community art, steeped in design and research methodologies. She is the Founder of Jaaga, an organization started in 2009 that builds collaborative communities to solve today's big challenges. Jaaga has a co-working community with an alumnus of over 500 people, a lab that serves enterprises through innovative tech solutions, a program focused on learning and a public arts program that has worked with more than 60 artists and supported many international residencies. Archana's focus is on taking research and creative practices into community engagement through projects like Malleshwaram Accessibility Project, Urban Avantgarde, Neighbourhood Diaries and Hampi Craft Diaries.

Melinda Rackham wove tales of online intimacy, intrigue, and identity when the internet was young. Her desire to level hierarchies saw her present new artforms on prominent public platforms and found the critically engaging -empyre- forum. Melinda's recent playful performative interventions and poetic fictions explore art, environment, feminisms, and trauma, while her latest book *CoUNTess: Spoiling Illusions since 2008,* co-authored with Elvis Richardson, probes the persistence of gender asymmetry in the artworld.

Michelle Teran is an educator, artist, and researcher. She is practice-oriented Research Professor Social Practices at Willem de Kooning Academy (WdKA). Her research areas encompass socially engaged and site-specific art, transmedia storytelling, counter-cartographies, social movements, feminist practices, and critical pedagogy. Together with Marc Herbst, she co-edited *Everything Gardens! Growing from Ruins of Modernity*, one of a three-part publication (ADOCS and nGbK publishers) on how the global ecological crisis and its social repercussions raise questions regarding new forms of education. The English version of Ada Colau and Adrià Alemany's book *MortgagedLives* (original Spanish version *Vidas Hipotecas*), a translation project initiated by Michelle Teran and published by the Journal of Aesthetics & Protest, documents the Spanish right-to-housing movement, the PAH. She is editor of

Situationer, a transformative pedagogy reader (Research Center WdKA and Publication Studio Rotterdam publishers) that brings together experimental practices of learning otherwise.

Mare Tralla is an interdisciplinary artist, organizer, and activist. She employs and combines a variety of media, from video, photography, performance, painting, to interactive media. She was one of the very few conducting a feminist revolution in the field of contemporary art in Estonia in the 90s. As an activist she is involved with Act Up, London, No Pride in War coalition and LGSMigrants. Her recent socially engaged performative projects deal with queer experiences, gender issues, HIV stigma, investigate sustainability and economics.

Igor Vamos is a media artist and co-founder of the activist duo Yes Men and the Yes Lab, an institute aimed at facilitating creative activist projects and the development of creative activism worldwide. As Mike Bonanno, he has starred in the documentary hit *The Yes Men*, and wrote, directed, produced, and starred in the award-winning feature documentary *The Yes Men Fix the World*, official selection at Sundance, Toronto, Berlin, and dozens other international film festivals. In addition to the films, Vamos has been published widely and created numerous international performances and activist interventions. He is Associate Professor of Art and Technology at Rensselaer Polytechnic Institute.

Ivar Veermäe is an artist focused on artistic research, combining documentary and staged work both in real life and through 3D animations. Veermäe had solo exhibitions in Edith-Russ-Haus, Oldenburg, Gallery im Turm, Berlin, Tallinn Art Hall Gallery, Freies Museum Berlin, and City Gallery of Tallinn, among others. His work has been exhibited in group exhibitions at Riga Biennale, Venice Architecture Biennale, transmediale Festival in HKW, Moscow Biennale for Young Art, BIENALSUR in Buenos Aires, the Bozar in Brussels, the ZKM in Karlsruhe, the Art Museum of Estonia, Art Hall of Tallinn, the Estonian Contemporary Art Museum, the Latvian Centre for Contemporary Art, the Kulturhuset Bronden in Denmark, the Kunstverein Wolfsburg, the KunstvereinKassel, the Pinnacles Gallery in Australia. His videos are being screened at the Rencontres Internationales in Paris and Berlin, in HeK Basel, transmediale Festival, AND Festival in Manchester, EMAF in Osnabrück, Kasseler Dokfest, Crosstalk festival in Budapest, in Virtual Memorial, Cambodia among others.

BIBLIOGRAPHY

Brown, Adrienne M. *Emergent Strategy: Shaping Change, Changing Worlds*, Chico: AK Press, 2017.

Center for Systems Science and Enginering, *COVID-19 Dashboard by CSSE*, John Hopkins University, https://coronavirus.jhu.edu/map.html.

Cramer, Florian, and Michelle Teran. 'Letters from Dystopian and Utopian Futures of Arts Education.' In *Hoger Beroepsonderwijs in 2030: Toekomstverkenningen En Scenario's Vanuit Hogeschool Rotterdam*, ed. D. P. Gijsbertse, H. A. Van Klink, C. Machielse, and J. H. Timmermans, Rotterdam: Hogeschool Rotterdam Uitgeverij, 2020, pp. 427–464.

Crary, Jonathan. *24/7: Late Capitalism and the Ends of Sleep*, London: Verso Books, 2013.

Gumbs, Alexis Pauline. *Undrowned*, Chico: AK Press, 2021.

Han, Byung Chul. *The viral emergenc(e/y) and the world of tomorrow*,https://elpais.com/ideas/2020-03-21/la-emergencia-viral-y-el-mundo-de-manana-byung-chul-han-el-filosofo-surcoreano-que-piensa-desde-berlin.html.

Herbst, Marc, Michelle Teran, and Lígia Milagres. 'Everything Gardens: Working Notes Towards a Solidarity Economy.' In *PARK.Reader*, 2021. https://doi.org/https://doi.org/http://park.levart.no/2021/01/19/everything-gardens.

hooks, bell. *All about Love: New Visions*, New York, NY: William Morrow, an imprint of HarperCollins Publishers, 2018.

Latour, Bruno. *What protective measures can you think of so we don't go back to the pre-crisis production model?*, Versopolis, 2020. https://www.versopolis.com/times/opinion/846/what-protective-measures-can-you-think-of-so-we-don-t-go-back-to-the-pre-crisis-production-model.

Schulman, Sarah. *Conflict Is Not Abuse: Overstating Harm, Community Responsibility and the Duty of Repair*, Vancouver: Arsenal Pulp Press, 2017.

'Social Practices COVID-19 Teaching Resources - Beyond Social,' 2020. https://beyond-social.org/wiki/index.php/Social_Practices_COVID-19_Teaching_Resources.

Spade, Dean. *Mutual Aid: Building Solidarity during This Crisis (and the next)*, London; Brooklyn, NY: Verso, 2020.

LIST OF ILLUSTRATIONS

Figure 1: Back at my home studio, with my cat Murmullo (photo by Anita Crescionini).

Figure 2: Billboard of canceled flights, Santiago de Chile airport.

Figure 3: Temporary studio in Valparaiso (with cats Rucio and Koshka).

Figure 4: Graffiti in a staircase in Recreo, Valparaiso where I got stuck waiting for a flight to Montevideo.

Figure 5: Waiting for flight news in Valparaiso with Rita (photo by Valentina Montero).

Figure 6: Mare Tralla doing a film shoot in a London park during lockdown, with a one-person film crew.

Figure 7: Covid Plants Action, front garden activism, a part of Free the Vaccine campaign. We planted and dedicated plants to COVID-19 vaccine researchers. The images were used on social media. We also sent direct messages to the researchers, thanking for their work and asking them not to sell out to Big Pharma and instead support the pledge for affordable global vaccine access. Here, Mare is planting potatoes for the Jenner Institute researchers, who developed the AstraZeneca vaccine (Lockdown, spring 2020).

Figure 8: Covid Plants action. Here is a zucchini plant dedicated to a researcher from Liverpool University. It has the hashtag #opencovidpledge on it.

Figure 9: Lorna Mills' studio.

Figure 10: Lorna Mills' collaboration with Kes.

Figure 11: John Duncan as Joe in Samuel Beckett's Eh Joe, produced and directed by Luz Maria Sanchez who also plays Voice. Streamed live from Mexico City and Bologna.

Figure 12: BACKFIRE OF JOY. Phew, John Duncan and Kondo Tatsuo live at Hosei University, Tokyo. Released by Black Truffle.

Figure 13: Detail of Patchwork (anarchist flag and secondhand underwear), 2020.

Figure 14: Video interview still, February 2021.

Figure 15: The Jaaga building made of pallet racks. Image source: Wikipedia.

Figure 16: Video interview still, February 2021.

Figure 17: Production shot 'Decisions, Decisions, Decisions,' studio !Mediengruppe Bitnik, Berlin, 2020.

Figure 18: Klasse Brenner, class meeting in Second Life, Stuttgart State Academy of Art and Design (ABK Stuttgart) where !Mediengruppe Bitnik taught as guest professors in 2019/2020.

Figure 19: !Mediengruppe Bitnik, Flagged for Political Speech, exhibition view Delta Lab Rijeka, 2020. Photo credits: Tanja Kanazir/Drugo More.

Figure 20: Jennifer Kanary tries to do yoga next to homeschooling during lockdown.

Figure 21: Jennifer Kanary, Drawing of the COVID-19 virus.

Figure 22: Labyrinth Psychotica VR workshop at a GGZ (mental care facility) just before the second lockdown.

Figure 23: Jennifer Kanary drawing made for INKTOBER 2020; Trying to be normal.

Figure 24: Sachiko Hayashi performing her motion controlled audio-visual work 'Still Untitled' (2018) Photo: Emanuel Schütt.

Figure 25: A still from motion controlled audio-visual work 'Still Untitled'" using Leap Motion, programmed in Max Jitter (2017-2018).

Figure 26: A still from gesture controlled audio-visual work 'Hard Candy,' using Myo armband, programmed in Max Jitter (2019).

Figure 27: Garnet Hertz showing custom Ugly Rudy Giuliani Christmas Sweater, December 2020.

Figure 28: I had brought an old Risograph machine into his garage and started producing a capstone project booklet titled 'Exploratory Interaction Design' with students. This project was abandoned.

Figure 29: Screenshot of a Snapchat from October 2020 talking about a YouTube video Garnet had made about speculative design and decolonization

Figure 30: I printed a six-foot tall inkjet Facebook 'care' emoji poster and stuck it in the dirty nook where I liked putting my backpack while skateboarding at Leeside Skatepark in Vancouver.

Figure 31: Alternate view of installed Facebook 'care' emoji poster at Leeside skatepark. This site ended up becoming used as a memorial for Lee Matasi, a skater, artist, and originator of the DIY skatepark in Vancouver. Matasi was killed by senseless gun violence in 2005.

Figure 32: During the pandemic, I also produced a risographed zine titled 'Two Terms: Critical

Making + D.I.Y' that I gave away to anyone that mailed me a physical item. These are some of the things people sent to me.

Figure 33: S()fia Braga, 'I Stalk Myself More Than I Should,' installation, SHARE Festival, 2020.

Figure 34: SSID: @tagme.

Figure 35: Screenshots from 'Die Verwandlung,' short movie for Instagram Stories, 2020.

Figure 36: Ben Grosser's home studio, March 2020.

Figure 37: A usually busy street at 9pm on Friday from March 2020 in Illinois, U.S.

Figure 38: U.S. COVID-19 death count visualization, Ben Grosser, 2020-ongoing.

Figure 39: Ben Grosser, 'The Endless Doomscroller,' 2020.

Figure 40: Tiny Domingos, Portrait in rot, digital edition, 2021.

Figure 41: Tiny Domingos, 'Sonnenuntergang am Tegeler See,' digital edition, 2021.

Figure 42: Tiny Domingos, Spross, digital edition 2021.

Figure 43: Daniela de Paulis' new home studio.

Figure 44: Facemasks, a gift from Daniela's parents.

Figure 45: Original image by Quentin Aurat for the 'All Women Crew' workshop, organized by Olats/Leonardo.

Figure 46: Moon reflected image. Credits: Quentin Aurat, All Women Crew participants and organizers, Daniela de Paulis, Dan Gautchi, Mario Armando Natali, Nando Pellegrini.

Figure 47: Vamos (or Bonnano, I can't remember which one I am) has found more fulfilling ways to enjoy life without leaving home.

Figure 48: Melinda Rackham, 'Remake Hoda Afshar,' 2020.

Figure 49: Melinda Rackham, 'Remake Julie Rrap,' 2020.

Figure 50: Ticket to cross the border between different Australian states.

Figure 51: Melinda Rackham, 'Remake VNS Matrix,' 2020.

Figure 52: Ivar Veermäe, Studio (with Lily), 16.04.2021.

Figure 53: Ivar Veermäe, 'Spielplätze' (work in progress), 2021.

Figure 54: Ivar Veermäe, 'Backgrounds' (Test), Grünheide, 2020.

Figure 55: Arcangelo Constantini, VitriNa SuBjeTiVa, Espacio Mexico Montréal, 2017.

Figure 56: 3sTu:DiøZō ACe_LeRaDø, #biom3k4niko series, 2021.

Figure 57: Meditatio Sonus, overview with audience, Muséo Oaxaca, 2020.

Figure 58: Screenshot 2020-04-27 18.47.14.

Figure 59: Screenshot 2020-03-31 13.02.26.

Figure 60: Screenshot 2020-03-13 12.42.48.

Figure 61: Community garden Prinzessinnengarten as seen from Moritzplatz, Berlin.

Figure 62: Prinzessinnengarten announcement board.

Figure 63: Miltos Manetas.

Figure 64: Studio view with Miltos Manetas' daughter Alpha.

Figure 65: Self-portrait with less privileged.

Figure 66: Street view of Miltos Manetas' studio in Bogota.

Figure 67: Performance still Nancy Mauro Flude (right) and Linda Dement, 'Cyberfeminist Bed Sheet Transfigured' (2020) in Tomorrow, Bett Gallery, Hobart Tasmania. Image courtesy of Jonathon Delacour.

Figure 68: Workstation in bedroom. Image: Nancy Mauro-Flude.

Figure 69: Prep list.

Figure 70: 'The Budget' performed a supporting role, including the host of non-financial items that underwrote the event, reconfiguring the zero-sum game of double-entry accounting, listing artists' cultural expertise, childcare, and planning meeting lunch items, and so on, regularly blanked by economists. Other notables are the asymmetrical lines of 'INCOME and NON BUDGET' rescued from its role as a background inevitability, hidden in annual reports. 'The Budget' was installed at the event as a featured artwork and item of merchandise (on sale at the door for $10). Also, it draws attention to intermediary workings that are often mistaken for the slippery prospect of transparency. Detail from 'The Thorny Question of Art and Economy A Conversation Piece' (2020). Image courtesy of Nancy Mauro-Flude.

Figure 71: Ouijic Agent number 13 JUSTICE in the hands of 'The Chosen One.' Under the guise of Ouijic Agents, gifted from the Advanced Centre of Excellence for Automated Decision Making, these beguiling robotic mop automata balls, self-contained electrical devices, powered by servo motors that simultaneously rotated and pushed, found a murky way to furnish prominence with another peripheral kin. Image detail, 'The Thorny Question of Art and Economy A Conversation Piece' (2020). Image courtesy of Jesse Barclay.

Figure 72: 'Womb of the World' (2020) recorded as internet scale one-channel video depicting a woman standing in the midst of elemental forces on a floating platform timtumili minanya/ River Derwent. Image courtesy of Nancy Mauro-Flude.

Figure 73: One of the media collaterals for Economythologies #MLX a techno-pagan-mystic visual system the stars + currency symbols + technological networks = economythologies.network. Shaee Illyas, a transdisciplinary designer, made a script to generate different variations of this mage for different collaterals, such as invitations, reports, backdrops, presentations, social media, website etc. Each iteration is different. Image: Shaee Illyas.

Figure 74: Lynn Hershman in front of 'Shadow Stalker' at the opening of Uncanny Valley at the de Young Museum, San Francisco, 2020.

Figure 75: Cover of the book for 'The Floating Museum.'

Figure 76: Drawing before I got my COVID-19 shot, ink, watercolor on paper, 8 x 10", 2021.

Figure 77: Adham Hafez, selfie with mask.

Figure 78: Scene from the KitKat Club by HaRaKa Platform, December 2020.

Figure 79: Archival map of downtown Cairo, Egypt. Presentation by Adam Kucharski.

Figure 80: Scene from the KitKat Club, with Lamia Gouda performing Asmahan, December 2020.

Figure 81: Superposition of images of the performance of 'Breathing' by Utterings.

Figure 82: Screenshot 'Distant Movements #6,' with clockwise Muriel Piqué, Annie Abrahams, and Daniel Pinhiero.

Figure 83: Projection of 'Breathing' by Utterings live performance at STWST48x6 MORE LESS in Linz, September 2020, photo by Sandra Brandmayr.

Figure 84: Screen printing on wallpaper at Oolite Printshop, Miami; 2021.

Figure 85: Collage of screen prints on wallpaper, 2021.

Figure 86: Untitled.

Figure 87: Untitled.

Figure 88: Providing domestic support to some needs. A flag encouraging people to stay home, produced in my garage.

Figure 89: Delivery. Delivery motorbikers have been joining a silent protest against the death of more than 400,000 people due to the lack of any public health plan.

Figure 90: Garbage. All kinds of actions are valid to raise further consciousness about the madness in the government.

Figure 91: Large-scale projections I did in support of the Yanomamis, with photos provided by artist Claudia Andujar. There are already 25,000 gold prospectors in Yanomami lands, taking all kinds of plague (including corona virus) to their lives.

Figure 92: Protest against closing of Brazilian Cinemateca, in São Paulo, a major institution devoted to the cinema archives.

Figure 93: Still frame of the feature film 'Lavra,' mostly edited during the pandemic, to be released in 2021.

www.ingramcontent.com/pod-product-compliance
Lightning Source LLC
Chambersburg PA
CBHW071457220526
45472CB00003B/837